Mutual Funds
Today...

Who's watching *your* money?

A guide for investors...
A wake up call for Mutual Fund Directors

By Dan Calabria

Limit of Liability/Disclosure of Warranty

Cover and Interior Design: Leading the Web, Inc.
Typesetting: Leading the Web, Inc.
© 2008 by Mutual Funds Bureau, LLC
Published by Mutual Funds Bureau, LLC

First printing: 2009

ISBN: 978-0-578-00786- 9780578007861

LCCN: 2009923251

Printed in the United States of America

ATTENTION CORPORATIONS, UNIVERSITIES, COLLEGES AND PROFESSIONAL ORGANIZATIONS: Quantity discounts are available on purchases of this book for educational, gift purposes, or as premiums.
For information, please contact: www.mutualfundsbureau.com

Table of Contents

Introduction

Full Disclosure

The U. S. Securities and Exchange Commission (SEC) requirement that publicly-traded companies release and provide for the free exchange of all material facts that are relevant to their ongoing business.

The general need in business transactions for both parties to tell the whole truth about any material issue pertaining to the transaction. (Investopedia.com)

The mutual fund segment of the securities industry has grown into a major player in the competition for your investment dollars, and with remarkable success. I'm a confirmed, vocal advocate for investing in mutual funds and when asked by those who know of my background if there isn't a better investment available for most people, my response has always been – mutual funds are the worst investment available, except for all the other investments in the market place.

I firmly believe that, but I'm also a purist. There are many ways to make fund investing more profitable and effective in order to realize better results for the average investor who seeks financial independence. However, the industry has not always lived up to its potential and has demonstrated that it is vulnerable to excesses from people who should know better. I've owned and own a number of well managed funds and I've learned that it takes a bit of time to determine that you own a well managed fund, but not very long to recognize a loser. I know - I've owned a few of those over the years. But let's focus on the present and use the past for educational purposes and as a guide to a sensible investment approach.

It was only a few years ago that the mutual fund industry dodged the bullet when it was deeply embarrassed by the so-called market timing and late trading scandals. The industry was lucky and shareholders were, as usual, very forgiving. Can it escape so easily the next time?

That's hard to say. However, I believe it's safe to say that if mutual fund investors are alert and properly represented by astute, informed boards of directors then such incidents will be rare. But fund investors must pay attention and hold their independent directors accountable for their role as "watchdogs" and fiduciaries on their behalf.

This book was written for two different kinds of people – those who own mutual funds and those who don't. What you're about to read will shed some light on the factors that are important in cutting through the hype and spin confronting you. It's intended to help investors put together a basic investment program based on sound, fundamental investment principles to help achieve their investment goals. It's no small task to determine which mutual fund to select for one's investment. How do you do it? A small part of the problem was made clear by a recent article in The Wall Street Journal, titled: "Exotic Stocks: Investors flee, but pros don't," subtitled, "Fund managers wax bullish on emerging markets they think will zig as U.S. zags." The article described the potential of investments in "developing markets," including "emerging markets" and something called "frontier markets," which included countries like "Vietnam and Kazakhstan." This represents one of the dilemmas faced by today's investors - the array and sheer number of mutual funds is mind boggling. And it's compounded by the incredible slicing, dicing and duplication of funds with similar investment objectives, all designed with the objective of increasing the fund manager's market share – I know, I was part of the crowd. That's the name of the game. Unfortunately, the investment goals of mutual fund shareholders are sometimes almost an afterthought.

That's why we might soon hear talk of "Frontier" funds – I can see it now, it won't take long before investors will be confronted with the "Outer Limits Funds," "Twilight Zone Funds," "Stone Age Funds," etc. We might even learn of the "Elbonian Funds." Why not? If Scott Adams, the creator of the always funny "Dilbert" comic strip, can create the country of Elbonia (where the national bird is the Frisbee) why not create a fund to take advantage of investment "opportunities" that are sure to develop there? Just think about investing in Elbonia once they invent the wheel! Full disclosure: I'm a Dilbert addict and look forward to reading it every day; it helps to put things in perspective.

Of course, the proliferation of mutual funds has become a little silly, but the creative people in the fund business know no limits in their efforts to increase market share. So how do current and prospective investors manage their investments for the future when faced with what has come to be known as a "flavor of the month" marketing machine? It's no small task.

1977 was a frustrating time in my career. I had decided to write a book about mutual funds and completed only a few chapters. However, as part of the book I compiled a "Directory of Mutual Fund Families." That directory was interesting, but it gave no indication of what the future held for the mutual fund industry in the decades ahead. For example, it listed a total of 348 equity and bond funds, 53 money market funds, 27 municipal bond funds and 61 closed end funds, a total of 489 mutual funds that were managed by 60 fund sponsors or investment advisers. Even though the Investment Company Act of 1940 was passed thirty seven years earlier, the mutual fund business was still a cottage industry compared to the sheer number and total assets of mutual funds today.

Let's admit the obvious – there are altogether too damned many funds in the marketplace today. Where and when will it end? How did we get here? Simple - the fund management business is very lucrative in that almost anyone can make money, lots of money, as long as you follow the rules and do what you say you'll do. It's almost always those who get too "sophisticated" or stretch the rules that get in trouble. Obviously not all funds have done a great job for their shareholders. But as long as you have a motivated sales network with the right incentive packages, almost anyone in the business can survive, if not prosper.

Here's a fund fact of life – not all well managed mutual funds are successful money making ventures for their investment manager. But there are an inordinate number of funds that have been created and aggressively marketed, not on the basis of their performance results, but on the basis of successful, aggressive marketing by highly motivated sales people, aka, brokers, advisers, consultants, financial planners, etc. As a result, the industry has learned that competitive, consistent, above average performance results alone do not necessarily translate into success measured by hundreds of millions of dollars in sales or billions of dollars in assets. In other words, in addition to good investment performance results, you had better have a sales/marketing program at least as good.

So today's mutual fund investor has a two-fold challenge in making an investment decision when selecting a fund or family of funds in which to invest – how to make his investment, and which funds to select for that purpose. In either case it's a formidable undertaking, especially when you consider that there are more than 8,000 mutual funds available today. That's not a misprint – the number of funds is way beyond what is needed primarily due to the duplication of funds offered by a variety of mutual fund management firms. This book will help guide you by providing information that's not as easy to obtain as it should be. So take it a step at a time and recognize that as with anything in life there are no guarantees. The information presented here will definitely help to avoid lots of unnecessary mistakes. Good luck!

Preface

The year was 1962 and things weren't exactly great. Trying to support a young family wasn't easy. Selling printing services in lower Manhattan wasn't pretty and watching the world go by wasn't the kind of pastime that promised prospects for a bright future. Then one night at a gathering of friends I learned that one of them was doing secretarial work for a small securities firm in lower Manhattan that sold mutual funds, a term that was unfamiliar to me. I got a brief description of what mutual funds were, which meant nothing to me until I learned that any time someone bought a mutual fund they were required by law to be given a prospectus, another term that was new to me. A light came on and I realized that prospectuses had to be printed - that was of interest to me.

That's how I met Murray Aaronson, the principal of the securities firm. He tried to convince me to join his small company and start selling mutual funds to the public. I loved Murray, but decided that was not the kind of selling that interested me. After several discussions (I never did get the order to print prospectuses), Murray said "You ought to go see the people at Dreyfus Fund." That was a name that meant something to me since most people with a pulse in metropolitan New York were familiar with the famous "Dreyfus Lion." It was the fund symbol that became famous based on the TV ad that showed the lion coming out of a New York City subway station and walking into the lobby of 2 Broadway where it climbed on a pedestal and became motionless. I'm sure many people were surprised to discover that there was no lion in the building lobby. But they sure came to know the Dreyfus lion as a symbol for something called a "mutual fund."

In early 1963, thanks to Murray Aaronson's introductory phone call, I went to work for the Dreyfus Mutual Fund organization as "Assistant Advertising Manager." While the title sounded great, the job primarily involved proof reading every document printed for the fund's marketing program, including prospectuses and shareholder reports. It was boring, with a capital "B." But it wasn't long before I came to understand what a mutual fund was all about, how it worked and the investment results that had been achieved. Those investment results were nothing less than a revelation for me.

When I originally told Murray about my job interview appointment, I was surprised by his advice. He told me that they weren't the easiest people in the world to work for, but no matter what, take whatever job they offered and then leave in two years. I did and I did. Within a year after I was hired I moved into a sales support desk job primarily dealing with broker dealers who sold the fund to the investing public. I found I really enjoyed working with those "pioneers" who in a sense were selling "religion" to an uninformed and under educated public. It was hard work and I realized that my intuition about selling to the public was correct. It took a special talent that I knew I didn't have.

In 1965, about one week short of two years, I joined the best investment organization I ever worked for, Oppenheimer & Co., which had one small mutual fund, the Oppenheimer Fund, with total assets of approximately $21 million, the equivalent of a day's sales for a single fund today. I was the third former Dreyfus employee to join Oppenheimer, having followed Don Spiro, the president of Oppenheimer's fund division, and Stan Egener, who I had worked with as his phone back-up at Dreyfus. That was the beginning of an 11 year period of hard work, with great people and compensation I had only dreamed of in the past. About a year later, my good friend Bob Galli also came over from Dreyfus to join Oppenheimer as in-house counsel for the Fund. A few years later Stan Egener left to form another mutual fund organization and I eventually became executive vice president of Oppenheimer Management Corp., responsible for national sales and a limited partner of Oppenheimer & Co., the parent company of the fund operation. I never worked so hard and had so much fun being part of an aggressive, outstanding research organization that was driven by the need to be one of the best firms on Wall Street. To describe it as exciting is an understatement and working at One New York Plaza at the tip of Manhattan was always a kick since I had been born and lived the first 13 years of my life about a dozen blocks from our offices. As the son of an Italian immigrant, it was the ultimate high.

Then I made the mistake of believing that I was ready for "bigger things," which resulted in a major career misstep. It was the first and only time I signed an employment contract locking me into a frustrating 2 year commitment. My new employer had made many promises, but I soon learned that they were primarily interested in being a caretaker for a small group of funds that management was not that interested in building. The "honeymoon" was over in just about a year and by mutual consent I agreed to stay on to the end of the 24 month period. (The Axe-Houghton Funds of Tarrytown, NY no longer exists.) With little to do I used the time to begin writing a book titled "How to Own a Mutual Fund," which was never completed. I have relied on some of that material as reference in placing certain events in perspective.

In 1979 I was offered the job of developing a direct, no-load sales program for the Lexington Funds, with successful results. After leaving Lexington, which seems to have gone into mutual fund limbo, I decided to start my own fund organization with a money market fund, Independent CashFlow Trust, which I subsequently sold to Van Kampen Merritt in Philadelphia. In 1986 I contacted my good friend John Galbraith who owned Templeton Funds Management Corporation in St. Petersburg, FL, the business management company for all of the Templeton Funds and accepted the job of president and CEO of the company, which was responsible for sales, accounting, administration and shareholder services for all Templeton Mutual Funds. In 1992 the company was acquired by the Franklin Funds and I accepted a severance arrangement. I felt I was ready to retire – which lasted about 6 months when I was called upon to help organize the Florida Tax Free Funds. After getting those funds underway I finally retired in 1995, and spent the next 11 years as an independent director of several mutual funds.

Over the many years I've been involved with these mutual fund companies, I've learned some things that will be helpful to both current and new fund investors. My goal is twofold, if only one young person who reads this book decides to pursue a career in the fund industry, I'll consider the book a success. However, if it motivates some readers to take advantage of mutual funds in planning for their financial independence then I will consider the effort to have been extremely successful.

Finally, I hope some of the issues discussed prompt the industry to be more sensitive to its obligations to fund shareholders, particularly those independent director/trustees who are charged with the role of "watch dogs" on behalf of their "employers," the shareholders. That role is best described as a fiduciary one, in representing the best interests of fund shareholders. For too long many fund shareholders have not been very well served by a "go along to get along" attitude on the part of some directors who are well compensated to represent them. After all, independent directors are paid by their shareholders for one purpose – to represent their interests, and only their interests. They exist for no other reason.

Acknowledgements

"Mutual Funds Today" has been sitting in cold storage for some time. It was originally conceived in 1977, after a very frustrating experience that involved working in a castle on the top of a hill in Tarrytown, New York. What was I thinking? Simple - I wasn't thinking. After all that has transpired I felt it necessary to write this book for the countless fund investors who have made mutual funds a part of so many people's live. So the first people to recognize for their role in this effort are mutual fund shareholders.

Second is my family, who had faith in the decisions I made and were always supportive. Then there are two young women without whom it would have taken much longer to complete the book (if ever!); Nicole Vikhlyantsev whose computer expertise and savvy made so much of the research and fact gathering become a reality, and Valerie Brehm who kept me on track in converting mutual fund jargon into plain English, cleaning up the errors and "getting it right."

Nicole and Valerie, this could never have happened without you both.

And finally, thanks to Scott Adams, creator of "Dilbert," for permission to use several of his fun strips that inject some humor into a serious subject.

Part I –
A Shareholder's Guide

Chapter One –
Mutual Fund Giants

There are many individuals who have made major contributions to the success and popularity of mutual funds. I'm proud and privileged to have known and worked for two of these individuals, while being a long time admirer of the third gentleman.

All three of these gentlemen are legends and true pioneers in the h story of mutual funds because their contributions were unique and essential to the widespread acceptance of mutual funds by the public. By way of introduction the following are snapshots of each of these gentlemen, which help to illustrate how they attained their well deserved fame and stature as industry legends.

Leon Levy, Oppenheimer Fund

When Leon Levy passed away in 2003 Forbes Magazine noted his passing in an obituary that described him in part as a "Wall Street genius and prolific philanthropist." That description was accurate but it doesn't come close to describing Leon. Having worked for the Oppenheimer Funds for 11 years I can tell you that he was a man devoid of pretense or hypocrisy. I believe those characteristics were part of what made him an investment genius – he did nct simply accept any of the buzz or hype that has always been so prevalent in Wall Street. He built what was arguably a premier research firm in Oppenheimer & Co. The Oppenheimer Fund was a major beneficiary of that research and a showcase of their work product as evidenced by the superior investment results enjoyed by its shareholders.

There are many factors involved in managing a mutual fund. Perhaps one of the best ways to gain some insight into how he managed the Oppenheimer Fund is to take a look back to 1975. The markets were still in the early stages of a recovery from the bear market of the early seventies when the 1975 Semi Annual Report for the fund included a question and answer interview with Leon which is reproduced here. As you will see, some of Leon's responses to questions also apply in the current investment environment and the challenges faced by investors today. As you read the interview it's important to remember that it took place more than 30 years ago. Nevertheless, there are certain fundamental points that are still applicable today. For example, bull markets vs. bear markets and when to invest; "getting even," selling at the wrong time, a mistake that some investors still make; the effects of a "market correction"; gasoline shortages and increased prices; the Dow Jones at 600; mutual funds as the "ideal investment," and the prediction that the Dow Jones Average would go to 1000. Here it is.

Semi-Annual Report, The Oppenheimer Fund

OPPENHEIMER FUND, INC.
SEMI-ANNUAL REPORT—JUNE 30, 1975

Semi-Annual Report, The Oppenheimer Fund, June 30, 1975

In April a year ago, we used these pages to excerpt a taped interview with Leon Levy, president of the Oppenheimer mutual funds, based on questions shareholders were asking at that extremely troubled time. Since stock market conditions are almost diametrically different today than they were then, a new informal dialogue has been taped. We hope you enjoy it and welcome your comments.

"Q. We've been in a very difficult recession, and the recovery is likely to be slow. How can we be having a bull market under such conditions?

LL. Well, it's an historical fact that a bull market usually anticipates an economic recovery by about six months. This bull market started in the last quarter of 1974. The recession bottomed out in the second quarter of 1975. For some while, the lead indicators of the economy have been hinting at a leveling off and reversal of the economic decline. I think it's safe to say that this bull market's head start on economic recovery is a pretty clear case of history repeating itself.

Q. Last May, for the first time in over a year, investors cashed in more mutual fund shares than they bought. How can this happen in the middle of a roaring bull market?

LL. All it means, really, is that investors who saw the value of their shares decline during the preceding bear market- and they are by no means limited to fund shareholders – are cashing them in now that shares are approaching their original cost. This is the phenomenon known as "getting even," and it unfailingly occurs in all bull markets. Unfortunately, "getting even" is a classic investor mistake. It stems from the fact that many investors believe there is some mystique to the price they paid for their stock. Of all the factors that might go into deciding whether to sell stock, cost of shares is the least relevant except, perhaps for tax purposes.

Q. I bought my shares just in time to get clobbered by the market. Now that I'm close to getting even, I suppose you're going to tell me to add to my shares rather than redeem them.

LL. Your supposition is correct. This bull market seems to have a great deal of momentum and, more than that, the potential to last a good many months more. So it doesn't make a heck of a lot of sense to cash in your shares right now. But a strong case can be made for building your share balance. I can think of very few things that cost less today than they did in 1968. But most common stocks and common stock-oriented mutual funds do. Seven years ago they were over-valued. Today, they are substantially under-valued, I think, even despite the sharp run-up since last October. Obviously the time to buy stock – and stock-type mutual funds – is when price is low relative to value.

Q. With stock prices up so sharply over such a sustained period, aren't we overdue for a severe market correction?

LL. Not necessarily. Major bull markets can last quite a while without significant interruptions. But even if one occurs, it's important to remember that it is exactly what the word suggests: an interruption. Once it is over the market begins to rise again, thus giving investors a second chance to buy stocks at attractively low prices. I might add that, even though this bull market has yet to experience the first serious correction, stock values remain attractive.

Q. Your friends jokingly describe you as a "chronic bull." How can you be so bullish all the time even when the market is at its lowest?

LL. You should hear what I call my friends sometimes. Seriously, though, over the decades, even generations, stocks have gone up in price a lot more than they've gone down. So if one has to choose between being a chronic pessimist or a chronic optimist, I think chronic optimism is the better choice. In self-defense, I should add that the degree of my optimism varies, meaning that I've been more bullish at some points than at others. My shareholder letter to you of last January is a case in point. Although the market at that time was hovering around the 600's, I suggested the Dow Jones Industrial Average would shoot up dramatically. Not many people were sticking their necks out quite that far last January. I'm still bullish now, of course, but to a different degree since a substantial portion of the market rise has already occurred.

Q. Bull markets often get their second wind when the small investor recommits his funds to common stocks. Any sign of this happening now?

LL. Mutual fund sales and odd lot sales indicate that this hasn't happened yet. The small investor usually takes a long time to get back into a market that is in a sustained bullish phase. Unfortunately, he often gets back too late to enjoy its real rewards – and maybe just in time to be victimized when the market begins to head south. I would guess that it will be many months before small investors return to the market in massive numbers.

Q. How do you tell when a bull market has peaked out?

LL. My guess is that we're many, many months away from that. But bull markets generally peak after several raises in margin requirements signs of really tight money, a booming economy with much higher employment, and indications of far more greed than fear on the part of the average investor. An increase in the number of new public issues of stock is another warning sign.

Q. Are we in for another gasoline shortage soon and if so, how would it impact the stock market?

LL. Most economists are predicting further rises in gas prices over the next year or two, but not a shortage…assuming no unforeseen developments occur. I would not expect that higher gasoline prices would have a substantive effect on the market.

Q. What's the worst investment mistake you ever made?

LL. I've been in the investment business so long, it is difficult to single out the ultimate blooper. I suppose the biggest mistake money managers make – and I'm no exception – is to resist the fact that there is a stage of the market cycle when most stocks are very overpriced. The danger is in trying to decide which stocks are exceptions at times when the exceptions are so few that the risk of guessing wrong is too high.

Q. Mutual funds have had their problems in recent years, yet you continue to regard them as ideal investments for most people. Why?

LL. The problems many mutual funds have had are generally "people" problems, not structural ones. In my opinion, there has never been an investment vehicle as ideally suited for the investor as a mutual fund. It provides professional management on a full-time basis. It broadly diversifies your capital no matter how small your investment may be. It lets you know at all times how your investment is doing. It supplies you with any number of useful services for expanding or making use of your investment dollars. It's about as liquid an investment as you're likely to find. And finally, while share prices do fluctuate, the probabilities are great that the per share value of most mutual funds will be higher at the end of any 10-year period than at its beginning.

Q. Which stock groups do you see fueling a continuation of this bull market?

LL. I think stocks of companies that have been hurt more than most by the recession, yet whose underlying long-term growth prospects are good, are likely to lead the next leg of the bull market. Producers and sellers of capital goods should be big beneficiaries as well as manufacturers of intermediate services and products.

Q. Although mutual funds have been promoted as a way to off-set long-term inflation, that's hardly been the case since 1970. Why so?

LL. It depends, I think, on what you mean by "long-term." Guided by the kinds of investment time goals most fund shareowners seem to have, I look at "long-term" as meaning 10 years or more. And in virtually every 10-year period of the almost two centuries since stocks have been traded in this country, stock prices have at least stayed even with and very often outpaced, inflationary trends. The last ten years have been a rare exception.

Q. If, as you say, this bull market is likely to be both sustained and steep, can you tell us how sustained and how steep?

LL. Well, there are just too many variables to make flat-out forecasts. But given the intensity of this market and the reverse intensity of the bear market that preceded it, it would not surprise me at all if stock prices in general continued to climb through most of 1976. If that should happen, it's a good bet that we would end up with a Dow Jones Industrial Average substantially above 1,000.

Leon Levy had the ability to use plain language relative to investing that was not the conventional method of communicating with shareholders in the investment business at that time. I believe that ability was a major factor in the success enjoyed by Oppenheimer Fund shareholders and why the organization achieved the success it enjoys to this day. We need more Leon Levys.

Templeton Mutual Funds Shareholder Services Guide

John Templeton - Templeton Funds

The fund industry was blessed with another pioneer in the person of John Templeton who filled that role in a new and different manner. But Templeton's was not an overnight success story. In fact he had sold his investment advisory business in 1969, including the funds then under management, left the United States and moved to the Bahamas, where he still resided until his death in 2008. The Funds were acquired and renamed the Lexington Funds. However, Templeton Growth Fund with total assets approximating $7 million, was not included in the sale apparently because the Lexington people felt that since it was a Canadian chartered fund, it would not be widely accepted by Americans. So John took the fund to the Bahamas where he continued to manage it with virtually no new sales. A few years later a fund industry executive, John Galbraith, who had been with Lexington, met with John Templeton and they agreed that Galbraith would organize a marketing effort for the fund in the U. S. That was the beginning of one of the greatest success stories in the fund business, a collaborative effort that developed into what was arguably one of the most successful partnerships in the history of mutual funds.

Galbraith was a veteran of World War II where he served as a Marine Corps pilot, flying DC3s in the Pacific. After the War he became a pilot for TransWorld Airlines (TWA) and eventually became a CPA, joined Waddell & Reed, a mutual fund group in Kansas City, MO, and subsequently joined the Lexington Funds in New Jersey. John Galbraith is the most knowledgeable, honest and trustworthy individual I have ever met and he enjoys that reputation throughout the fund industry. After he and Templeton agreed on a business partnership, John began building one of the most successful fund marketing and administrative organizations in the country. This eventually grew into full responsibility for sales, marketing, accounting and administrative services for all U. S. Templeton Fund shareholders.

It was a simple business arrangement, combining the two ingredients for success in the fund business. John Templeton focused his full attention on investment management of the mutual funds while Galbraith assumed all other business responsibilities for what became the Templeton Group of Funds, which had grown to +$17 billion prior to its acquisition by the Franklin Funds of California.

I was a beneficiary of that successful partnership when, after several years with the Lexington Funds, John Galbraith asked me to join the organization in 1986 as president and CEO of Templeton Funds Management Corp., the business manager for all U. S. Templeton Funds. Headquartered in St. Petersburg, FL we served all Templeton Fund investors – which grew to more than 800,000 shareholders.

How did the $7 million Templeton Growth Fund grow to be the premier international mutual fund organization? That's a story worth knowing because it was Templeton's pioneering effort involving investing in global markets that had been overlooked by most fund management companies. The goal was to seek out international investment opportunities by not limiting himself to just one country. Once again he had a remarkable ability to communicate his investment approach to the public – and they listened.

At Templeton we published a "Shareholder Service Guide" which included a commentary from John Templeton that we felt would help educate our shareholders about their investments and John's approach to investing. As you read this excerpt, note the clarity of his strategy and the compelling logic of the "Templeton Approach."

"At Templeton we have never been able to predict market cycles. However, we firmly believe that astute investors not only can live with market cycles, but can potentially profit by them if they use common sense when investing."

That was not just meaningless rhetoric. John continued describing the "Templeton Approach."

"We have no formulas.
We have no magic.
We don't know any way to beat the market.
We simply try to use common sense."

That common sense approach to investing was explained in a description of the "Templeton Approach to Investing," which was rigorously applied in the management of all Templeton Funds as follows:

"For 49 years, superior investment results have been achieved using the Templeton methods. The Templeton approach constantly seeks to improve its methods since our experience has demonstrated that every single investment selection formula will become obsolete, especially if it becomes too popular. Thomas Alva Edison said, "If you are still doing anything the same way as 20 years ago, then there must be a better method.

The Templeton Approach has always been flexible, open-minded and innovative. To remain ahead of the profession, Templeton Chartered Financial Analysts are continually devising and experimenting with five or more new investment selection methods for possible future use in helping various investors achieve their long-term goals. Sometimes several methods are used for the same fund in order to take advantage of rapidly changing opportunities in various nations and various types of investment assets.

We were pioneers in quantitative security analysis, in bargain hunting and worldwide investing because we believe that you cannot achieve results superior to other security analysts if you buy the same securities at the same time as other security analysts.

Under present conditions, well chosen stocks may provide the most effective, most flexible means to produce the greatest possible total return."

SOME OF THE METHODS USED BY TEMPLETON TO SELECT INVESTMENTS

"First, we are usually bargain hunters. We search for bargains. Now what are bargains? A bargain is a stock selling at a price that is unusually low in relation to our appraisal of its value. We appraise the value of individual stocks and find that some stocks are selling above our appraisal. Others are selling below. And we find some selling at much less than half what we think they're worth. In fact, there have been a good many times in past years when we bought stocks as low as one quarter of what we judged them to be worth.

Now, not everybody stops to think that you can't get a stock at a bargain price when it's popular. If you want to buy the same stocks that other people are buying, you are not likely to have a superior record. When many people are buying a stock, it is not likely to be a bargain – they have already pushed the price up. The only hope you've got to produce a superior investment record is to do something different from what the crowd is doing.

Second, we normally search worldwide. We believe that is common sense….and it has helped our record quite a lot. There were times when there weren't many bargains in the U.S.

It just stands to reason that if you're looking all over the world, you will find better bargains than if you're looking in one nation. The United States is so large and we're so accustomed to thinking of our own nation, that it really is unusual to know much about stocks anywhere else. But let's suppose you lived in Switzerland…would you dream of having one hundred percent of your assets in one country?

A basic principle of investing is to diversify; and so it is wise to diversify amongst nations, in addition to diversifying amongst industries and types of stocks or securities. There is almost always some stock market that is going to do better than the American market. So worldwide diversification seems to be only common sense.

Third, we are flexible. The fact that we've done well in an area for three or four years is a reason for thinking that maybe it is no longer the best place to be, that there may be somewhere else we can get better bargains. So, whenever we've been in one particular type of security or one particular nation for a while, we try very hard to look around the world to find something different to put your money into for the next several years.

Now, we're not always right; sometimes we're wrong. When we sell one stock in order to buy another, we know that, at least one-third of the time, we're going to be sorry we made that change. A year later we look back and the stock we sold in some cases did better than the stock we bought. That's the very nature of the business. Because of that, there always will be some bad years mixed in with the good. "

"It is our conviction that well-chosen common stocks selected with these principles in mind will provide the most effective, most flexible means for staying ahead of inflation. Since our approach to investing is characterized by common sense and patience, then the hallmark of our Funds must be consistent, long term, superior investment results that we have been fortunate to achieve in the past."

I'm not familiar with every money manager in the history of mutual funds, or the literature that all mutual funds provide to their shareholders. However, I do know that not many investment managers and funds have taken the time or made the effort to communicate their investment philosophy and approach as was done by the Templeton Fund Group. That's why we need more John Galbraiths and John Templetons.

Author's note: John Templeton passed away on July 8, 2008 at the age of 95. In his *Forbes Magazine* column of September 1, 2008, John W. Rogers, Jr., paid tribute to Mr. Templeton by recalling perhaps the most important principle of his "common sense" approach to investing:

"The time of maximum pessimism is the best time to buy."

In light of the current state of securities markets there are few more appropriate reminders of Mr. Templeton's investment wisdom.

John C. Bogle - Vanguard Funds

The third pioneer who took a different approach has proven to be remarkably successful thanks to his foresight and persistence against deep skepticism and some derision from those who should have known better. John Bogle founded the Vanguard Group in 1975, during a very difficult period for mutual funds. Bogle's quest took on what was the conventional wisdom of the time when money managers then as now sought to outperform a broad measure of stocks represented by an index of those stocks. The Dow Jones Average and the Standard & Poor's Stock Index (S&P 500) were the indexes against which most funds measured their performance. If you could outperform the index then the cost of a management fee would be justified. Today the number of indexes has grown significantly in what seems to be a search for an index that can be consistently bested by a manager. That search continues to this day.

My guess, and it's only a guess, is that Bogle may have wondered why anyone would try to best an index of stocks when you could own that index by buying the stocks that comprise the index in the form of a mutual fund. One of the advantages of this approach was the ease of putting together a diverse group of stocks representing a cross section of the U. S. stock market, holding that portfolio of stocks, while avoiding buying and selling individual positions in an attempt to predict future prices of the stocks. This obviously would reduce transaction costs whenever a stock was sold and replaced by another stock. Additionally, by owning a "fixed" number of securities, it was not necessary to employ an army of portfolio managers and securities analysts. The effects of this approach resulted in significant cost savings to shareholders of the fund, which has proven itself ever since John Bogle founded the Vanguard Funds in 1975.

But Bogle did more than build a better mouse trap. The Vanguard Funds also served as an example that wide diversification and lower costs could also dramatically improve performance results, much to the chagrin of many in the industry. I don't mind admitting that I was one of those who scoffed at the concept. I had always believed that lower costs were not the criteria for good, if not better performance. Of course my perspective was the result of my experience with Oppenheimer Funds and Templeton Funds which had well above average long term performance records. I was convinced that the human element would prevail in the attempt to achieve superior performance. However, that was not the case with the overwhelming majority of mutual funds.

Bogle proved his point times over and his address before the Practising Law Institute ("PLI") in 2000 was an eye opener for many in the industry. Having first served on a fund board in the 1970s I was particularly pleased to see how Bogle concluded his remarks in that speech with "10 Commandments for Fund Directors," which is spot on. Many readers might be seeing this for the first time, including many independent fund directors. Mutual fund investors can take heart that someone finally had the courage to "go public" and recognize that the emperor had no clothes. That's what these "10 Commandments" proved by spelling out what appeared to have been overlooked by many in the industry. This excellent advice targeted to independent mutual fund directors was a long time in coming if for no other reason than it made a point of the sole reason for the existence of independent directors – to represent the interests of their fund's shareholders who are in fact their employers. Here are Bogle's "Commandments" which comprised the conclusion of his address to PLI in 2000.

Reprinted with permission of The Bogle Financial Markets Research Center.

"10 Commandments for fund directors"

1. **Thou shalt retain thine own independent counsel.**

   Recommended by the Securities and Exchange Commission, this step seems so obvious and so essential that it is hard to imagine why it hasn't been mandatory ever since this industry began in 1924. Just imagine, in any other business, the anomaly of a firm being represented not by its own counsel but by counsel for its largest supplier of services, who depends on it for its very existence. Yes, I read all the arguments against independent counsel – there aren't enough lawyers, they won't be as experienced, they won't be the best, they won't have enough financial incentives, and, believe it or not, in the face of the failings I've described, the industry (says it) "is not aware of any problems that have arisen as a result of current practices." Although I have no doubt that the present proposal can be sharpened, these makeweight arguments must be disregarded and the independent counsel proposal implemented.

2. **Thou shalt elect an independent director as thy fund chairman.**

   The present fund chairman, by and large, is chairman or president of the fund's management company. But it must be clear that the management company is a business corporation, and the primary responsibility of its chairman is to keep the business running soundly and to earn the largest possible profit for its owners. The fund chairman's primary responsibility is, in a sense, precisely the same...but for a completely different constituency: to keep the fund running soundly and to earn the largest possible profit for its owners. The two responsibilities directly conflict: The more the manager charges in fees, the less remains for fund shareholders. Only by separating these two distinct responsibilities can we possibly begin the process of bringing management fees and profit margins under control. After all, when the fund chairman negotiates fees with the management company chairman, and they are the same person, we hardly can expect shareholders to come first. Warren Buffett put it perfectly: "Negotiating with oneself rarely produces a barroom brawl."

3. **Thou shalt get the facts about performance.**

Demand full, fair comparisons. Consider risks, peers and appropriate market indexes. Look at cumulative returns over extended periods, and don't forget after-tax returns.

4. **Thou shalt get the facts about costs.**

For each fund you serve as a director, follow the money. Review the Adviser's profit and loss statement. How much did the fund pay? How much was spent on investment management? How much on marketing and administration? (Press hard on exactly how those expenditures on advertising – directly or indirectly, through 12(b)-1 plans – benefit the shareholder.) What was the manager's pretax profit margin – before and after marketing costs – on each fund you serve? On all funds in the complex? This information should be readily accessible. You can't intelligently consider fund fees without knowing where the money goes.

5. **Thou shalt compare the dollar fees thy fund pays with those of competitors.**

This industry has done a marvelous job at one thing: placing public focus on fee rates rather than the fee dollars. It brags that the cost of mutual fund ownership has fallen to 1.35% of assets, from 2.26%, since 1980. With the total dollar costs paid by all funds (excluding sales charges) soaring to $65 billion in 1999, from $800 million in 1980, it takes some kind of brass to make that argument. Expense ratio comparisons are fine as far as they go, but they don't go far enough. It is dollars that fund shareholders pay and dollars that the managers extract. A 1% expense ratio may look low – indeed it is almost universally acclaimed as low – but on a $25 billion fund, it produces $250 million for the manager every year, $1 billion over four years. Make sure you know how the dollars your fund spends compare with the dollars spent by its peers.

6. **Thou shalt challenge thy fee consultants.**

   Many fund managers retain fund consultants to provide comparative data to the board. But like executive compensation consultants, fund consultants know what their job is: to justify existing compensation (fee) levels and to provide a basis for compensation (fee) increases. So demand that the consultants calculate dollar fees as well as fee rates. While you're about it, demand that they include data for index funds and data for funds run by differently structured (low cost) fund organizations.

7. **Thou shalt keep an eagle eye on portfolio turnover.**

   Consider the level of fund turnover and demand to see the attendant costs of brokerage commissions and demand to see the attendant costs of brokerage commissions and market impact, the amount of gains realized, the extent of short-term gains and the dollars-and-cents burden in unnecessary federal, state and local taxes borne by shareholders. Find out how turnover affected performance: Did it help? Did it hurt? By how much? Ask for a simple examination of the results of the portfolio held at the year's outset, assuming that no changes have been made all year. Ask for an explanation of the frequent rotation of portfolio managers and demand to know the extent and cost of anticipated portfolio changes when a new manager is appointed.

8. **Thou shalt not ignore incentive fees.**

   We all – fund officials, directors, managers, shareholders – expect, or at least hope for, outstanding performance. Don't pay for expectations or hopes. Pay for achievement, a standard easily accomplished by adopting a fee schedule that awards premium fees for performance that exceeds agreed-upon benchmarks and assesses penalty fees for performance that falls short. While the equity of such a system seems self-evident, incentive fees have almost vanished from the mutual fund scene.

9. **Thou shalt consider redemption fees.**

   One of the easiest and fairest ways to mitigate the use of mutual funds as speculative vehicles for short-term gains, and to return them to their traditional use as investment vehicles for long-term accumulation, is the imposition of reasonable redemption fees. Today equity fund redemptions are running at an astonishing 50% annualized rate. Yet, largely as the result of a redemption fee of 2% in the first year and 1% for the next four years, the funds in the industry's first tax-managed series, now in their sixth year, have an annual redemption rate running just 5%. Surely there are lessons to be learned from this potential 90% reduction in redemption activity. (Alas, even as it effectively excludes short-term investors, the redemption fee retards marketing. So you serve the shareholders at the expense of the manager.)

10. **Thou shalt evaluate thy funds as if it were thine own money.**

Bring this attitude to your work as a director: Is this the way my money should be run? Is my performance satisfactory? How about my tax efficiency? How about continuity of my portfolio management? How much would I be willing to pay for this service? When performance lags, how patient would I be? When would I terminate my own fiduciary relationship and move to another? In all, behave as if you were a large shareholder and assume that the assets were important to you. Better yet, actually own shares of the funds you serve as trustee. The investment of a significant portion of your own assets in the funds you serve is the single most meaningful step you can take in demonstrating both your commitment and your independence.

Those are hardly radical changes, and most require no new laws or regulations. A statement of these principles by the Investment Company Institute, or the newly formed Mutual Fund Directors Education Council, or by the SEC – or even a speech by a senior SEC official – would start the ball rolling, and it would not soon stop. It's high time to begin the process.

It's important to note that four of these "Commandments" have been implemented in some form or other since Bogle made his comments. Those four relate to independent counsel, independent board chairs, redemption fees and ownership of fund shares by directors. My guess is that more than a few of the remaining "Commandments" have also been implemented to some extent by many fund boards. Bogle also made reference to the inordinate rate of mutual fund redemptions, which may have been the precursor of what became the market timing scandal a few years later.

I cannot imagine a single mutual fund shareholder among the current 94 million investors who own mutual funds objecting to any of these "Commandments." In fact, I would imagine any shareholder who is not comatose or brain dead would wonder why these principles are even a subject of discussion. After all, aren't independent mutual fund directors their representatives? Aren't they often described as the "watchdogs" of the mutual fund industry? Don't they work for the shareholders? Aren't they paid handsomely for what some have described as a part time job? Those questions are not meant to be disrespectful or insensitive to the many reputable directors on fund boards today. However, it's distinctly possible that not enough independent directors truly understand their fiduciary role as the shareholder's representative – even employee. Let's never forget that the directors are paid from the total assets of the mutual funds they serve. The management company bears none of the costs of the independent directors, including their annual retainer fees, travel and lodging costs to and from regular meetings, including industry conferences and emeritus programs (where they exist) that provide for the continuation of a director's fees after retirement, usually at a reduced rate. Therefore, a very strong case can be made that in some cases shareholders are not always served commensurate with the cost of retaining the directors whose sole job is to represent them, and only them.

Yes, John Bogle was truly the pioneer of a unique concept in the mutual fund industry that proved its value over time. In addition, he has also done an outstanding job of what could be described as serving as the "conscience" of the mutual fund industry.

Levy, Templeton and Bogle, all legends, were directly responsible for the growth and acceptance of mutual funds. Their wisdom is even more important today for both fund shareholders and independent directors. As the industry faces new challenges the principles they espoused can be the foundation for continued success and growth provided that independent directors, investment advisors and regulators fully understand their respective obligations and responsibilities to fund shareholders. The following chapters provide evidence that we can learn from the past and secure the place of mutual funds as the best alternative for investors to achieve financial independence.

Chapter Two - Lies, Damned Lies and Annuities

Concerning annuities, the more things change, the more they remain the same. The history of annuities demonstrates beyond the shadow of a doubt that they may be appropriate for a very narrow, defined group of people with a precise goal – usually the goal of not "outliving their incomes." This need invariably requires a fixed stream of income, that will not be reduced – or increased, i.e., "guaranteed." Someone once described a "guarantee" as follows: the issuer (insurance company or bank certificates of deposit) guarantees that no matter how much they make with the money you give to them, they guarantee they will never pay you more than x%. It's as simple as that. In fact, it's one of the reasons why most insurance companies and banks survive in a competitive environment.

Do annuities "work?" Sure. You can receive an income you can't "outlive," but at what cost? Regardless of how long you live, the dollars you receive each year will be worth less and less, thanks to inflation. The real question is will an annuity provide a steady stream of income that will keep pace with inflation – the relentless increase in the cost of living? How will an annuity protect your "guaranteed" monthly income from declining in purchasing power? A long time ago, insurance companies ran full page advertisements in popular magazines touting annuities as the answer to retirement needs. The following are four examples over a 31 year period that provide an eye opening revelation – these are exact replicas of those ads with the names of the insurance companies deleted. It's not certain if these kinds of ads appeared after 1966, but they might have. However, you won't find these kinds of ads running today. In fact they haven't appeared in some time, for obvious reasons.

Take a look at the 4 ads on the following pages that appeared in 1935, 1939, 1955 and 1966. As you read each of these advertisements you'll see what looks like a sensible approach to investing for retirement. Then we'll review the pertinent text in each ad.

On $100 a Month

You can live in the famous HOT SPRINGS *Region*

● Of the many attractive localities, where it is possible to live on $100 a month, Hot Springs, Ark., has a special appeal. By the time you are ready to retire from active work, its famous hot spring baths might prove a great boon to you physically.

Here in a land of scenic beauty—a favorite playground of the American people—and where there's just enough cold weather to make it welcome—you could have a cozy home, and live comfortably on a very moderate income.

That's the kind of life you can lead, when you're ready to retire. Whether it's Hot Springs, or another of the nation's wonder spots—or perhaps your own home town—it would be possible to live comfortably on $100 a month. And what a great satisfaction it is to know that at 55, or later, you can have that income, or more, for the rest of your life! That's what you can do if you own ████████ ████ *retirement insurance.*

Decide now that you will have a worry-proof income for your less productive years . . . a sure, dependable check every month from one of America's oldest, strongest life insurance companies. Mail us the coupon below for the booklet—"EARNED LEISURE." Play safe with your future!

Without obligation, please send me your booklet "EARNED LEISURE."

Name ....

Address ....

City .... Age ....

T-2- -25- 35

The assets of the ████████████ *as reported to state insurance departments, now total a billion dollars—a great estate administered for the mutual welfare and protection of more than 600,000 policyholders.*

An advertisement that will help you get the things you want

IF YOU WANT an income for life—that will support you after you reach 55 or 60—here are facts you should know.

Let's assume you are 40 now. Perhaps you are saving regularly—hoping you will have enough money some day to let you retire.

But will you? Let's see. In order to retire on $150 a month, you will have to save $45,000 and invest it at 4%. If you can get only 3%, you must save $60,000 to get the same income! Can you set aside that much in the next 15 years? It's a good way to retire, but it takes too much money for most of us.

That's why the ▮▮▮▮▮ Retirement Income Plan was started. It is now being used by over 38,000 people. Through this Plan, you can get a guar-

anteed income for life, you can guard against emergencies, you can avoid investment risks and uncertainties. And you can do all this with much less money than other investment plans require.

Get $150 a Month for Life

Here's how it works. Suppose you are 40 now, and you qualify for the following ▮▮▮▮▮▮▮▮ Plan which pays you $150 a month for life, beginning at age 55. Here is what the Plan provides:

1. A check for $150 when you reach 55, and a check for $150 every month thereafter as long as you live.

2. A life income to your wife in case of your death before age 55, and

3. A monthly Disability Income to you if, before age 55, total disability stops your earning power for six months or more.

Of course, you need not be 40 now. You may be older or younger. The income need not be $150 a month. It can be any amount from $10 to $200 a month or

more. And you can have it start at any age: 55, 60, 65 or 70. Similar Plans are available to women.

You don't have to be rich to retire this way. Since you start the Plan 15 years or more before you need the retirement income, you receive all the benefits of compound interest, long-range investments and *mutual* operation. You get a retirement income for far less money than ordinary investments require.

Send for Free Booklet

Let us mail you an important booklet giving the complete facts about the Retirement Income Plan. In a simple, illustrated way, this booklet shows you exactly how thousands of people are providing their own life incomes, tells you how the Plan protects against such emergencies as death or disability. Send the coupon below and we will mail you this booklet without cost or obligation. Discover for yourself the secret of getting your own life income!

COPYRIGHT 1939, BY ▮▮▮▮▮▮▮▮ INSURANCE COMPANY

May 15, 1939

Retire in 15 Years - Advertisement

How I retired in 15 years with $250 a month

November 21 1955

"Sometimes I have to smile. It's hard to believe that I'm retired today—retired with a life income. You see, I never had more than my salary, never inherited a dime, or even had luck in business! Yet a check for $250 a month arrives on the dot. And I'm my own boss for keeps!

"I left the office two years ago. And when I explained how I was doing it, though I was only 55, more than one of my friends said he only wished I'd told him years before. He'd be retiring, too.

"There's only one secret. Seventeen years ago, back in 1938, I had saved a little money. So I went into partnership with a friend. We thought it was going to pay off very well.

"Well, it didn't. But it was the most profitable investment I ever made. It showed me that there was no easy way for *me*, with *my* limited experience, to make a lot of money.

"I had to find a way that was systematic and sure. I was 40 then.

"It was shortly after that that I read an advertisement that told of a modern way for people of moderate means to retire. It didn't call for any great capital. It simply required fifteen or twenty working years ahead. One thing I liked particularly was that my family was protected with life insurance from the first day I took out my plan. (This, surely, was better than any ordinary savings method!) And the income was guaranteed—whatever happened to the business world—each month, every month, from the day it began as long as I live. The plan was called the ▮▮▮▮▮▮▮ Retirement Income Plan.

"The ad offered more information. So, I mailed in the coupon. It brought a booklet describing the various plans.

"Soon after, I applied and qualified for a ▮▮▮▮▮▮▮ Plan. And from that day on I've honestly felt like a rich man. Because I knew I wouldn't just simply live and work and die. I had a future I'd really enjoy. And that's what I'm doing today—with many, many thanks to my ▮▮▮▮ ▮▮▮▮ check for $250 a month that means financial independence for life."

Send for Free Booklet

This story is typical. Assuming you start at a young enough age, you can plan to have an income of $10 a month to $3,000 a year or more—beginning at age 55, 60, 65 or older. Send the coupon and receive, by mail and without charge, a booklet which tells about ▮▮▮▮▮▮▮ Plans. Similar plans are available for women—and for employee pension programs. Don't put it off. Send for your copy now.

COPYRIGHT 1955, BY ▮▮▮▮▮▮▮ INSURANCE COMPANY

Retire in 15 Years - Advertisement

Vol. 60. No. 3

January 21 1966

"How we retired in 15 years with $300 a month"

"Look at us! We're retired and having the time of our lives. A fish story? It sure isn't! Let me tell you about it.

"I started thinking about retiring in 1950. Nancy thought I was silly. It all seemed so far away. 'And besides,' she said, 'it makes me feel old.' It didn't seem silly to me, though. We'd just spent the afternoon with Nancy's aunt and uncle. Uncle Will had turned 65 during the war, and, by 1945, his working days were over.

"Now, life seemed to be standing still for them. They couldn't take even the short weekend trips that their friends could easily afford; they couldn't visit their children as often as they'd like.

"A pretty grim existence, I thought. But why? He'd had a good job. Then Nancy reminded me . . . they'd never planned ahead. During her uncle's working years, his paycheck was spent almost as soon as it arrived.

"Fortunately, they had put some money aside for a rainy day. But they hadn't planned ahead enough to make those retirement days sunny!

"Not for me, I decided. When it's time for me to retire, I want to be able to do the things we've always dreamed of doing instead of counting every penny.

"I showed Nancy a ▮▮▮▮ advertisement I'd seen in Life magazine a week or so before. It described their retirement income plan, telling how a man of 40 could retire in 15 years with a guaranteed income of $300 or more for life!

"Nancy agreed it was a great idea. The thought of retiring at 55 didn't make her feel old at all! So I filled out the coupon that day and sent it right off.

"A few days later the booklet describing the ▮▮▮▮▮ Plans arrived. I picked the right one for us and signed up right away. Three months ago my first check arrived—right on time.

"Last month we moved down here to Florida, and we love it. Nancy looks great with her tan, and she's thrilled at the thought of keeping it all year long!

"My tan suits me fine, but I'm really hooked on the fish. Whether I catch one a day or ten (or none), I'm having the time of my life, because we saved for a sunny day with ▮▮▮▮▮."

Send for free booklet

This story is typical. Assuming you start early enough, you can plan to have an income of from $50 to $300 a month or more—beginning at age 55, 60, 65 or older. Send the coupon and receive by mail, without charge or obligation, a booklet which tells about ▮▮▮▮▮ Plans. Similar plans are available for women—and for Employee Pension Programs. Send for your free copy now. In 15 years you'll be glad you did!

Retire in 15 Years - Advertisement

<u>February 25, 1935</u>

"On $100 a month you can live in the famous Hot Springs Region."

"...and live comfortably on a very moderate income."

"...it would be possible to live comfortably on $100 a month"

"...you can have that income, or more, for the rest of your life!"

"...you will have worry-proof income..."

<u>May 15, 1939</u> (4 years later)

"If you want an income for life that will support you after you reach 55 or 60..."

"...you can get a guaranteed income for life, you can guard against emergencies, you can avoid investment risks and uncertainties."

"Get $150 a month for life"

"You don't have to be rich to retire this way."

<u>November 21, 1955</u> (16 years later)

"How I retired in 15 years with $250 a month"

"...retired with a life income."

"and I'm my own boss for keeps!"

"And the income was guaranteed...each month, every month, from the day it began as long as I live."

"...check for $250 a month that means financial independence for life."

January 21, 1966 (11 years later)

"...How we retired in 15 years with $300 a month"

" When it's time for me to retire, I want to be able to do the things we've always dreamed of doing instead of counting every penny."

"...with a guaranteed income of $300 or more for life!"

Do you see a pattern here? Over a 31 year period the ads boasted of a guaranteed $100 a month in 1935, then $150 a month four years later in 1939, which is an increase of 50%! In 1955 the "guaranteed" ad promised $250 a month and then $300 a month 11 years later in 1966, this time the increased monthly income promised was *"only"* 20% higher! There's a message here that must be understood – inflation is built into our economic system. Rather than provide a long history of inflationary increases in the U.S., perhaps the best example is your answer to the following question:

"Do you want to make more money next year than you made last year?"

Unless you're among the mega wealthy, your answer has to be "Yes." And that's the key to the problem we face – if we want our income to increase each year, the price of the goods and services we produce must increase. It's a no brainer. Armed with that simple fact of life, what is the only sensible avenue to your financial independence? It's simple, you have to continue to earn money and save it by investing in a vehicle that reflects the inevitable price increases in the goods and services we consume.

Is that vehicle a sure thing? No. Is it guaranteed? No. Is it free? No. Is it Social Security? Hell No! However, if you're certain that the cost of food, energy, electricity, clothing, autos, medical services and taxes will *not* increase, you have it made. Your problems are solved. Just ask anyone you know who is retired if they agree with you. That's why we have to look at the numbers. Those numbers are simple. On average we can expect real inflation to increase 3% a year. Taxes could cost you at least 3% a year, including income taxes, social security taxes and sales taxes – and that's probably a low estimate. But let's add 3 and 3 for a total of a 6% increase a year, which means if you do nothing your *purchasing power* could go down each year on average 6%, i.e., your one dollar will decline in *purchasing power* to 94 cents. How many years of doing nothing do you think it will take to put you on welfare and food stamps?

Need more evidence? The February 27, 2008 edition of *The Wall Street Journal* carried an op-ed, *"Inflation May Be Worse Than We Think,"* by David Ranson, head of research at H. C. Wainwright & Co. Economics. As Mr. Ranson explains,

"Why does this (inflation) matter? The accompanying graph shows how rapidly the purchasing power of income declines from an ongoing inflation of 4%. After nine years an income of $100,000 is worth only $70,000. After 17 years its purchasing has been cut in half, and after 30 years by about 70%."

With life expectancies steadily increasing this is a challenge faced by everyone. Take a look at the graph and do the math. Then get to work on facing the inevitable.

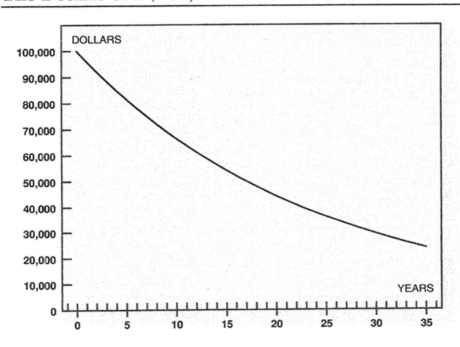

The Decline of a $100,000 Income at 4 Percent Inflation

Decline of $100K

In reading this chart you can see that based on the historical average rate of inflation of about 3%, a retired person's purchasing power is reduced by half in 23 years. However, if the rate of inflation increases to 4%, purchasing power is cut in half in 18 years. Inflation is not a pretty picture.

It doesn't have to be that way. You can begin to work at avoiding that scenario by finding an investment that makes sense, is affordable, will be managed by some of the best investment professionals in the world today, people it's unlikely that you could afford to have working for you. They are the people who will search worldwide to find profitable investments that have the potential to grow more than 6% a year on average, which will help you offset inflation and build your investment capital. Is it guaranteed? Absolutely not. But it does give you a chance to win the fight against the decline in the purchasing power of your dollars, whereas guaranteed investments almost assuredly will result in a loss of purchasing over a period of time. You don't have to be a rocket scientist to figure it out. But you have to put the odds on your side, which is simply not possible with guaranteed investments.

So let's accept the fact that guarantees like annuities, bank CDs, etc. actually guarantee the erosion of your purchasing power, your standard of living and your financial independence. However, if you have a "chicken little" complex and you absolutely must have a guarantee as part of your investment program, then limit "guarantees" to 10% of your investment portfolio. As the future unfolds, you'll congratulate yourself on being smart enough to have avoided risking your financial well being in an investment that is guaranteed to always pay off…for banks and insurance companies.

Seminar Soldiers – A Potential Train Wreck

Maybe you've received one of those invitations for a "free" lunch or dinner and a discussion of "investments." If you haven't received them but you have retired parents, it's quite likely that they have received them, frequently. The similarity of the language used in these invitations is pretty interesting. Here are some examples:

> **"Safely make more money in turbulent markets"**

> **"Eliminate risk from your investments"**

> **"Considerably increase your income"**

"Increase income, reduce taxes and guarantee you'll never run out of money without market risk or fees"

"Extract hundreds if not thousands of dollars out of your IRA, completely free of taxes over your lifetime"

"How you can avoid taking required minimum distributions even if you're over age 70-1/2"

"How you can benefit from the performance of the markets without market risk or fees"

"Learn to reduce your tax bill; recover your investment losses; avoid paying taxes on your Social Security; maximize asset protection and tax relief"

"No Cost...No Obligation"

Wow! After reading these "invitations" the first thing that should come to mind is why are they willing to give me a "free" lunch or dinner? If they can do only half of what's advertised, people should be lined up outside these "experts" offices clamoring for their presumed "expertise." So what's going on here?

First let's agree – there's no such thing as a "free lunch," or dinner. In fact such "free" events can be pretty expensive depending on how persuasive the host is, and how gullible you are.

In almost all cases these are billed as either "Investment Seminars" or "Estate Planning Seminars." Of course some of these seminars might be informative. On the other hand, they may be worth exactly what they "cost" you, or worse. The fact is that some of these gigs may be far more expensive than you dreamed, especially when they involve insurance based products. It's probably a safe bet that most experienced investors do not consider insurance based products as investments. Everyone knows that they should have adequate life insurance to prepare for premature death or disability. That just makes sense. However, when making an investment everyone should know that all investments involve an element of risk – they can go up or down in value. While real investments can't protect or "guarantee" against loss, they do offer the potential for reasonable gains over time. But if you're trying to double your money over a short period of time your best bet is Las Vegas – at least you might have fun while trying.

What about our "free lunch" friends? What are they selling -- and you can bet they're selling something. The bait is usually avoiding taxes or reducing estate taxes to which fewer and fewer investors are subject. However, the appeal of "tax-free income" and "guaranteed returns without stock market risk" should cause your internal caution lights to start blinking, big time. What to do? First, beware of several important factors, including cost, liquidity and access to your money, <u>without penalties</u>. We know that bank CDs are guaranteed by the FDIC subject to a maximum dollar amount, and they will mature after a specific period of time, or a maturity date. But if you have to take your money out before that time you are subject to a penalty. That's only fair since you're getting a specific return on your money provided you keep it there for a specific period of time, which you know when you buy the CD.

In too many cases the speakers at these "free" food deals are insurance product salesmen, who earn very handsome commissions on different kinds of annuity products and often conveniently "forget" to explain some of the fine print in insurance contracts, especially those involving annuity products. You should know that there are a number of different kinds of annuities and not all are appropriate for older investors, the targeted audience for these "freebies." For example, you can buy an annuity that "guarantees" a stream of income for life or for a specific period of time. However, should your circumstances change your options may be severely limited, and very costly. What happens if you need your money? That's when you learn the real meaning of "free," based on stiff withdrawal penalties. In addition, when you die, whatever principal you "invested" can be "inherited" by the insurance company – and they won't even show up for your funeral – which means there might be nothing available for your survivors. Figure it out – that's not "free." So how can they afford those "free" lunches and dinners? The math is simple. If they can get 100 people to attend these functions during a one week period and they only sell one $100,000 annuity (not a large amount of money for today's seniors) the commission could be 10%, or higher. That's $10,000. If the cost of the freebie is $15 per person, that's $1,500. Therefore, they can collect a net of $8,500 on a single sale! Not a bad return on their investment. Now you know why you're getting a "freebie." And remember, one sale out of a hundred prospects is not impossible, and a good salesman can do better than that.

What to do? If you really need that free meal, go for it. But if you care about your finances be very careful of what looks like it's too good to be true, because it's almost always just that – too good to be true!

However, if you do attend one of these gigs, be sure the sponsor is a major brokerage house or a local independent investment broker because then you know you're dealing with a company that is regulated by either the New York Stock Exchange or the National Association of Securities Dealers. The regulatory function of both these organizations has been combined and is now known as the Financial Industry Regulatory Authority ("FINRA"). Why should that matter to you? Primarily because you then have the opportunity to check out the "financial adviser" (or whatever they call themselves). You should also know that anyone who is registered with the Exchange or the Association is finger printed as a requirement of their license to sell securities. And there's a reason for that – to protect the investing public.

Additional information about investment scams is available in an online booklet on the SEC's website: www.sec.gov/investor/seniors.shtml. Attendees should also ask the speaker/sponsor for their "CRD" number (Central Registration Depositary), a computer database jointly owned by state regulators and FINRA. All licensed securities representatives, regardless of the titles they assign themselves, have a unique CRD number. Once you have that number you can access any record of disciplinary incidents on the Internet and learn if the individual or the firm has a disciplinary record that you should know about. You can also call a "hotline" for this purpose, 800-289-9999, and there's no cost for this information - it really is free! If no CRD Number is available, then eat if you must, but get the hell out of there as fast as possible. And you don't have to leave a tip.

Finally, don't - do not - rely on "guaranteed investments" to solve your future financial requirements. The so-called guarantees don't work, never have, and never will. Invariably they are the source of perpetual frustration. Informed investors must own equities and common stocks, and be participants in the continued growth of our economy and global progress that is inevitable – it cannot be stopped. And the best way to be part of that growth and progress is to invest in well managed mutual funds.

"The Great Annuity Rip-Off"

We know what inflation can do to the value of your dollars. Decades old insurance company advertisements have driven that point home. In addition, Treasury Secretary Henry Paulson recently described the coming "Fiscal Train Wreck" in the form of overwhelming demands of Social Security and Medicare. And despite all this, the annuity peddlers continue to misguide and mislead investors who are legitimately concerned about their future financial survival. But remember, annuities have proven what they are with their own advertisements.

Readers should know that the disadvantages of annuities are not imaginary – they are real. Some might assume that my career in the mutual fund industry might be prejudicial against annuities. However, there are other credible, objective sources that have been outspoken in their criticism of annuities – how they're promoted and sold, and how they work. One of those sources is *Forbes Magazine.* *"The Great Annuity Rip-off"* is the title of an article that appeared in the February 9, 1998 issue of *Forbes Magazine,* which has granted permission to reprint the following article.

That's right, the article was written in *1998,* ten years ago!

NOTE: Tax rates, etc., are those that were in effect in 1998, and should ***not*** be assumed to be applicable today.

Recent tax law changes should have wiped out sales of variable annuities, but they are as hot as ever. How gullible can investors get?

The Great Annuity Rip-off

TAKE THIS QUIZ. ARE YOU:

- Contributing the max to your IRA and 401 (k)?

- Very sure you won't need the money until you are past 59-1/2?

- Confident you won't have an occasion to either give appreciated securities to charity or leave them to heirs?

- Going to invest in either junk bonds or a high-turnover stock portfolio?

- Prepared to lock up the money for a decade or more and/or annuitize the payout?

- Going to buy a no-load contract?

- Certain that your tax rate will be lower in retirement?

If all your answers are yes, consider owning an annuity.

DO YOU WANT PROOF POSITIVE that investors are irrational? Here it is: Sales of variable annuities went up 16% last year, to $85 billion.

A variable annuity is a mutual fund-type account wrapped in a thin veneer of insurance that renders the investment earnings tax-deferred. The tax deferral is just about the only good thing you can say about these investment products. Almost everything else about them is bad: the high -- sometimes outlandishly high -- costs, the lack of liquidity, the fact that the annuity converts low-taxed capital gains into high-taxed ordinary income. That tax deferral comes at a very high price.

The last of those three drawbacks just became bigger. The 1997 tax law cut capital gains tax rates while leaving ordinary income tax rates high. So the benefit of wrapping an annuity around your stock portfolio has just about vanished.

That tax change should have stopped annuity sales cold. The salespeople who push these things should have moved on to products more suitable for their clients, like plain old mutual funds. Shares of the leading variable annuity vendors -- such as Hartford Life, Nationwide Financial Services and SunAmerica -- should have collapsed.

None of these things has happened. Their shares are up 30% and more over the last year. What on earth is going on?

It's the old story: Annuities are sold, not bought. And a good salesman can get a lot of mileage out of the apparent tax advantages of a tax-deferred annuity. This investment product, he will tell you, is like an IRA, except that there is no $2,000 limit on contributions. You can put in $1 million if you want. Leave the money in as long as you want. It compounds tax-deferred.

The statement is true, up to a point. But unlike a deductible IRA or a 401(k), which is bought with pretax dollars from your paycheck, a deferred annuity gives you no tax deduction when you buy it.

Nor is an annuity anything like one of those new Roth IRAs. The Roth IRA is tax-exempt (if you meet certain criteria). An annuity is merely tax-deferred -- meaning that you have to reckon with the tax collector someday on your earnings.

In a typical transaction a stockbroker (or financial planner or insurance salesman) persuades you to salt away, say, $20,000 in an annuity policy that is a mutual fund in all but name. Indeed, the portfolio choices for your account will often be clones of popular mutual funds (like Fidelity Contrafund). Your choice of portfolios is usually wide: stocks, bonds, money markets, foreign securities.

But with an annuity there's an extra layer of fees. In addition to the investment fee on the portfolio there's a "mortality and expense risk" charge, typically 1% or more a year. This covers the cost of the "insurance" you are getting.

Insurance? It's there, a pale imitation of life insurance. The insurance guarantees that when you die, the value of your account will be at least as great as the money you originally put in -- unless you get a contract that steps up the insurance coverage over time, all you are insured for is the starting value. If the account has indeed grown, you still get only the value of the account, no more, no less; the insurance pays nothing. To collect on the insurance, that is, you have to pick a rotten investment -- and then drop dead before the investment recovers. Is that what you had in mind? We doubt it.

What is the actuarial value of that life insurance? It is safe to say that with the vast majority of annuities sold today, almost all the money you are assessed for "mortality and expenses" winds up in either the salesman's or the insurance company's pocket.

Assuming you don't die, the account accumulates. Say it grows to $32,000 and you decide to cash out. The $12,000 increase in value is taxed as ordinary income, at federal rates of up to 41% (taking into account a surcharge that relates to itemized deductions) plus state and local levies; for a New York City taxpayer that can add up to higher than 50%. That's true even if much of the gain is from stock price appreciation. If those same stocks were held in a mutual fund the price appreciation would be taxed at about half those rates, assuming the fund shares are held for at least 18 months.

Annuities are costly to own. Expenses -- portfolio management fees, plus that "mortality" charge -- average a hefty 2.1% a year. That's half again what it costs to own the average mutual fund, and ten times what it costs to own the Vanguard Index 500 fund. Surrender charges are common, starting out typically at 7% if you cash out in the first year and declining to 0% in the seventh year. Also, if you cash out before you reach 59-1/2; you have to pay a tax penalty, except under certain narrow circumstances.

There are a handful of exceptions to the rule that annuities are costly. The College Retirement Equities Fund sells very low-cost annuities, but only to schoolteachers and professors in the TIAA-CREF pension system. Vanguard, T. Rowe Price and Jack White sell annuities with no surrender fees and low annual expenses -- but they don't sell very many.

The rest of the business pretty much belongs to people who live on commissions: insurance agents, stockbrokers and commission-paid financial planners. They get a payout of up to 7%, which they share with their firm. Where else can they pocket that kind of money? Not in load mutual funds, where the average commission is something like 4%. Certainly not in stocks or bonds, where commissions are facing stiff competition. "The salesman has a new hammer, and everybody starts looking like a nail," says Charles Haines, a fee-only financial planner in Birmingham, Ala.

If the terms are so terrible, then why do people buy the salesman's pitch? Because they are mesmerized by the words "tax deferral." Does this sound familiar? A generation ago a different crop of investors was mesmerized by the words "tax shelter" -- and ended up with worthless railcar leases and cattle farms.

But just what is this tax deferral worth? Get out a pencil and do some arithmetic. Say you've got $20,000 to salt away for retirement in 20 years and you want to put it in stocks. If you own the Vanguard Index 500 fund, most of your return takes the form of unrealized appreciation in the fund's shares. You will get income dividends of only 1.5% a year, which will create a tax burden equal to maybe 0.7% of assets annually.

Capital gains payouts on the Vanguard fund have been extremely modest. When you cash out, the accumulated gain in fund shares is taxed at low capital gains rates.

Now look at the Prudential Discovery Select stock index account. Sure enough, this will spare you the 0.7% tax bill. But at what cost! The annuity's total expenses run 1.8% of assets annually. That is 1.6 percentage points above the cost of the Vanguard fund, more than wiping out your current tax savings.

If this were the end of the matter, the annuity mightn't be too bad. But now look at what happens when you cash out. Let's assume an average annual return of about 7%; the account quadruples in 20 years, to $80,000. In the ordinary Vanguard index fund you would have a long-term capital gain of a bit less than $60,000 (less, because your reinvested dividends get counted in your purchase price). On that you would owe federal tax of $12,000. At Prudential the whole gain is ordinary income. You'd owe something close to $24,000.

The taxable mutual fund has another advantage over the supposedly tax-favored annuity. You could escape the $12,000 capital-gain tax altogether by either giving the fund shares to charity or leaving them in your estate. No such option is available to an annuity holder. Transfer or bequeath an annuity to anyone but your spouse and you trigger recognition of the full appreciation as income.

Any prospective customer who takes the time to understand annuities runs away screaming. A recent report by consulting firm Cerulli Associates puts the matter as delicately as it can: "Information about variable annuity purchases reveals that they do not appear to be based on educated decisions."

Consider the experience no-load fund giant T.Rowe Price had when it sent potential customers software to help them determine whether variable annuities were right for them. The program factored in the investor's age, income, tax bracket and investment horizon -- and it regularly told potential buyers that they would be better off in a plain old fund. An educated consumer, as it turned out, was not a good prospect for annuities.

If folks really knew what they were buying, how could you explain the $21 billion of annuities sold in 1996 that went into IRAs? IRAs, already tax-sheltered, benefit not a whit from the annuities deferral feature.

A case can be made for buying one particular kind of variable annuity inside an IRA. This is the kind that converts a lump sum into a monthly payout that lasts only as long as you do; what you are paying for is not a tax shelter, which is already there, but rather an assurance that you won't outlive your capital. But of that $21 billion worth of IRA annuities sold in 1996, only 1% were these monthly payout contracts.

"This is one of the biggest disgraces in the entire securities industry," fumes investment adviser Joseph Ludwig of Tandem Financial Services, in Canton, Mass. One of the victims: Ludwig's own son-in-law, Barry Joseph. Before marrying, Joseph bought a Metropolitan Life annuity inside his IRA. "I honestly thought I bought a mutual fund," says Joseph. "The salesman never mentioned the word annuity to me."

After Congress lowered the tax rate on capital gains, the annuity industry commissioned a study by Price Waterhouse on the implications. A stunning specimen of spin, the study concluded that the new tax rates would have a negligible impact on the number of years it takes for the benefits of tax deferral to overcome the higher costs of variable annuities relative to mutual funds.

But Patrick Reinkemeyer, editor of Morningstar's variable annuity report, says Price Waterhouse made some dubious base assumptions. Among them: that variable annuity investors will be taxed at the rock-bottom 15% federal income tax rate when they withdraw their money in retirement, and that the investments will earn 13.6% per year, the average for mutual funds from 1987 to 1996.

Richard Toolson, an accounting professor at Washington State University, has done his own calculation of break-even points. For someone in the 36% income tax bracket who has to choose between a low- turnover index fund and an annuity portfolio earning the same pretax return, it would take more than 40 years for the annuity to earn back even a low 0.5% mortality charge. Yes, the salesman is right when he says that "annuitizing" your investment when you retire (taking monthly payouts over a long period) keeps the taxman at bay a while longer. Still, 40 years is a long time.

And a 0.5% fee is not easy to find. The *average* mortality charge in the annuity industry is 1.3%; with that kind of fee, says Toolson, the annuity buyer never comes out ahead, even if his tax bracket has gone way down by the time he cashes in the annuity. Toolson didn't even figure in the freebie that owners of stocks or fund shares get when they donate or bequeath the property.

Not counting academics lucky enough to be eligible for CREF, is there anybody who in his right mind should even consider owning an annuity? Glenn Daily, a fee-only insurance consultant in New York City, offers a few examples.

Case one: Someone who owns an underwater cash value life insurance policy. Say you have poured $100,000 into a universal life policy and it now has a cash value of $85,000. Insurance policy losses are almost never tax-deductible, but if you transfer the $85,000 to an annuity, the first $15,000 of profit you make on the annuity is tax-free.

Case two: a retiree who has just barely enough money to live on and needs one of those monthly payout annuities.

Case three: potential targets of lawsuits. Three-quarters of the states, among them New York, Washington, Florida and Texas, protect assets in variable annuities from creditors, to one degree or another. Doctors worried about malpractice suits, for example, might do well to stash some money in variable annuities.

If you fall into one of these three categories, look for a no-load annuity and don't pay a penny more than you have to in expenses. What if you've bought a high-cost annuity already and regret it? Cut your losses. Wait until the surrender charge period is over and then roll your account into a no-load, low-expense annuity via a tax-free "Section 1035" exchange.

Imprisoned

YOUNG WIDOWS. Baby boomer couples. Small business owners. Top executives. The investment landscape is littered with victims of aggressive variable annuities salespeople.

Ronald Rog, a financial planner in Bohemia, N.Y., has a widowed client who'd been persuaded by an insurance agent to tie up half her $1 million inheritance in variable annuities. After running through her liquid assets by age 52, she was forced to cash out the annuities and buy bonds and dividend-paying stocks for income - paying taxes, surrender fees and penalties, since she was under 591/2. "That was criminal," says Rog. "It's absolutely unbelievable what people will do for that 7% commission."

Lexington, Mass. financial adviser William Baldwin tells of a couple in their 40s who'd been shoveling $7,000 per year, nearly all their savings, into a high-fee variable annuity. When it came time to exercise some in-the-money stock options, they didn't have enough cash to do it. Baldwin had them stop funding the annuity and roll the balance, $57,000, into a no-load annuity with Vanguard. They had to pay surrender charges, but the lower expenses of the Vanguard contract should overcome these fees in eight years.

Peggy Ruhlin, a Columbus, Ohio financial planner, advised her clients with annuities to stop funding them three years ago when talk of a capital gains tax cut was in the air. Still, she marvels at the creativity of some salespeople. One tried to convince a client who owns a business to choose a variable annuity for the firm's new 401(k) plan. There was no tax justification for such an investment; since a 401(k) is already tax-deferred, the tax deferral built into an annuity is irrelevant. The annuity was simply the most convenient vehicle for the 401(k) custodian to recoup the considerable overhead costs on a small-business thrift plan.

A New York marketing executive, who asks that his name not be used, confides that he feels burned by the broker who put one quarter of his portfolio - about $500,000 - into three variable annuities. "I feel like I'm in prison with them," he says. Just 57, he can't get out without paying a tax penalty, not to mention ordinary income taxes on any gains. So he rolled one into Schwab's no-load annuity, and is waiting for the surrender fees to expire on the others from Putnam and Nationwide - so he can roll those over, too.

"I don't blame anyone but myself," he says. "I was really depending on the face that smiled the best and the heart that seemed the warmest."

What is this insurance worth?

BUY A $10,000 Imperium variable annuity from American Skandia and you run up an annual 1.4% fee for "mortality and expenses." Stay in there for ten years, assume a little growth, and you could easily be spending $1,500 on the insurance element of your contract.

What do you get for this outlay? Not much. The death benefit is nothing like $10,000. Rather, it guarantees that if you die while holding the annuity, you or your heirs will collect an account balance at least equal to $10,000.

In any given year only 0.4% of variable annuity contracts are surrendered on account of death or disability. Of those, only a fraction have losses that trigger a death benefit. And among those losing accounts, the loss is never the full $10,000; it might be only $500 or $1,000.

The longer you stay in an annuity, of course, the less likely it is that the death benefit will pay off. After ten years of growth, you would expect that $10,000 account to be more like $20,000 - and highly unlikely to ever drop below $10,000. Otherwise, why buy the darned thing?

Sellers of variable annuities are not obligated to tell you what they do with your mortality and expense money. Aurora Consulting's Thomas Mitchell, an independent actuary in St. Louis, estimates that the actuarial value of the death benefit averages in the neighborhood of 0.2%. Enhanced death benefits that keep pace with the account's earnings cost slightly more, plain vanilla death benefits slightly less. A larger chunk of the money is for the insurance company's profits and overhead.

For an annuity sold by a commissioned salesperson, about half of the mortality fee goes to pay the distribution costs. The sponsor of the annuity will pay an upfront commission of up to 7%, then recoup the money with the mortality charge.

"Most people would balk at paying someone $700 for selling them a $10,000 variable annuity," says insurance consultant Glenn Daily, "but they are apparently quite willing to let the annuity company pay the same $700 on their behalf and repay the loan over time - with high interest."

The performance game

"ANNUITIES BEAT Major Indexes In Stellar Year," blared the headline in the January 12, 2008 article in *The Wall Street Journal.*

Balderdash. As the text of the article made clear, only the best annuities beat the market. As the *Journal* article did not say, the average annuity is nothing you would want. Morningstar calculates that the average annuity subaccount invested in U.S. stocks last year delivered a return (net of fees) of 21%. The S&P 500 earned 33%, including dividends.

FORBES doesn't rate variable annuities. Why? They're stupid investments for nine and a half people out of ten. The only folks who benefit from these things most of the time are the people who sell them.

GOOD MORNING FLORIDA!

On May 10, 2008 the Tampa Tribune editorialized on the subject of annuities, which included the following excerpts –

"Florida has its share of unscrupulous insurance agents who have been talking retirees into bad deals…

A bill was passed named for a couple from Venice, they're in their 80s, and were sold an annuity that came with a big fee if they converted it to cash within 15 years…

The new bill will add transparency to the sale of policies and reduce but not eliminate, abuses…

Florida Chief Financial Officer, Alex Sink, advocated a tougher bill. 'I'm disappointed that we were unable to make it a felony to intentionally deceive a senior in an inappropriate annuity product' she announced...

Sink is right that the worst abuses are the same as thievery and that that the guilty agents deserve time behind bars."

Amen Ms. Sink. However, the insurance company and its executives that accept these kinds of annuities should also be held accountable for their conduct. This stuff could never happen without their knowing consent.

<u>*NOTE:*</u> In fairness, *The Wall Street Journal* recently ran an article that described "Inflation-linked annuities" that were described as "Annuities that increase payouts every year, based on either inflation or a percentage chosen by the investor." One of the selling points for this approach is that "as investors get older they get a payout that keeps pace with inflation. However, initial payments are much lower than classic annuities," which sounds like you're paying for keeping pace with inflation. As explained by John Heywood, a principal at Vanguard, "If the maximum payout is your biggest focus, you don't want to buy an insurance-protected annuity because that's going to reduce your payout on day one." Remember, there's always a cost for a guarantee, it's just that some are more obvious than others.

More information about annuities.

The Securities & Exchange Commission's website offers a plain language explanation of annuities that includes additional information that you should know. Look for *"Variable Annuities: What You Should Know,"* titled "<u>Variable Annuity Charges</u>." The full text is available at www.sec.gov/investor/pubs/varannty.htm

---

Social Security, A "Fiscal Train Wreck"

That's how Treasury Secretary Henry Paulson described the future of Social Security and Medicare. He said that in March 2008 and he just might know what he's talking about. Trustees of both Social Security and Medicare again reported that the so-called Social Security "Trust Fund" will be <u>*depleted*</u> by 2041, a little more than 30 years from now. Everyone in their 30s and 40s had better start paying attention. But wait, it's even worse for Medicare, which is expected to be wiped out by 2019 – about ten (10) years from now. That means everyone had better start paying attention or seniors had better make sure not to get sick in the future.

That's the fiscal train wreck coming at us, full speed. It involves 78 million baby boomers who will begin to retire and start drawing benefits. What to do? The easiest way to handle this is exactly what our politicians are doing – kick the problem down the street. And many of those who refuse to pay attention will do what so many Social Security and Medicare participants do now – moan, groan and complain about how unfair the "government" is and the "government" should pay more and tax the "wealthy." One has to ask why people who made a conscious decision to ignore the coming train wreck would be surprised when it finally arrives and then target the government for criticism – a government cannot give anyone anything without first taking something from someone else. Does that make sense? Who decides who should pay and how much, and who gets paid and how much? Believe it or not there are people who claim that socialism, so-called national health care, is the solution. This despite the fact that the preponderance of people seeking medical assistance come to the United States, while few Americans are lined up to buy airline tickets to foreign countries to obtain quality health care. Doesn't that tell us something about socialism's approach to health care?

It's been said that everyone is entitled to their own opinion, but not their own facts. That's why it's essential to look at the history of Social Security over the last 40-50 years. Reasonable people will recognize that what was intended as a "safety net" morphed into an entitlement program. As a result, the Social Security system is cracked. If it makes you feel better, call it a hairline crack. In any case, that crack will not disappear but will only grow larger and more dangerous. The "crack" is simple to understand. When the system was created in the 1930s, we had 16 workers contributing for every retiree. Now we are at the point where it will soon be 2 workers contributing for every retiree. Can you do the math? It won't work, i.e., it's a fiscal train wreck. As a result, it's plain to see that based on simple math this serious problem won't go away. What to do?

A few years ago a presidential commission was formed to address the problems facing the Social Security system. One of the suggestions made was to permit individuals to place a small portion of their social security taxes in a government regulated account in the participant's name, which could be invested in several index funds with different objectives selected by the participant. Unfortunately, this sensible idea was met with a broadside of propaganda, led by the AARP of Washington. It was one of the most dishonest and hypocritical campaigns in recent memory that was based on distortion and misinformation. AARP decried what they termed was a "risky" idea because it permitted individuals to invest in several different index funds. What was lost in the propaganda campaign, and no one had the courage to point out, is the fact this same AARP sponsors and offers upwards of forty (40) mutual funds to its members. Apparently no one thought to ask if the AARP mutual fund prospectuses describe those funds as "risk free."

Some delusional people have described Social Security as "the most successful government program ever." The truth is that if any insurance company operated on the same basis as the current social security system, they would be run out of business and their executives jailed for fraud.

It's essential to remember that today's monthly social security checks are being paid for by people who are still working and paying off mortgages, while raising families and trying to prepare for their children's education and their own retirement. Well, what's wrong with that you say? Nothing, according to AARP and its Beltway friends. Clearly AARP feels it has to operate on the belief that Social Security payments must be increased by having more taxes deducted from working people to pay retired people and those payments should be increased every year. You have to wonder how many children of AARP members realize that an organization supported by their parents is lobbying to convince Congress that there's nothing wrong with taking more money from them, younger working people, to give to older retired people.

Of course, there's nothing really wrong with the concept, except that it's based on the Willie Sutton formula for success. It was Willie Sutton who, when asked why he robbed banks replied, "That's where the money is." It seems that the nice folks at AARP have learned that the Willie Sutton approach works quite well. In polite circles such as political lobbying sessions, this is referred to as "intergenerational wealth transference." Hey, it sounds good, and you don't need a gun and a getaway car. The truth is that simply raising the payroll tax by any amount, and/or raising the current cap on income subject to that tax (effectively a double hit on the most productive members in the work force) brings to mind what has been said about people who keep doing the same thing over and over again, expecting a different result, i.e., it's the definition of insanity.

The fact is that this approach is exactly how we arrived at this point today. When will we face reality and act responsibly by correcting known flaws in the system with a concept that has proven itself repeatedly in the past? We need only look at IRA Plans, 401k Plans and 403B Plans to see that informed people are capable of preparing for the future when given the opportunity to do so sensibly and conveniently. A few years ago a Wall Street Journal editorial described how a number of countries have addressed the challenge they faced in providing a sound, sensible and effective government-backed retirement system. As an example, they cited Chile (not exactly the financial/investment capital of the world) that started a program in 1980 that involved "mandatory savings by workers, usually in an individual private account." The results have been no less than remarkable. At the outset, about 25% of eligible workers participated. Now more than 90% of eligible workers are covered. This program and its proven benefits, flexibility and significant payouts is real, not a theoretical proposal based on political rhetoric. It works.

The editorial went on to list the success of similar programs in Australia and, hold on now, Sweden, which arguably has one of the most socialist economies in the West. So how about it? Don't we deserve something more than the do-nothing approach, or worse, the ineffective scheme of increasing taxes, again, invariably recommended by some politicians? Or worse yet, the smarmy lobbying of special interest groups pandering to their members at the expense of non-members of the group.

Social Security Private Accounts – Isn't it about time that we really look at sensible, responsible solutions to the challenges we face in fixing a broken system? We should permit and encourage private accounts within the system by phasing them in over time in order to avoid future tax increases or raising the earnings cap, both of which represent nothing less than discriminating against our most productive workers. In addition, we should consider extending the time period for determining the amount of Social Security payments to retirees from the current 40 quarter employment requirement to a more realistic qualifying period. Most important, we must change the terribly flawed basis for determining annual Social Security increases and replace it with an index that's more appropriate to a retirement program. The Beltway crowd always has trouble with ideas that they can't demagogue, but we have a problem in need of a sensible solution – a solution that's more important than just winning the next election.

Here's a question everyone should be made to answer:

"If you were given the job of creating a government sponsored and controlled national retirement program, would you propose a system that is identical to the current social security program?"

Despite what some people may like to think, Social Security and Medicare are not the solution to financial independence. As presently configured, it just won't work and it can only get worse – "a fiscal train wreck."

Investment News

Because it's so important, and a problem we will undoubtedly face in the not too distant future, I requested permission to reprint an editorial on this very subject that appeared in the March 17, 2008 edition of *Investment News,* ("The Leading News Source for Financial Advisers"). As you will see, this is a subject which is much on the minds of people involved in the investment industry.

VIEWPOINT

This baby isn't Babar

IN THIS ELECTION YEAR, no one is discussing the elephant-in-the-room problem that is devouring an ever larger share of the nation's federal budget – Medicare. Medicare spending swallowed $367.5 billion, or 13%, of the federal budget in 2007, and it is expected to grow by 6.5% a year for the foreseeable future.

This year, Medicare spending will exceed the program's inflow, which comes from a tax of 1.45% on taxpayer income. And, just 10 years from now in 2018, the Medicare Trust Fund is expected to run out of money.

The current unfunded Medicare obligation is estimated at $71 trillion. Despite the looming catastrophe, Congress averts its eyes from the monster gobbling up more and more federal resources, as do the presidential candidates of both parties.

The Medicare program is slipping into the red even before the great bulk of the baby boomers begin to retire. The first baby boomers reach eligibility for Medicare in 2011, and the numbers swell every year thereafter. By 2030, the number of Americans over 65 will grow to 73 million, from 40 million today.

If the program is not soon changed drastically, today's younger workers will have to foot the bill in the form of an enormous tax increase and they won't be happy.

A great deal of time, preparation and negotiation will be necessary to prepare the public for the painful choices that must be made if Medicare is to survive.

In the short term taxes will have to be raised. In the longer term, a combination of Medicare benefits cuts and tax increases, and perhaps other spending reductions, will be needed to preserve the system for retirees.

At present, the government is attempting to cut costs to keep the system going by cutting reimbursements for doctors and hospitals. The result is that more and more doctors are refusing to treat new Medicare patients, and hospitals continue to try to pass more and more of their costs on to private insurers. This is not a viable long-term strategy, or even a short-term strategy

At the very least, President Bush or Congress, should establish a bipartisan commission to consider changes in Medicare to preserve it.

A new bipartisan commission focused solely on Medicare could prepare the way for significant changes. It might also serve to educate boomers about Medicare. As reported in last week's issue of *Investment News,* most baby boomers are largely unfamiliar with Medicare's benefits, and what they cost.

Medicare Part B premiums can be as high as $405 a month per beneficiary, there is a $1,024 deductible for the first 60 days of hospital care, and co-pays can rise to as much as $512 a day after 90 days of treatment.

It's time to educate workers and retirees about Medicare, its benefits and its total costs, and it's time for the president and members of Congress to honestly discuss the size and shape of the elephant in the room, and the damage it could cause if it is not soon harnessed.

————

The conclusion of this editorial points to the problem which is twofold: lack of knowledge and concern on the part of the investing public and the irresponsible conduct of elected officials whose only concern is their own re-election; both of these problems need to be addressed.

Part II – Selecting your Funds

Chapter 3 - Getting Started, Money Market Funds

Let's put things in perspective. Everyone, and I mean everyone, should have a money market mutual fund account for a whole host of reasons. Most investors may not realize that the first money market fund was introduced in 1972.

Initially many people scoffed at the idea of a money market fund, including me. This was based on thinking who would want to "invest" in a type of bank account? Nevertheless, Bruce Bent, one of the creators of this new concept just pressed forward and money funds began to take root, with virtually every major fund organization offering their own money fund. The idea was simple – give average investors the opportunity to pool their monies in order to buy large denomination certificates of deposit and commercial paper, which were normally beyond the reach of individual investors. And so the concept took hold and good thing! Equity markets were in a difficult cycle and fund sales were at best anemic. Money market funds provided investors with a possible way to ride out down cycles in the market and "park" their money while participating in high current interest rates with liquidity and stability of principal. The fact is that money market funds proved to be a life saver for the mutual fund industry.

So we have some history for money funds which includes several terrible mistakes in the 70's that were made by investment "managers" who simply did not understand the rules, or thought they could bend the rules. Isn't it amazing how problems always seem to arise from some bright bulb trying to increase or "enhance" yields? Well it happened with money market funds back then as it has recently happened with some now infamous income fund managers. It didn't work back then and it doesn't work today. Soon money market mutual funds will have proven themselves over 4 decades, while they continue to do the job for which they were designed.

Commerce Magazine Interview

One of the best explanations of what a money market fund is and how it works appeared in *Commerce Magazine,* the monthly magazine that was published by the North Jersey Chamber of Commerce in 1980, which included an interview in which I answered a series of questions. At that time money funds were still relatively new, but interest rates were at historic highs and an investor could open a money fund account and enjoy the advantages of liquidity, stability and current high yields. After reading the interview you'll have a good idea of why you should own a money market mutual fund.

Commerce Magazine Interview

COMMERCE

June 1980   **one dollar**

Heights Plaza

Horizon North at Norwood

Elmwood Park Plaza

Ivanhoe

Alfred Building bus

COMMERCE MAGAZINE – Interview 1980

Unless you own one of the five Lexington Mutual Funds you're probably not aware that one of the country's better investment advisors is located right here in northern New Jersey - specifically, Englewood Cliffs.

While for its entire existence, Lexington Management Corporation has maintained a commendable level of investment management results, at the same time keeping a low profile in terms of marketing, this appears to be changing based on the overwhelming reception to the Lexington Money Market Trust - the only New Jersey-based money market mutual fund.

All five of the Lexington Funds have been under Lexington's management since their inception. Lexington Management Corporation was known as Templeton, Dobrow & Vance until 1969 when Piedmont Management Company, an Insurance/Financial Holding Company, acquired the firm and the investment advisory and distribution function for the Lexington Funds.

Since 1969, the firm has introduced three more funds and earlier last year, 1979, they acquired the Lexington Money Market Trust from an old line New York advisory company.

The thrust of the firm's marketing efforts is targeted to offering a complete spectrum of investment products to the small- to medium-size corporate benefit plan market, as well as serving the individual investor. They hope to do this by offering superior, personalized service and a full complement of no-load mutual funds, including a fund which specializes in gold mining companies and gold bullion which is currently being negotiated.

The theme at Lexington is best described by its marketing executive, Dan Calabria. "Our goal," he said, "is to offer our clients 'Lifelong Money Management' through a broad range of investment funds which offer a diversified spectrum of investment objectives - all available without sales charges or commissions. In addition, built into our package is the convenience of being able to exchange holdings of one fund for another to satisfy investment objectives or adapt to a different market climate. And this can even be done by phone. As a result, our investors can literally tailor their investment portfolios to suit their needs at different times. The key here involves conveniences, diversity and flexibility - which we feel are vital to the concept of 'Lifelong Money Management.'"

The marketing approach now employed by Piedmont is one which involves direct contact with almost 30,000 investors in the Lexington Funds, including pension, profit sharing, Keogh and IRA plans. As a result, more and more people are becoming aware of the Lexington Funds and the fact that they have developed a most attractive "track record" of investment results.

Dan Calabria...interview conducted mid-April, 1980

Q: What is a money market fund?

A: It is the gathering together of a group of people who pool their investment dollars together in order to give them buying power, which they can then use as a group to buy large blocks of money instruments at very favorable rates.

Q: Define money market instruments.

A: For the most part, these would consist primarily of any one of three different instruments. Bank certificates of deposit and acceptances, but only from banks with total assets in excess of one billion dollars; government securities in the form of bills or notes; and last, but certainly not least, commercial paper, which are simply short-term corporate "I.O.U.'s" issued by major corporations.

Q: Why only banks with a billion dollars in deposits?

A: In our case we wanted to be sure we were investing in the strongest banks in the country. We felt it was necessary to provide the kind of stability people need for their short-term cash reserves.

Q: What are the advantages of investing in money market funds?

A: I think there are probably three major advantages: yield, liquidity, and stability. 1) You earn high current yields; 2) You have the use of your money at any time without penalty; and 3) You have the relative safety in the marketplace that is unique with the exception of a bank account; but there you're not going to get the other two advantages.

Q: In regard to lack of guarantees, what kinds of investments are being made by the fund now? Wouldn't the guarantee reflect the nature of the investment?

A: It would and it does. As to the guarantee factor in the money market field, if things were to get to such a state wherein any of us would be concerned, there is no reason why we couldn't put the trust one hundred percent in government paper. As a matter of fact, just ten days ago we adjusted a substantial part of the fund - $1 million in treasuries -- and moved it up to about $12 million-equivalent to 30 percent of the fund in governments and we may continue to emphasize governments depending on what happens in the money market. We have the ability to change our investments in order to be as safe as possible. If we ever got to the point that we believed the state of the economy warranted it, we could literally be invested entirely,

100%, in government paper. Then you would have the government backing the entire portfolio.

Q: *What is the average length of maturity of the portfolio?*

A: Under 20 days at this time.

Q: *What is the minimum amount required to open an account in the Trust?*

A: It's $1,000 to start an account; $100 or more for additional investments at any time.

Q: *What about withdrawals?*

A: It depends on how you do it. If you are using our free check writing privilege, the minimum check is $500; if you're using the telephone, the minimum withdrawal is $200; by mail, any amount.

Q: *Is there a limit on frequency of withdrawals?*

A: The only requirement we have is that any monies that are invested by check must remain on deposit 15 days before you can exercise your check writing or telephone redemption-in order to allow sufficient time for your check to clear.

Q: *How about cash or its equivalent?*

A: The equivalent of cash, e.g., "wired" or "federal" funds can be put in today and taken out tomorrow, using your commercial bank account.

Q: *How and why did money market funds get started?*

A: Money market funds got started in 1972 and interestingly enough they were started by two fellows who had no prior mutual fund experience. All they had was an idea which turned out to be a great one. They envisioned a short-term investment vehicle where money could be moved in and out while earning current high interest rates -- and where the risk factor would be almost negligible. They started a fund in 1972 and for almost two years people in the industry were skeptical about the idea -- and even slightly amused. They asked questions such as "What are they doing? . . . "What do they know?" ... "Who let them in?"... "What's it all about?" Well, within that two-year period there were five more money funds started; and at that point in 1974, everybody sort of fell into line; and it was just a question of time before, as a management company, you had your own money fund. There are about 84 money funds in existence today. In my opinion, this particular vehicle, which was created by two people from outside our industry, literally saved the mutual fund industry. Today there are more assets in money funds than there are in the rest of the entire mutual fund industry.

Q: I think most people understand what mutual funds are. Isn't a money market fund basically a mutual fund?

A: Basically it is. It is simply a mutual fund in terms of the basic format of the investment vehicle. But is it like other mutual funds? No, it is absolutely not like other mutual funds. There is no bid or asked price. The price of the fund is its Net Asset Value. There is no fluctuation in the value of your investment in the fund. And, other than a money market fund, there is no other kind of fund that pays daily dividends.

Q: So it is only the same in concept?

A: Yes - in form.

Q: Do you find there is a broad range in your "typical customer" category?

A: It can range anywhere from individuals who have some money set aside for their children, on up to any number of major corporations with hundreds of thousands -- perhaps even a couple of million dollars in their pension plan to invest.

Q: Do some local corporations participate in your fund?

A: We have a number of local companies as well as companies from out of state that invest in the Trust.

Q: What kind of interest options do you have?

A: Basically you have two options regarding the daily dividends that are paid: 1) You can take them out in cash every month as they are declared, or 2) You can reinvest them and in effect have your money compounding for you daily. Unlike any other investment vehicle that I know of, the money market fund actually reinvests your dividends every day so that you have daily compounding as opposed to monthly, quarterly, or semi-annually, and that does make a difference.

Q: How big is your fund?

A: At the moment, $43.5 million.

Q: What was it a year or two ago?

A: Well, as a matter of fact, a little more than a year ago is when we acquired it. In January of 1979 we acquired what was then known as 'Bannner Ready Resources Trust" from the Lionel D. Edie Company;

in effect, what we bought was a shell, just the corporation itself. We changed the name; put in the "seed" money of $100,000, and started from there.

Q: How do you attract customers?

A: Our approach is very simple, and frankly, limited because of our size, but it has proved very effective. All of our advertising has been done on radio. We selected a radio program in New York based on a telephone call-in format devoted to questions on investments. We are the exclusive money fund advertising on this program and our ads run six days a week. People call us up after hearing about us on this show. We have recently expanded our campaign to similar programs in Philadelphia and Miami.

Q: Who in your firm makes the investment decisions?

A: Our portfolio is managed on a day-to-day basis by Peter Briggs. Pete has had approximately 30 years experience in the bond market, both long and short term. He consults on a daily basis with the president of Lexington Management Corporation, Grover O'Neill, who is an economist. This combination of background and experience gives us a very real edge in this market.

Q: What is the relationship between Lexington and Piedmont? How is the company structured?

A: We're sister companies. Lexington is the management company, the investment adviser. They provide the day-to-day management and research for our funds as well as our institutional accounts (approximately $400 million) and we are the marketing organization for the funds. We plan to combine these two functions under Lexington sometime this year. Since we are now a completely no-load organization, there is no longer the need for a separate distributor. We are the only New Jersey-based money market fund.

Q: Why did you decide to locate in New Jersey?

A: As a matter of fact, the company has been in existence here since 1938. Lexington was organized in 1969 and was formerly known as Templeton, Dobrow & Vance, an investment counseling organization. The name was changed to Lexington Management Corporation.

Q: What happens to money market funds if the economy shifts and interest rates come down again?

A: Well, first of all, we do expect interest rates to come down. We don't know how far down they'll go and we don't know when it's going to happen, but certainly the current trend will be reversed. When that happens you must keep in mind that money funds are relative to other alternative forms of investment. At that point in time, bank CD's are going to be paying a lower rate; treasuries, commercial paper and everything else will decline; so it's always a question of "How good is my money fund yield relative to what else is available to me?" And the one thing we haven't seen come into the competitive area is a vehicle that compares with money funds in terms of the liquidity and conveniences offered. So interest rates are relative: it's the services that you get from the money fund that are the extra advantages; and we don't see anything coming close to us at this point.

Q: Do you think the deregulation of bank interest which was recently passed by Congress and signed by the President will affect the volume of investment in money market funds?

A: Possibly. But, again, we must realize that those people who understand what a money fund is don't make a decision based on whether to have money in a bank or a money fund. Rather, their decision is based on how much to have in a bank account and how much to have in a money fund because you're really talking about two different kinds of dollars.

Q: Was that legislation passed as a response to the success of the money market funds, in your opinion?

A: I think in part it was, yes. I think it also was in part due to inflation itself. You can't have an inflation rate of +18 percent and expect the banks to continue to pay 5 percent and do business. The ceiling had to be lifted so it would be more in line with what's happening in the economy.

Q: Any predictions about when interest rates will drop and in what sequence of events?

A: Very, very tough question, especially in light of the fact that we're in an election year. I can't make that prediction; it depends on what happens politically. If the incumbent wants to "turn on" his campaigning, he could possibly turn things around in a matter of weeks in the money market.

Q: What caused the interest rates to go up so precipitously?

A: I think the major cause, while it's very difficult to get people in power to admit this, is the fact that as long as Washington continues to print money and spend money beyond what it is taking in, we're going to have a rate of inflation that is totally out of line with what we have experienced in the past. And the fundamental problem is not anywhere else but in Washington. Some people look at money funds and say, "They are contributing to inflation and high interest rates." That's not true at all! Interest rates being paid by money funds are the result of inflation, not a cause of inflation. And that's what some people have lost sight of.

Q: So, if the government continues to inflate the money supply, that would in effect be good for the funds, would it not?

A: Good for the funds but not good for us as individuals or the economy as a whole, that's for sure!

Q: So you're suggesting that inflation is caused by Washington creating more money because of deficit spending.

A: Yes, that's my opinion.

Q: What are the advantages or disadvantages of a big, major fund as compared to your fund? Are there any?

A: A couple of weeks ago the Federal Reserve issued a ruling whereby money funds from March 14 forward would have to reserve 15 percent of any new investments in a non interest bearing account. A week later they amended the ruling to exclude any money funds with under one hundred million dollars. So for the first time, at least in my career, being smaller has proved to be beneficial to us.

Q: If I were an investor in your fund and you escalated to a hundred million dollars, what would happen to my rate of return if everything remained constant with respect to today's standards?

A: We did make a calculation when the news was first announced and at that point we took a look back at the months of January and February and analyzed what would have happened to our yield had the Federal Reserve requirements been in effect. Based on that analysis our yield would have been lower by three-tenths of one percent.

Q: What is that on an annual basis?

A: Hardly worth speaking about.

Q: Why then did the large funds, or all but 14 of them to be accurate, refuse to accept people's money at this point?

A: The problem that a fund faces is its responsibility to its existing shareholders versus its responsibility to new shareholders. And the problem that they had to wrestle with was: If they were to continue to remain open and take in new dollars, and this, in effect, reduced the fund's yield, would they be properly serving the original share-holders? And would the original shareholders have cause to criticize management for not having served them properly? Many felt that in order to avoid the problem they would just stop selling, or start a new fund.

Q: How does your company make money?

A: We, as every other mutual fund management company, earn our money on the basis of a management fee, which in our case is one-half of one percent based on total assets of the Trust collected on a monthly basis.

Q: One-half of one percent of what? Please clarify.

A: As an example, for every $1,000 invested in the Trust the man-agement fee of 1/2 % is equivalent to $5 for the entire year.

Q: What is the current rate of return?

A: As of today it's 15.18%

Q: What is the trend?

A: The trend has been up. The prime rate has risen practically every week and currently is at 20%. Incidentally, we really don't think the rate is going to stay at this level too long.

Q: So the prime rate is the barometer for yields?

A: Generally speaking, the prime rate is the barometer; and gener-ally speaking, if you want to know what your money fund is yielding - practically any money fund - you will usually be two points behind the prime. However, we've recently had so many successive increases in the prime that the money funds have been lagging behind. But they'll catch up.

Q: How much paperwork is involved in investing in your money funds?

A: That's relatively simple. In every case, an application contain-ing the name and address and social security number of the owner must be signed, with a check, and sent to us. The only part that is a little bit unusual is that those individuals who want check writing privileges, or telephone redemption privileges, have to fill out autho-rization forms on which their signatures have to be guaranteed. We require them to sign the form in the presence of an officer of a bank where they are known or in the presence of the manager of a stock exchange firm thus guaranteeing the signature. This is really for the investor's protection.

Q: Do you expect any more government regulations adversely affecting your industry in the near future?

A: We hope not. Although there is no guarantee, there is every possibility that they can increase the reserve requirements. There is no prohibition against it because what they have done is to set this up under an emergency act passed back in 1969. So I don't know what else is in the works there.

Q: What was the rationale for requiring 15 percent to be set aside?

A: I don't know why they picked 15 percent versus 20 or 10. The rationale behind the reserve requirement was supposedly to prevent dollars from leaving banks. The only problem is, and the problem I have difficulty with, is the fact that money funds are still miniscule compared to the total money supply. I think if they really did an analysis of this, they'd find that the amount of money going into money funds is negligible compared to the amount of money that is going into treasuries, which have become very attractive.

Q: How many people have entered into the money funds in the last year?

A: It's in the millions.

Q: You mentioned earlier that you had a lot of corporate accounts opening up. Why are they doing it?

A: One of the main advantages is the fact that in this inflationary economy every corporate financial officer is aware of the fact that he must make every dollar work for him seven days a week. In some cases, that's not possible. In many cases, if you have an excellent relationship with the banking organization that you work with, there are ways that can be worked out; you have to be large enough to do it. A small to medium sized corporation's options are limited. However, with a money fund they could literally earn interest on their cash balances 365 days a year. For example, a company that maintains an average cash balance of $10,000 a year at an average yield of 10% can pick up an extra $1,000 a year in interest on their money fund account. Now that doesn't seem like a great deal of money, but in many cases it can pay the rent for a month or a couple of month's phone bills or something like that. And that's where we're at in this kind of an economy, looking for ways to get unproductive dollars to pay for certain fixed expenses. That's why a money market fund makes sense.

Q: Are many corporations in the money funds today?

A: I believe so. Most informed corporate officers are involved in money funds in one form or another. For example, compare the advantages of a company that does business with an organization in California. When they purchase an item from them and send their check in payment for the merchandise they would write the check against their regular checking account. In some cases that check might take two or three weeks to clear. With a money fund you can do exactly the same thing and while the check is clearing you're earning interest on it until the day it clears the money fund's custodial bank. And if you do that often enough throughout the course of a year you'll find out that in some cases the cost of products you are buying is actually reduced by earning interest on your payment checks.

Q: Who is your custodial bank?

A: Our custodian bank is State Street Bank and Trust Company in Boston.

Q: Why in Boston?

A: There are literally a handful of banks in the country that are set up to work with mutual funds - even fewer with money funds in terms of conveniences and the volume of business being done. Based on our investigation, State Street had all the necessary programs and systems required to service our shareholders, which made the decision easy for us.

Q: How does the investor keep track of the daily rate of return?

A: We keep him informed through a monthly statement of the account with the prior seven days' average yield. In addition to that, we ask our shareholders to either call us collect or on our 800 line to get the current yield on the Trust whenever they want that information.

Q: Do people call every day?

A: Yes!

Q: Are their calls answered personally?

A: Yes. We don't use any answering machines or answering services. We're proud of this. Whenever you call Lexington, you speak to a real person who is trained to respond directly to specific questions.

Q: Do you have any new products planned?

A: As a matter of fact, we are waiting for SEC clearance of the Lexington Tax Free Daily Income Fund, a tax free money market fund, which offers all the conveniences of a money fund with the advantage of tax-free yields. It's perfect for the high tax bracket investor.

————

NOTE: *While this interview took place in 1980, the basic principles that apply to money market funds remain unchanged.*

Chapter 4 - The Next Steps

Now that you have a good idea of what a money market fund is, the question for those who don't own a money fund is, why not? You can own a taxable money fund or a tax free money fund – there are no excuses. The fact is that a money fund should be the first mutual fund an investor owns. However, even a money fund can be misused. For example, too many investors have between 10% to as much as 100% of their 401k or IRA plans invested in a money market fund. Why? Why invest in a tax sheltered account to shelter 2 to 4% in yield when you can be invested in equities and shelter 6, 8 or 10%, and some years even more, in capital appreciation? The tax shelter is there for two purposes – to avoid current income taxes and take advantage of tax deferred, compound earnings.

So step one is to own a money market fund to serve as the foundation for a sensible, long term investment program – it's the first step in intelligent management of your own money. But which fund(s) should you own? As discussed earlier there are entirely too many mutual funds available today – more than 8,000! However, that total includes almost 3,000 money funds. Once you open your money fund account you will immediately eliminate almost all money market funds, which will be of no interest to you and serve only as distractions. (See Chapter 5 for how to select a fund.) What about the remaining 5,000 funds? You can eliminate most of them because they are simply duplicates of each other. Let's look at some mutual fund industry statistics. According to the 2007 edition of the "Mutual Fund Fact Book," published by the Investment Company Institute, at the end of 2006 nearly half of all US households owned mutual funds in 2006 compared to less than 6 percent in 1980. That represents an increase in household ownership from 5.7% in 1980 to 48% in 2006, an increase of about 800%. During the same period the number of mutual funds grew from 564 to 8,120, an increase of more than 1,500%! During this period total mutual fund assets grew from $1.3 billion to more than $10.4 *trillion!* (Currently total fund assets exceed an estimated *$9 trillion!)* And that includes a period in the stock market that survived a number of very serious economic problems and market declines. Today more than $9 trillion is invested in a little over 8,000 mutual funds.

Let's put this in some perspective. Many of us eat cereal for breakfast. The next time you visit a supermarket take a look at the cereal aisle. It can be overwhelming with dozens and dozens of different brands in a variety of sizes. Now just imagine a supermarket that carried 8,000 different cereals (or beers). Silly, isn't it? Why do we have so many mutual funds today and who is selling them? Do you really think we need 8,000 different brands and varieties of funds for investors? Of course not. And yet the fund industry has grown by duplication and imitation to a size that boggles the mind. How do we cut the numbers down to a level where we can make an informed selection? We've already taken the first step by eliminating almost 3,000 money funds, bond funds, and "hybrids," simply by selecting one money fund that satisfies your needs. The next step is a little more involved, but not so complicated that you can't create a mutual fund portfolio designed for your goal of long term growth of capital.

SOME FOUR LETTER WORDS

There are a few *four letter words* you must contend with when making any investment.

"Risk" is **_not_** one of *"those"* four letter words. In fact without risk, no corporation would ever be able to turn a profit simply because they take risks every day creating and promoting new products, making investments in new technology, etc. You get the idea. Any attempt to create wealth involves taking risks. The difference is the _kind_ of risks taken. There is risk when you invest in anything, including mutual funds. However, if you're totally risk averse, don't invest in mutual funds. Put your money in banks and annuities and the banks and insurance companies will love you, but don't expect them to reward you for your loyalty.

NOTE: There is a difference between investment risk and speculation – look it up.

"Debt" is another four letter word and it's possible that more people are doing more harm to their financial future by going into debt with credit cards and other borrowing than people who invest in a mutual fund with less than superior performance. Debt is certainly acceptable and beneficial when you buy your house because that house is really an investment and historically real estate values have increased over time. But credit card purchases for feel good, non-essential products makes no sense whatsoever – except to the credit card companies, which are usually owned by...banks. Gee, who would have thunk it?

"Dumb" is also one of *"those"* four letter words. It's most applicable to those people who blithely ignore the reality of taxes and inflation while paying no attention to their future well being. That's dumb and often causes investors to be prey to con artists and investment scams that are always out there waiting for the opportunity to separate you from your money. Are you "dumb?" Not if you're reading this.

But if you've been dumb in the past, you can recover from that malady and get yourself on track with a sensible long term investment program.

Summary: You can and should accept reasonable risk in any investment – that's risk, _not speculation,_ or guarantees that have proven ineffective over the long term. You must avoid excessive debt and limit your debt to a reasonable percentage of your income. With the exception of your home mortgage, one way of controlling debt is to limit the total amount of credit card spending to the extent that you can pay your credit card bill in full each month. Think about it – paying interest rates of 18, 19, up to 22% and carrying charges on credit card purchases can only be described as _Dumb_. With all the information available today there's no excuse to be dumb about investing. You have an army of mutual fund sales people and fund websites available to assist you in learning and understanding the basics of successful long term investing, which is far from rocket science.

So it's up to you – take the time now, pay attention to your finances and select one or more mutual fund organizations for your investment dollars. Then take advantage of the most valuable asset you have, and that's time. It's the one thing that cannot be bought, borrowed or replaced and it will make the difference in your future financial independence.

"Four Letter" Words and More

©Scott Adams/Dist. By United Feature Syndicate, Inc.

Let's take a look at another factor you have to contend with today.

"Hype, PR AND BS"

Welcome to the world of mutual fund marketing today. It's a fun place to be provided you don't take some of this stuff seriously and never, as in *NOT EVER, make* an investment decision based on this stuff.

From the "Fund Track" column in a recent edition of *The Wall Street Journal* - the subject was the challenge of overcoming net redemptions and one possible alternative. The title of the column was "Morgan Stanley Tries to See What Sticks," which speaks directly to what you need to be aware of in making investment decisions. In some quarters this is more commonly described as "throw enough stuff against the wall and see what sticks." This is an approach in the industry that has proven successful – provided that the emphasis is on gaining market share and not necessarily on managing shareholder investments for consistent, above average performance results. Perhaps the best example appears daily in the *Journal,* under the caption "Mutual Fund Scorecard." It's a very concise, snapshot of performance results of a limited number of mutual funds based on investment objectives and the total assets of the funds. The investment objective is highlighted and described in plain English and includes the performance results of each of the listed funds for the year-to-date, one, three and five-year periods.

The first section of the chart consists of the "10 biggest funds" with the same investment objective. The second part of the chart includes "Year-to-date top performers." However, this group includes the top 10 performers among *all* funds with the same investment objective, not just the 10 largest funds. The last chart consists of five funds that comprise the "Year-to-date bottom performers" among all funds with the same investment objective.

It was interesting to track just several days at random to see what the "Scorecard" reveals. Here's what I found on three different dates, May 22, May 30 and June 3, 2008. This was not based on scientific sampling, just 3 dates selected at random.

<u>May 22</u> – Health & Biotechnology Funds.

Among the "<u>10 biggest</u>" listed are 3 Fidelity Funds (Fidelity Select Health, Fidelity Select Med Equip, and Fidelity Sel Bio Tech). The "<u>Year-to-date top performers</u>" included Fidelity Sel Med Equip and Fidelity Sel Bio Tech. The "<u>Year-to-date bottom performers</u>" included Fidelity Sel Medical and Fidelity Adv Health;A.

<u>Summary</u>: In this "Scorecard" we find Fidelity has 3 Health & Biotechnology Funds in the "Ten largest"; 2 funds in the "top performers," and 2 funds in the "bottom performers." The result is Fidelity has a total of five (5) different Health & Biotechnology funds included in the list with 3 among the "10 biggest"; 2 among the "top performers," and 2 among the "bottom performers."

<u>May 30</u> – Natural Resources

There are three (3) Fidelity funds listed in this category with all three included among the "<u>10 biggest</u>" – Fidelity Sel Energy, Fidelity Sel Nat Gas and Fidelity Adv Energy;T. Two of the Fidelity Funds, Sel Nat Gas and Sel Energy are included among the "top performers," and two of the Fidelity funds, Fidelity Adv Energy;T and Fidelity Sel Energy are included among the "bottom performers."

<u>Summary</u>: In this Natural Resources "Scorecard" we find Fidelity has a total of three (3) different Natural Resources funds included in the list with all 3 funds among the "10 biggest"; 2 among the "top performers," and 2 among the "bottom performers."

<u>June 3</u> – Multicap Growth

Of the "<u>10 biggest</u>" funds listed in this category, five (5) of them are Fidelity products – Fidelity Contrafund, Gro Company, Cap App, OTC and Independence. One of these funds made the "top performers," Fidelity Independence, while none of the Fidelity Multicap Growth funds were among the "bottom performers."

<u>Summary</u>: In the Multicap Growth category only one of the 5 qualifying Fidelity Funds made it as a "top performer," while none of their funds was in the "bottom performers."

So what's the point? Simple – the name of the game is marketing and if you're lucky enough to be invested in some funds with above average performance then accept the fact that part of your selection was, at least in part, based on luck as is demonstrated in the summaries above. But which of the funds with the same objective should you chose? All of them? I don't think so. In fact, you might be well advised to avoid this "shotgun" approach to fund selection altogether. The fact of the matter is that it's not unreasonable to assume that when you hire a company to manage your mutual fund, you should not be put in the position of guessing which of those funds with identical objectives will be the better performer. In addition, why are there so many "flavors" of the same fund within the same management group? Why isn't there one Multicap Growth fund to take advantage of economies of scale and eliminate duplicative expenses while relying on the portfolio managers to focus on what they believe are those stocks in that segment of the market with the best prospects for growth? I guess because there's no requirement for a management company to do so... it's only the shareholder's money involved. However, another important factor might be in play here. Since management companies of some size employ a small army of attorneys on their staff, why not keep them busy filing new mutual fund prospectuses? After all, the initial capital required to register a mutual fund is a mere $100,000 per fund, which amounts to a rounding error at this level.

But wait – what if the fund doesn't work out, it fails to perform as planned? Not to worry, just shut it down or, if it has enough total assets, just merge it into another existing fund, which invariably will be blessed with knee jerk approval of a compliant board of directors. No, we won't discuss the independent director's fiduciary obligation to fund shareholders at this time. However, it's an important question that raises the more serious issue of "independence" of those appointed as "watchdogs" on behalf of shareholders, and getting paid quite handsome fees for presumably representing shareholder's best interests.

Variety is NOT always the spice of life.

©Scott Adams/Dist. By United Feature Syndicate, Inc.

The mutual fund industry is prone to excess in its marketing efforts that almost seem designed to distract shareholders from monitoring their investments in favor of promoting the latest flavor or fad. Some recent examples include:

BRIC funds – Funds that invest primarily in Brazil, Russia, India and China which are believed to have great potential as long term investments. However, a major concern when investing in foreign countries is the type of government in control of those countries. The fact is that governments controlled by autocrats can confiscate entire industries and companies and bid farewell to foreign investors in a heartbeat. So is there potential for profitable investing in these countries? You bet, but there are also the additional risks of foreign regulations, changing currency rates and confiscation or nationalization of entire industries that is over and above typical risks in most mutual funds.

Commodity Funds – They're hot, hot, hot and being billed as "diversifiers." However, the history of specialty funds is that after the market for such investments cools down they are not very rewarding as long term investments, and often go into extended periods of hibernation, or end up in the mutual fund graveyard.

130/30 Funds – Comprise a portfolio of securities, 100 of which are straight stock investments and 30 stocks that are sold short. My opinion? You want Vegas, make a reservation and book a flight; you'll have lots more fun.

Quantitative Funds – Here the managers apply information from internal algorithms that are applied to thousands of stocks to try to determine the prices of those stocks in the future. Whatever happened to crystal balls? Spare me – some of these folks need to get out more.

Buy-Write Funds – This is one of those concepts that are usually available in a *closed end* fund that employ options to generate income. I have no idea why, but investors bought $5.3 billion of closed end funds in 2007.

NOTE: A word about closed end funds. Lots of people are <u>sold</u> closed end mutual funds – I don't think many average investors buy them. Here are a couple of questions you should ask anyone who recommends a closed end fund to you:

"What was the price of XYZ Closed End Fund when it was initially offered to the public?"

"What is the price of the fund now?"

Then ask why it's selling at a discount.

Those are <u>not</u> Dumb questions.

Where to Start – Fund Allocator

©Scott Adams/Dist. By United Feature Syndicate, Inc.

The first decision you have to make is whether you want to do it yourself or find a professional to guide you through the process. There are more than enough competent and qualified professionals from which to choose depending on how you want to pay for their services. Some charge reasonable commissions and some charge a reasonable annual fee. Just remember, whatever the nature of their compensation that is not the sole basis on which you should make your selection. You should recognize that finding an honest, capable and reliable professional adviser is a challenge. They're out there, but you have to find them. The best advice on finding that adviser is to rely on friends. Talk to them, as many whose judgment you respect, and ask them who they use for this purpose. Talk to them and keep talking to them until you've met with a few potential advisers from which you select the one who impressed you as most knowledgeable and experienced. Then follow his or her advice and be sure that part of their service includes a simple year end analysis, including beginning and ending account values. But let's assume that you prefer to do it yourself which involves a simple illustration.

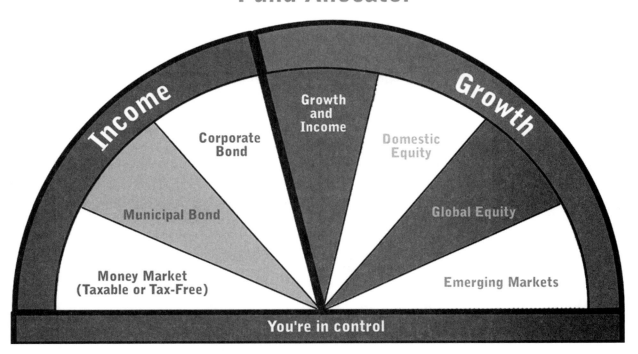

While there are seven categories of funds in the "Allocator," it's simpler than that. You already know that you must own a money market fund for yield, liquidity, convenience and stability, plus free check writing. Does that mean you will no longer need a local banking relationship? Of course not. Your local bank should be considered as a convenient service for identification purposes, a source of ready cash and some bill paying for smaller expense items. It's also important for reference purposes that might be required for a variety of reasons. The idea is to make a slight change in your local banking relationship and habits. Instead of them using you as a source of steady income, i.e., bank fees, float, etc., you should use their services as an accommodation for your investment program. They should no longer be a "gatekeeper" that pays you "rent" for your money, but a facilitator that provides services to you. What about debit cards? Use them if you must, but be aware of the limitations, restrictions, costs and possible penalties that vary from one bank to another, as well as some other possible pitfalls.

Unless you're _over 80 years of age_, without an investment portfolio or other source of income, and you rely entirely on social security – then you should consider placing _no more_ than 10% of your assets in income products, either municipal or corporate bond funds. Any additional amounts invested in income products simply reduces the amount of dollars available to work for you in equities where the total returns have been more rewarding over the long term.

That leaves four selections for allocation of the major portion of your investment assets. I'm a strong advocate for equity securities ,i.e., you are likely to do better in straight equities than in a growth/income fund which is mandated to include a combination of stocks and income producing securities in the portfolio. Why reduce your potential gains with an income allocation if you already have about 10% or more of your portfolio in money market and/or income funds? However, I understand that some people prefer the comfort of periodic dividends from their investments. So go ahead, do it if you must, but recognize that you're lowering your potential for maximum growth of your investment. And remember, every now and again something happens that should give investors pause before putting too much of their "serious" money in income funds.

REALITY CHECK – "Stretching" For Higher Yields

The April 22, 2008 edition of *The Wall Street Journal*, provided a cautionary tale in its "Fund Track" column that reported the plight of the Regions Morgan Keegan funds. The column was titled "Seven Bond Funds Get New Management." Now that's definitely **_not_** routine news. Briefly, this is what happened. Two of the seven funds mentioned posted returns of -70% and -73% losses over the 12 month period through March 31, 2008. The funds were primarily invested in mortgage backed securities; including low quality mortgage and complex securities like collateralized debt obligations. Apparently, they decided that's where the "best" yields were.

Part of the fallout included total assets of one of the funds dropping from approximately $1 billion in July 2007 to about $104 million currently – that's almost a 90% drop in assets!! Some investors had a similar experience a few years ago during the tech stock boom, but it's extremely unlikely that investors seeking income could have or should have expected these kinds of results.

Unfortunately it did happen, which resulted in the investment adviser hiring an outside investment management firm effectively outsourcing its investment management responsibilities.But something else also occurred which was really surprising – the entire board of directors of the funds was replaced with a new board. Now that's extremely unusual, but certainly appropriate since a strong case could be made that the board was remiss in fulfilling its oversight responsibilities relative to their duty as the shareholders' "watchdog" in overseeing the activities of the investment manager. By the way, if you're a fan of or invested in one of those "high yield," 'enhanced" funds, or whatever marketing label is used, maybe you should call your income fund's toll free 800 number and ask them how the fund performed over the following periods: the last six months of 2008 and for the 12 months ended December 31, 2008. Hopefully you won't be surprised, or worse, shocked by what you learn.

Another example of "stretching" for higher yields involves Charles Schwab Corp.'s Yield Plus Fund, an ultra short bond fund offering high yields. According to The Wall Street Journal the fund was advertised as a vehicle created for conservative investors looking for a slightly higher yield while preserving their capital. At the end of February '08 the fund had more than half of its assets in mortgage-backed securities. At the end of the first quarter of '08 the fund's NAV per share declined more than 18%, which resulted in class action suits filed in New York, Massachusetts and California. By the end of April it was down 26%. It's been reported that this has led to Charles Schwab holding several telephone conference calls with advisers who sold the fund to their clients.

The *Journal* reported that Schwab was offering settlements to investors in the fund representing pennies on the dollar for losses suffered by some investors according to attorneys seeking class action status.

Meanwhile, one of the closed end fund kings, Nuveen Investments is hard at work in an attempt to "liquify" *$15 billion* worth of shares of preferred auction-rate securities designed to boost fund yields. These involved preferred securities that were sold to individual investors as a higher yielding alternative to money market funds and were issued by 100 of its funds.

Nuveen is also reported to have been working the phones with financial advisers who placed client's monies in the funds.

Once again we have some unhappy examples of the search for enhanced or higher yields from presumably "safe" investments, this time in the form of mutual funds.

*This is a good time to remind everyone that if it sounds too good to be true, it's probably **too good to be true**!*

One more thing –

For an excellent review of mutual fund basics in a plain language tutorial, including a brief glossary of terms "straight from the horse's mouth," the Securities & Exchange Commission's own website, check out the reprint of that tutorial beginning on page 95. You'll find it worth the time to review this information which also includes some cautionary advice. For additional information visit the SEC's website at: www.sec.gov/investors/pubs/inwsmf.htm

---

How To Select Your Mutual Fund(s)

©Scott Adams/Dist. By United Feature Syndicate, Inc.

The Basics – Do It yourself

Here are some factors to consider before making your allocation decisions.

- What is my investment objective and do the selected funds match my objective?

- How much time do I have?

- Am I willing to accept greater risks for potentially greater returns?

- Which are the six mutual fund organizations that appeal most to me?

- Have I visited their websites?

- Are the websites written in plain English or by lawyers who are primarily concerned with protecting their client, not necessarily informing me, the investor?

- Have I called the fund group's toll free number and spoken to a customer service person, and then asked to be transferred to one of their retirement specialists?

- Is the fund managed by one person or a team of managers?

- What was the fund's portfolio turnover rate for the last two full reporting years? (Portfolio turnover rate is stated as a percentage. If the fund has a portfolio turnover of 100% in a one year period it means that all the stocks in the portfolio have been replaced during that one year period.)

If you're a long term investor do you benefit from high portfolio turnover? First, it's expensive – every time a stock is sold and replaced with another stock commissions are incurred, which are a direct charge to the fund for each and every transaction. In other words you, the shareholder, pay those commissions. Second, every time a stock is sold it could trigger a "taxable event," i.e., a gain or a loss for income tax purposes, which you have to report on your tax return. Obviously, portfolio turnover is another factor to consider in making your fund selections.

> **Reality Check** – If you're not willing to invest a small amount of time to learn this information then don't go any further – "hire" a broker or financial planner/adviser to do this work for you. And if he doesn't do a good job for you, "fire" him or her.

Before selecting and investing in any mutual fund(s) for any purpose including your personal portfolio, IRA, 401k Plan, custodial plan for a child, etc., you need to use this checklist to get the answers to several "must ask" questions, **_before_** you invest. It should be obvious that using blind faith in making investment decisions makes no sense. It's your money and your future. You don't owe any mutual fund anything – they owe you lots of hard work, research, plain language communications and consistent, above average performance results. But you need to do some leg work to help put the odds in your favor when "hiring" a mutual fund management company to work for you. That means "ya gotta ask!" Here are the questions that will provide you with part of the basis for making your choice.

1. Who are they?

2. What do they say they will do?

3. What do they do?

4. Have they done what they say they do?

5. How well have they done what they say that they do?

There's an important principle in investing that cannot be ignored – if you don't understand an investment or the people doing the investing for you are unable to explain what it is they're doing...*Don't Invest!* If you don't know the answers to the 5 questions above, *Don't invest!* Keep your money in your local bank that promises a specific return on your dollars, backed up by the Federal Deposit Insurance Corporation. No kidding, it's that simple.

Here are the reasons why you need to work through the 5 questions above, which can be done by phone, by letter to the fund company CEO (information usually available on the website or by phone), or by email on the fund's website.

1. You must know who will manage your mutual fund(s), the actual portfolio manager(s) and how long they've been managing the specific fund. How long have they been in the mutual fund management business? Does the portfolio manager have any of his personal money invested in the fund? If so, how much does he/she have invested in the fund?* Was the fund initially offered by the management company, was it acquired or the result of a merger with another fund, and if so, when?

   *Check it out – recently Morningstar, the fund rating company (www.morningstar.com), announced it would soon publish details of a portfolio manager's investment in the fund(s) he/she manages.

   A sub-title to the description of their findings was "So many funds, so many goose eggs." They compiled information for ownership levels for the top 300 funds, of the 6,000 funds they cover. Here's a capsule of their findings: U.S. stock funds – 47% report no manager ownership; foreign stock funds, 61% have no ownership; taxable bond funds, 66% have no ownership; balanced funds, 71% have no ownership, and municipal bond funds, 80% have no ownership. In fairness, corporate bond and municipal bond funds may not be appropriate for younger managers, depending on their ages and states in which they live. Morningstar intends to run the information for all the funds they cover in the near future.

Reality Check – this begs the old question about "eating your own cooking."

2. Exactly what is the objective of the fund in which you're interested? Don't just accept a prospectus of the fund which was written by lawyers for lawyers and carefully crafted to protect the investment manager. Remember, it's your money and if they want you to hire them, they should be willing to honor the principle of "Full Disclosure." If they are either unwilling or unable to respond to these questions, end the discussion and move on to another company that will. If you feel the information you seek is not in the material they send to you, write them with your specific questions.

3. Are they an investment management organization? Is managing money either their sole or at least their primary business? Or are they an arm of a brokerage house with a mutual fund division or subsidiary, or a bank or insurance company with retail brokerage subsidiaries? Remember, you're looking for a real, full time investment management company, not an asset gathering company.

4   & 5. What about their performance record covering the most recent calendar quarter, the last 12 months, and the last 3, 5 and 10 year periods, including the results of the benchmark against which the fund's results are measured? These are vitally important details, which are an important part of your investment decision. The key to comparing performance results is discussed in Chapter 5. But for now you must understand that raw performance results, (*absolute performance results*), alone are not adequate for purposes of comparison. You also need *relative performance results,* which compares the fund's performance to similar funds with the same investment objective for identical time periods. All of this information is readily available and updated regularly for the same time periods. Any mutual fund that is unwilling to provide this information to you should be avoided – period.

The response you receive to your questions may include literature or brochures that address one or more of these questions. Some of the best fund managers have excellent explanatory literature that will answer many of your questions. That doesn't mean they will all have the best performance record - very few do. But at least they do more than just pay lip service to the concept of "full disclosure." Finally, if the response you receive consists of stacks of printed documents, commonly known as a "paper dump," don't waste your time in an attempt to wade through the material to find the answers to these specific questions, the answers to which should be readily available from the fund. In addition to providing direct answers to your questions, some of the best fund organizations have excellent websites that can be a convenient source of information and can be very helpful to you.

In conclusion, before you just send in your money, including your name, address and social security number to a fund, you need more than just a prospectus that's replete with legal mumbo jumbo, more commonly referred to as disclaimers and all sorts of hedged statements, which provide none of the information you need to make an informed investment decision. In this regard, it is earnestly hoped that the SEC will recognize that what passes for prospectuses are not informative, waste paper and more often than not are completely ignored by investors. Anyone in the industry who disputes this can go public with their defense of the present system at any time with an inexpensive website and tell the world that the present system is the best we can do.

Selecting an Investment Adviser

©Scott Adams/Dist. By United Feature Syndicate, Inc.

You may not want to take the time or make the effort to gather the information discussed, which is understandable. Happily, there's another alternative – you can "hire" an adviser, broker, financial planner, etc. This is at least as important as picking the right funds to match your investment goals, and it can be done. Part of this decision involves how you want to pay the adviser you select, a fee based on an annual charge or fees based on transaction charges. Regardless of which compensation method you select, if you get the right person, the cost will be more than worth it. But take your time, there's no rush and never forget that you're not making a lifelong commitment. It's an arrangement that works only as long as you are satisfied that the results you achieve are worth the cost.

The following pages are reproduced from the SEC's website titled *"Investment Advisers: What You Need to Know Before Choosing One."*

SEC – Basic Information/Glossary

U.S. Securities and Exchange Commission

Investment Advisers:
What You Need to Know Before Choosing One

The SEC receives many questions about investment advisers—what they are and how to go about choosing one. This document answers some of the typical questions we receive from investors about investment advisers. This Q&A is for the benefit of investors. You should not rely on it to determine if you need to register as an investment adviser.

Q: What is an investment adviser?

A: Investment advisers are in the business of giving advice about securities to clients. For instance, individuals who receive compensation for giving advice on investing in stocks, bonds, or mutual funds, are investment advisers. Some investment advisers manage portfolios of securities.

Q: What is the difference between an investment adviser and a financial planner?

A: Most financial planners are investment advisers, but not all investment advisers are financial planners. Some financial planners assess every aspect of your financial life—including saving, investments, insurance, taxes, retirement, and estate planning—and help you develop a detailed strategy or financial plan for meeting all your financial goals.

Others call themselves financial planners, but they may only be able to recommend that you invest in a narrow range of products, and sometimes products that aren't securities.

Before you hire any financial professional, you should know exactly what services you need, what services the professional can deliver, any limitations on what they can recommend, what services you're paying for, how much those services cost, and how the adviser or planner gets paid.

Q: What questions should I ask when choosing an investment adviser or financial planner?

A: Here are some of the questions you should always ask when hiring any financial professional:

- What experience do you have, especially with people in my circumstances?

- Where did you go to school? What is your recent employment history?

- What licenses do you hold? Are you registered with the SEC, a state, or the *NASD*?

- What products and services do you offer?

- Can you only recommend a limited number of products or services to me? If so, why?

- How are you paid for your services? What is your usual hourly rate, flat fee, or commission?

- Have you ever been disciplined by any government regulator for unethical or improper conduct or been sued by a client who was not happy with the work you did?

- For registered investment advisers, will you send me a copy of both parts of your Form ADV?

Be sure to meet potential advisers "face to face" to make sure you get along. And remember: there are many types of individuals who can help you develop a personal financial plan and manage your hard–earned money. The most important thing is that you know your financial goals, have a plan in place, and check out the professional you chose with your securities regulator.

Q: How do investment advisers get paid?

A: Before you hire any financial professional—whether it's a stockbroker, a financial planner, or an investment adviser—you should always find out and make sure you understand how that person gets paid. Investment advisers generally are paid in any of the following ways:

- A percentage of the value of the assets they manage for you;

- An hourly fee for the time they spend working for you;

- A fixed fee;

- A commission on the securities they sell; or

- Some combination of the above.

Each compensation method has potential benefits and possible drawbacks, depending on your individual needs. Ask the investment advisers you interview to explain the differences to you before you do business with them, and get several opinions before making your decision. Also ask if the fee is negotiable.

Q: Do investment advisers have to register with the U.S. Securities and Exchange Commission?

A: Depending on their size, investment advisers have to register with either the SEC or the state securities agency where they have their principal place of business. For the most part, investment advisers who manage $25 million or more in client assets must register with the SEC. If they manage less than $25 million, they must register with the state securities agency in the state where they have their principal place of business.

Q: How do I find out whether an investment adviser ever had problems with a government regulator or has a disciplinary history?

A: Most investment advisers must fill out a form called "Form ADV." They must file their Form ADVs with either the SEC or the state securities agency in the state where they have their principal place of business, depending on the amount of assets they manage.

Form ADV consists of two parts. Part 1 contains information about the adviser's education, business, and whether they've had problems with regulators or clients. Part 2 outlines the adviser's services, fees, and strategies. Before you hire someone to be your investment adviser, always ask for, and carefully read, both parts of Form ADV.

You can get copies of Form ADV from the investment adviser, your state securities regulator or the SEC, depending on the size of the adviser. You can find out how to get in touch with your state securities regulator through the *North American Securities Administrators Association, Inc.'s* web site or by calling (202) 737-0900. Ask your state securities regulator whether they've had any complaints about the adviser, and ask them to check the *CRD*.

If the SEC registers the investment adviser, you can get the Form ADV by sending an email to the SEC's Office of Investor Education and Advocacy at *publicinfo@ sec.gov*. You also can make a request by sending a fax to (202) 777-1027. Please note that you will have to pay a photocopying charge of $0.24 per page, plus tax and postage. In addition, at the SEC's *headquarters,* you can visit our Public Reference Room from 10:00 a.m. to 3:00 p.m. to obtain copies of SEC records and documents.

Q: What should I do if the financial professional claims that he or she is "certified?"

A: If the professional you're considering claims to be a CFP® certificant, you should also visit the website of the *Certified Financial Planner Board of Standards, Inc.* to see if the professional is, in fact, certified as a CFP® professional and whether the professional's certification has been suspended or revoked by the CFP Board. You can also call the CFP Board at (888) 237-6275 to obtain other disciplinary information about the professional.

Q: Are investment advisers required to have credentials?

A: While some investment advisers and financial planners have credentials -- such as CFP® certification or CFA (chartered financial analyst) -- no state or federal law requires these credentials. Unlike federally registered advisers, many states do require their advisers and representatives to pass a proficiency exam or meet other requirements.

Investment advisers and financial planners may come from many different educational and professional backgrounds. Before you hire a financial professional, be sure to ask about their background. If they have a credential, ask them what it means and what they had to do to earn it. Also, find out what organization issued the credential, and then contact the organization to verify whether the professional you're considering did, in fact, earn the credential and whether the professional remains in good standing with the organization. For information on various financial professional credentials and the entities that issue them, please visit NASD's (now FINRA) website and read *Understanding Financial Professional Designations*.

Conclusion

For more information about choosing investment advisers see *Get the Facts: The SEC's Roadmap to Saving and Investing*, *Invest Wisely*: *Advice from your Securities Regulators* and *Ask Questions* at *http://www.sec.gov/investor/pubs/invadvisers.htm*

> We have provided this information as a service to investors. It is neither a legal interpretation nor a statement of SEC policy. If you have questions concerning the meaning or application of a particular law or rule, please consult with an attorney who specializes in securities law.

Modified: 08/01/2007

As you can see, this excerpt from the SEC's website provides a wealth of information available to you simply by clicking on the link.

It's good "stuff" so take the time to read it and you'll be glad you did.

Mutual Fund Fees & Expenses

This is a subject that gets lots of press and while important, it should not be the sole basis for selecting a mutual fund. Before making a decision, you may want to compare the costs of investing in those funds you're considering for investment. The easy and most obvious part of your decision is the cost of acquisition, which could be zero, i.e., a no load fund, or a percentage of the amount you invest, recognizing that sales charges are reduced based on the amount invested. The SEC's website can be enormously helpful. Reprinted

below is a copy of "Calculating Mutual Fund Fees and Expenses" from their website.

U.S. Securities and Exchange Commission

Calculating Mutual Fund Fees and Expenses

Fees and expenses are an important consideration in *selecting a mutual fund* because these charges lower your returns. Many investors find it helpful to compare the fees and expenses of different mutual funds before they invest.

You can compare the fees and expenses of up to three mutual funds, or the share classes of the same mutual fund on the NASD's *Mutual Fund Expense Analyzer*. You can also compare the fees and expenses of up to three *ETFs* using the same program. You can use this analyzer to compare the costs of different mutual funds in a matter of seconds. That's because the tool automatically provides fee and expense information for you. Simply enter each fund's ticker symbol or select the fund through the drop down menu. If you can't remember the full name of the fund, you can also search for the fund using key words.

A mutual fund's fees and expenses may be more important than you realize. Advertisements, rankings, and ratings often emphasize how well a fund has *performed in the past*. But studies show that the future is often different. This year's "number one" fund can easily become next year's below average fund. On the other hand, independent studies show fees and expenses can be a reliable predictor of mutual fund performance.

Of course, selecting a mutual fund involves more than just picking one with low fees and expenses. Before you invest in any mutual fund, decide whether the investment goals and risks of the fund are a good fit for you and determine how it will affect the *diversification* of your entire portfolio. You can read about a fund's goals, risks, and costs in its *prospectus*.

The SEC's online, interactive Mutual Fund Cost Calculator can also help you compare the costs of different mutual funds and understand the impact that many types of fees and expenses can have over time. You can find this "classic" calculator at: *http://www.sec.gov/investor/tools/mfcc/mfcc-intsec.htm*. Unlike NASD's Mutual Fund Expense Analyzer, you'll need to enter fee and expense information manually from a prospectus or other disclosure document when using this tool.

http://www.sec.gov/investor/tools/mfcc/mfcc-int.htm

If you're so inclined you'll find this calculator helpful in learning about fund expenses that you, as a shareholder, pay for and how they affect your investment results.

However, if costs are a major concern to you, the SEC points out that a more convenient tool for comparing fund expenses between various funds can be found on the FINRA website. (FINRA is the acronym for Financial Industry Regulatory Authority, formerly known as The National Association of Securities Dealers or NASD.) If you visit FINRA's website you'll be pleased to find how simple it is to get the cost information and comparison for virtually any fund and ETF (Exchange Traded Fund) by simply "filling in the blanks." Remember, there's a huge difference between open end mutual funds and ETFs, which are unmanaged and subject to commission charges for any and all transactions, and don't offer the same degree of diversification. FINRA's "Mutual Fund Expense Analyzer" can be accessed at *www.finra.org/index.htm* then go to "Investor Tools" and click on "Mutual Fund Expense Analyzer."

A word about mutual fund operating costs and expenses – everyone wants to pay as little as possible for anything they might purchase, and that's fine. But it's not something to obsess over, because there's no such thing as a free lunch. Every business must earn a reasonable profit to survive and produce the product people want. That said we cannot ignore excessive costs, which by definition will be different for everyone. For example, if a fund's operating expense costs are as low as 6/10ths of 1%, but it fails to produce consistent above average investment results, the low cost is of no real benefit to the investor. On the other hand, if a fund has operating costs of 3%, that means that the first 3% in the increase in the value of your shares just gets you even – and that's every year. That's where these calculators may prove helpful in doing the kind of research which could result in your finding that any numbers of funds with "high operating expenses" have in fact consistently outperformed any number of funds with lower expenses. It's been my experience that there is no direct correlation between "costs" and comparative investment results. Some funds are more "expensive" than others, and worth it, while others that may boast lower "costs" may not always meet your performance requirements – just use your judgment.

Reminder – When selecting a mutual fund for your serious dollars, costs should not be the sole determining factor, except for index funds, which are unmanaged and may have identical portfolio holdings. In that case, you may find some fund managers are better at running their business, which results in lower operating costs.

Conclusion - Unless you insist on getting involved in the laborious job of accessing the SEC website and pulling information and financial statements for each fund in which you're interested (good luck!), you now have the ability to access that information from an objective, authoritative source that makes the job of cost comparison simple and convenient.

SEC's Plain English Mutual Fund Tutorial

Invest Wisely:
An Introduction to Mutual Funds

Over the past decade, American investors increasingly have turned to mutual funds to save for retirement and other financial goals. Mutual funds can offer the advantages of diversification and professional management. But, as with other investment choices, investing in mutual funds involves risk. And fees and taxes will diminish a fund's returns. It pays to understand both the upsides and the downsides of mutual fund investing and how to choose products that match your goals and tolerance for risk.

This brochure explains the basics of mutual fund investing — how mutual funds work, what factors to consider before investing, and how to avoid common pitfalls.

> ➤ Key Points To Remember
> ➤ How Mutual Funds Work
> ➤ Factors to Consider
> ➤ Avoiding Common Pitfalls
> ➤ If You Have Problems
> ➤ Glossary of Key Mutual Fund Terms

Key Points to Remember

- Mutual funds are **not** guaranteed or insured by the FDIC or any other government agency — even if you buy through a bank and the fund carries the bank's name. You can lose money investing in mutual funds.

- Past performance is not a reliable indicator of future performance. So don't be dazzled by last year's high returns. But past performance can help you assess a fund's volatility over time.

- All mutual funds have costs that lower your investment returns. Shop around, and use a mutual fund cost calculator at www.sec.gov/investor/ tools.shtml to compare many of the costs of owning different funds *before* you buy.

How Mutual Funds Work

What They Are

A mutual fund is a company that pools money from many investors and invests the money in stocks, bonds, short-term money-market instruments, other securities or assets, or some combination of these investments. The combined holdings the mutual fund owns are known as its portfolio. Each share represents an investor's proportionate ownership of the fund's holdings and the income those holdings generate.

Other Types of Investment Companies

Legally known as an "open-end company," a mutual fund is one of three basic types of investment companies. While this brochure discusses **only** mutual funds, you should be aware that other pooled investment vehicles exist and may offer features that you desire. The two other basic types of investment companies are:

Closed-end funds — which, unlike mutual funds, sell a fixed number of shares at one time (in an initial public offering) that later trade on a secondary market; and

Unit Investment Trusts (UITs) — which make a one-time public offering of only a specific, fixed number of redeemable securities called "units" and which will terminate and dissolve on a date specified at the creation of the UIT.

"Exchange-traded funds" (ETFs) are a type of investment company that aims to achieve the same return as a particular market index. They can be either open-end companies or UITs. But ETFs are not considered to be, and are not permitted to call themselves, mutual funds.

Some of the traditional, distinguishing characteristics of mutual funds include the following:

•	Investors purchase mutual fund shares from the fund itself (or through a broker for the fund) instead of from other investors on a secondary market, such as the New York Stock Exchange or Nasdaq Stock Market.
•	The price that investors pay for mutual fund shares is the fund's per share net asset value (NAV) plus any shareholder fees that the fund imposes at the time of purchase (such as sales loads).
•	Mutual fund shares are "redeemable," meaning investors can sell their shares back to the fund (or to a broker acting for the fund).
•	Mutual funds generally create and sell new shares to accommodate new investors. In other words, they sell their shares on a continuous basis, although some funds stop selling when, for example, they become too large.
•	The investment portfolios of mutual funds typically are managed by separate entities known as "investment advisers" that are registered with the SEC.

A Word About Hedge Funds and "Funds of Hedge Funds"

"Hedge fund" is a general, non-legal term used to describe private, unregistered investment pools that traditionally have been limited to sophisticated, wealthy investors. Hedge funds are not mutual funds and, as such, are not subject to the numerous regulations that apply to mutual funds for the protection of investors — including regulations requiring a certain degree of liquidity, regulations requiring that mutual fund shares be redeemable at any time, regulations protecting against conflicts of interest, regulations to assure fairness in the pricing of fund shares, disclosure regulations, regulations limiting the use of leverage, and more.

"Funds of hedge funds," a relatively new type of investment product, are investment companies that invest in hedge funds. Some, but not all, register with the SEC and file semi-annual reports. They often have lower minimum investment thresholds than traditional, unregistered hedge funds and can sell their shares to a larger number of investors. Like hedge funds, funds of hedge funds are not mutual funds. Unlike open-end mutual funds, funds of hedge funds offer very limited rights of redemption. And, unlike ETFs, their shares are not typically listed on an exchange.

You'll find more information about <u>hedge funds</u> on our website. To learn more about funds of hedge funds, please read NASD's Investor Alert entitled <u>Funds of Hedge Funds: Higher Costs and Risks for Higher Potential Returns</u>.

Advantages and Disadvantages

Every investment has advantages and disadvantages. But it's important to remember that features that matter to one investor may not be important to you. Whether any particular feature is an advantage for you will depend on your unique circumstances. For some investors, mutual funds provide an attractive investment choice because they generally offer the following features:

- **Professional Management** — Professional money managers research, select, and monitor the performance of the securities the fund purchases.

- **Diversification** — Diversification is an investing strategy that can be neatly summed up as "Don't put all your eggs in one basket." Spreading your investments across a wide range of companies and industry sectors can help lower your risk if a company or sector fails. Some investors find it easier to achieve diversification through ownership of mutual funds rather than through ownership of individual stocks or bonds.

- **Affordability** — Some mutual funds accommodate investors who don't have a lot of money to invest by setting relatively low dollar amounts for initial purchases, subsequent monthly purchases, or both.

- **Liquidity** — Mutual fund investors can readily redeem their shares at the current NAV — plus any fees and charges assessed on redemption — at any time.

But mutual funds also have features that some investors might view as disadvantages, such as:

- **Costs Despite Negative Returns** — Investors must pay sales charges, annual fees, and other expenses (which we'll discuss below) regardless of how the fund performs. And, depending on the timing of their investment, investors may also have to pay taxes on any capital gains distribution they receive — even if the fund went on to perform poorly after they bought shares.

- **Lack of Control** — Investors typically cannot ascertain the exact make-up of a fund's portfolio at any given time, nor can they directly influence which securities the fund manager buys and sells or the timing of those trades.

- **Price Uncertainty** — With an individual stock, you can obtain real-time (or close to real-time) pricing information with relative ease by checking financial websites or by calling your broker. You can also monitor how a stock's price changes from hour to hour — or even second to second. By contrast, with a mutual fund, the price at which you purchase or redeem shares will typically depend on the fund's NAV, which the fund might not calculate until many hours after you've placed your order. In general, mutual funds must calculate their NAV at least once every business day, typically after the major U.S. exchanges close.

Different Types of Funds

When it comes to investing in mutual funds, investors have literally thousands of choices. Before you invest in any given fund, decide whether the investment strategy and risks of the fund are a good fit for you. The first step to successful investing is figuring out your financial goals and risk tolerance — either on your own or with the help of a financial professional. Once you know what you're saving for, when you'll need the money, and how much risk you can tolerate, you can more easily narrow your choices.

Most mutual funds fall into one of three main categories — money market funds, bond funds (also called "fixed income" funds), and stock funds (also called "equity" funds). Each type has different features and different risks and rewards. Generally, the higher the potential return, the higher the risk of loss.

Money Market Funds

Money market funds have relatively low risks, compared to other mutual funds (and most other investments). By law, they can invest in only certain high-quality, short-term investments issued by the U.S. government, U.S. corporations, and state and local governments. Money market funds try to keep their net asset value (NAV) — which represents the value of one share in a fund — at a stable $1.00 per share. But the NAV may fall below $1.00 if the fund's investments perform poorly. Investor losses have been rare, but they are possible.

Money market funds pay dividends that generally reflect short-term interest rates, and historically the returns for money market funds have been lower than for either bond or stock funds. That's why "inflation risk" — the risk that inflation will outpace and erode investment returns over time — can be a potential concern for investors in money market funds.

Bond Funds

Bond funds generally have higher risks than money market funds, largely because they typically pursue strategies aimed at producing higher yields. Unlike money market funds, the SEC's rules do not restrict bond funds to high-quality or short-term investments. Because there are many different types of bonds, bond funds can vary dramatically in their risks and rewards. Some of the risks associated with bond funds include:

Credit Risk — the possibility that companies or other issuers whose bonds are owned by the fund may fail to pay their debts (including the debt owed to holders of their bonds). Credit risk is less of a factor for bond funds that invest in insured bonds or U.S. Treasury bonds. By contrast, those that invest in the bonds of companies with poor credit ratings generally will be subject to higher risk.

Interest Rate Risk — the risk that the market value of the bonds will go down when interest rates go up. Because of this, you can lose money in any bond fund, including those that invest only in insured bonds or Treasury bonds. Funds that invest in longer-term bonds tend to have higher interest rate risk.

Prepayment Risk — the chance that a bond will be paid off early. For example, if interest rates fall, a bond issuer may decide to pay off (or "retire") its debt and issue new bonds that pay a lower rate. When this happens, the fund may not be able to reinvest the proceeds in an investment with as high a return or yield.

Stock Funds

Although a stock fund's value can rise and fall quickly (and dramatically) over the short term, historically stocks have performed better over the long term than other types of investments — including corporate bonds, government bonds, and treasury securities.

Overall "market risk" poses the greatest potential danger for investors in stocks funds. Stock prices can fluctuate for a broad range of reasons — such as the overall strength of the economy or demand for particular products or services.

Not all stock funds are the same. For example:

- *Growth* funds focus on stocks that may not pay a regular dividend but have the potential for large capital gains.

- *Income* funds invest in stocks that pay regular dividends.

- *Index* funds aim to achieve the same return as a particular market index, such as the S&P 500 Composite Stock Price Index, by investing in all — or perhaps a representative sample — of the companies included in an index.

- *Sector* funds may specialize in a particular industry segment, such as technology or consumer products stocks.

How to Buy and Sell Shares

You can purchase shares in some mutual funds by contacting the fund directly. Other mutual fund shares are sold mainly through brokers, banks, financial planners, or insurance agents. All mutual funds will redeem (buy back) your shares on any business day and must send you the payment within seven days.

The easiest way to determine the value of your shares is to call the fund's toll-free number or visit its website. The financial pages of major newspapers sometimes print the NAVs for various mutual funds. When you buy shares, you pay the current NAV per share plus any fee the fund assesses at the time of purchase, such as a purchase sales load or other type of purchase fee. When you sell your shares, the fund will pay you the NAV minus any fee the fund assesses at the time of redemption, such as a deferred (or back-end) sales load or redemption fee. A fund's NAV goes up or down daily as its holdings change in value.

Exchanging Shares

A "family of funds" is a group of mutual funds that share administrative and distribution systems. Each fund in a family may have different investment objectives and follow different strategies.

Some funds offer exchange privileges within a family of funds, allowing shareholders to transfer their holdings from one fund to another as their investment goals or tolerance for risk change. While some funds impose fees for exchanges, most funds typically do not. To learn more about a fund's exchange policies, call the fund's toll-free number, visit its website, or read the "shareholder information" section of the prospectus.

Bear in mind that exchanges have tax consequences. Even if the fund doesn't charge you for the transfer, you'll be liable for any capital gain on the sale of your old shares — or, depending on the circumstances, eligible to take a capital loss. We'll discuss taxes in further detail below.

How Funds Can Earn Money for You

You can earn money from your investment in three ways:

1. **Dividend Payments** — A fund may earn income in the form of dividends and interest on the securities in its portfolio. The fund then pays its shareholders nearly all of the income (minus disclosed expenses) it has earned in the form of dividends.

2. **Capital Gains Distributions** — The price of the securities a fund owns may increase. When a fund sells a security that has increased in price, the fund has a capital gain. At the end of the year, most funds

distribute these capital gains (minus any capital losses) to investors.

3. **Increased NAV** — If the market value of a fund's portfolio increases after deduction of expenses and liabilities, then the value (NAV) of the fund and its shares increases. The higher NAV reflects the higher value of your investment.

With respect to dividend payments and capital gains distributions, funds usually will give you a choice: the fund can send you a check or other form of payment, or you can have your dividends or distributions reinvested in the fund to buy more shares (often without paying an additional sales load).

Factors to Consider

Thinking about your long-term investment strategies and tolerance for risk can help you decide what type of fund is best suited for you. But you should also consider the effect that fees and taxes will have on your returns over time.

Degrees of Risk

All funds carry some level of risk. You may lose some or all of the money you invest — your principal — because the securities held by a fund go up and down in value. Dividend or interest payments may also fluctuate as market conditions change.

Before you invest, be sure to read a fund's prospectus and shareholder reports to learn about its investment strategy and the potential risks. Funds with higher rates of return may take risks that are beyond your comfort level and are inconsistent with your financial goals.

A Word About Derivatives

Derivatives are financial instruments whose performance is derived, at least in part, from the performance of an underlying asset, security, or index. Even small market movements can dramatically affect their value, sometimes in unpredictable ways.

There are many types of derivatives with many different uses. A fund's prospectus will disclose whether and how it may use derivatives. You may also want to call a fund and ask how it uses these instruments.

Fees and Expenses

As with any business, running a mutual fund involves costs — including shareholder transaction costs, investment advisory fees, and marketing and distribution expenses. Funds pass along these costs to investors by imposing fees and expenses. It is important that you understand these charges because they lower your returns.

Some funds impose "shareholder fees" directly on investors whenever they buy or sell shares. In addition, every fund has regular, recurring, fund-wide "operating expenses." Funds typically pay their operating expenses out of fund assets — which means that investors indirectly pay these costs.

SEC rules require funds to disclose both shareholder fees and operating expenses in a "fee table" near the front of a fund's prospectus. The lists below will help you decode the fee table and understand the various fees a fund may impose:

Shareholder Fees

- **Sales Charge (Load) on Purchases** — the amount you pay when you buy shares in a mutual fund. Also known as a "front-end load," this fee typically goes to the brokers that sell the fund's shares. Front-end loads reduce the amount of your investment. For example, let's say you have $1,000 and want to invest it in a mutual fund with a 5% front-end load. The $50 sales load you must pay comes off the top, and the remaining $950 will be invested in the fund. According to NASD rules, a front-end load cannot be higher than 8.5% of your investment.

- **Purchase Fee** — another type of fee that some funds charge their shareholders when they buy shares. Unlike a front-end sales load, a purchase fee is paid to the fund (not to a broker) and is typically imposed to defray some of the fund's costs associated with the purchase.

- **Deferred Sales Charge (Load)** — a fee you pay when you sell your shares. Also known as a "back-end load," this fee typically goes to the brokers that sell the fund's shares. The most common type of back-end sales load is the "contingent deferred sales load" (also known as a "CDSC" or "CDSL"). The amount of this type of load will depend on how long the investor holds his or her shares and typically decreases to zero if the investor holds his or her shares long enough.

- **Redemption Fee** — another type of fee that some funds charge their shareholders when they sell or redeem shares. Unlike a deferred sales load, a redemption fee is paid to the fund (not to a broker) and is typically used to defray fund costs associated with a shareholder's redemption.

- **Exchange Fee** — a fee that some funds impose on shareholders if they exchange (transfer) to another fund within the same fund group or "family of funds."

- **Account fee** — a fee that some funds separately impose on investors in connection with the maintenance of their accounts. For example, some funds impose an account maintenance fee on accounts whose value is less than a certain dollar amount.

Annual Fund Operating Expenses

- **Management Fees** — fees that are paid out of fund assets to the fund's investment adviser for investment portfolio management, any other management fees payable to the fund's investment adviser or its affiliates, and administrative fees payable to the investment adviser that are not included in the "Other Expenses" category (discussed below).

- **Distribution [and/or Service] Fees ("12b-1" Fees)** — fees paid by the fund out of fund assets to cover the costs of marketing and selling fund shares and sometimes to cover the costs of providing shareholder services. "Distribution fees" include fees to compensate brokers and others who sell fund shares and to pay for advertising, the printing and mailing of prospectuses to new investors, and the printing and mailing of sales literature. "Shareholder Service Fees" are fees paid to persons to respond to investor inquiries and provide investors with information about their investments.

- **Other Expenses** — expenses not included under "Management Fees" or "Distribution or Service (12b-1) Fees," such as any shareholder service expenses that are not already included in the 12b-1 fees, custodial expenses, legal and accounting expenses, transfer agent expenses, and other administrative expenses.

- **Total Annual Fund Operating Expenses ("Expense Ratio")** — the line of the fee table that represents the total of all of a fund's annual fund operating expenses, expressed as a percentage of the fund's average net assets. Looking at the expense ratio can help you make comparisons among funds.

A Word About "No-Load" Funds

Some funds call themselves "no-load." As the name implies, this means that the fund does not charge any type of sales load. But, as discussed above, not every type of shareholder fee is a "sales load." A no-load fund may charge fees that are not sales loads, such as purchase fees, redemption fees, exchange fees, and account fees. No-load funds will also have operating expenses.

Be sure to review carefully the fee tables of any funds you're considering, including no-load funds. Even small differences in fees can translate into large differences in returns over time. For example, if you invested $10,000 in a fund that produced a 10% annual return before expenses and had annual operating expenses of 1.5%, then after 20 years you would have roughly $49,725. But if the fund had expenses of only 0.5%, then you would end up with $60,858 — an 18% difference.

A mutual fund cost calculator can help you understand the impact that many types of fees and expenses can have over time. It takes only minutes to compare the costs of different mutual funds.

> **A Word About Breakpoints**
>
> Some mutual funds that charge front-end <u>sales loads</u> will charge lower sales loads for larger investments. The investment levels required to obtain a reduced sales load are commonly referred to as "breakpoints."
>
> The SEC does not require a fund to offer breakpoints in the fund's sales load. But, if breakpoints exist, the fund must disclose them. In addition, a NASD member brokerage firm should not sell you shares of a fund in an amount that is "just below" the fund's sales load breakpoint simply to earn a higher commission.
>
> Each fund company establishes its own formula for how they will calculate whether an investor is entitled to receive a breakpoint. For that reason, it is important to seek out breakpoint information from your financial advisor or the fund itself. You'll need to ask how a particular fund establishes eligibility for breakpoint discounts, as well as what the fund's breakpoint amounts are. NASD's <u>Mutual Fund Breakpoint Search Tool</u> can help you determine whether you're entitled to breakpoint discounts.

Classes of Funds

Many mutual funds offer more than one class of shares. For example, you may have seen a fund that offers "Class A" and "Class B" shares. Each class will invest in the same "pool" (or investment portfolio) of securities and will have the same investment objectives and policies. But each class will have different shareholder services and/or distribution arrangements with different fees and expenses. As a result, each class will likely have different performance results.

A multi-class structure offers investors the ability to select a fee and expense structure that is most appropriate for their investment goals (including the time that they expect to remain invested in the fund). Here are some key characteristics of the most common mutual fund share classes offered to individual investors:

- **Class A Shares** — Class A shares typically impose a front-end sales load. They also tend to have a lower 12b-1 fee and lower annual expenses than other mutual fund share classes. Be aware that some mutual funds reduce the front-end load as the size of your investment increases. If you're considering Class A shares, be sure to inquire about breakpoints.

- **Class B Shares** — Class B shares typically do not have a front-end sales load. Instead, they may impose a contingent deferred sales load and a 12b-1 fee (along with other annual expenses). Class B shares also might convert automatically to a class with a lower 12b-1 fee if the investor holds the shares long enough.

- **Class C Shares** — Class C shares might have a 12b-1 fee, other annual expenses, and either a front- or back-end sales load. But the front- or back-end load for Class C shares tends to be lower than for Class A or Class B shares, respectively. Unlike Class B shares, Class C shares generally do not convert to another class. Class C shares tend to have higher annual expenses than either Class A or Class B shares.

Tax Consequences

When you buy and hold an individual stock or bond, you must pay income tax each year on the dividends or interest you receive. But you won't have to pay any capital gains tax until you actually sell and unless you make a profit.

Mutual funds are different.   When you buy and hold mutual fund shares, you will owe income tax on any ordinary dividends in the year you receive or reinvest them. And, in addition to owing taxes on any personal capital gains when you sell your shares, you may also have to pay taxes each year on the fund's capital gains. That's because the law requires mutual funds to distribute capital gains to shareholders if they sell securities for a profit that can't be offset by a loss.

> Tax Exempt Funds
>
> If you invest in a tax-exempt fund — such as a municipal bond fund — some or all of your dividends will be exempt from federal (and sometimes state and local) income tax. You will, however, owe taxes on any capital gains.

Bear in mind that if you receive a capital gains distribution, you will likely owe taxes — even if the fund has had a negative return from the point during the year when you purchased your shares. For this reason, you should call the fund to find out when it makes distributions so you won't pay more than your fair share of taxes. Some funds post that information on their websites.

SEC rules require mutual funds to disclose in their prospectuses after-tax returns. In calculating after-tax returns, mutual funds must use standardized formulas similar to the ones used to calculate before-tax average annual total returns. You'll find a fund's after-tax returns in the "Risk/Return Summary" section of the prospectus. When comparing funds, be sure to take taxes into account.

Avoiding Common Pitfalls

If you decide to invest in mutual funds, be sure to obtain as much information about the fund before you invest. And don't make assumptions about the soundness of the fund based solely on its past performance or its name.

Sources of Information

Prospectus

When you purchase shares of a mutual fund, the fund must provide you with a prospectus. But you can — and should — request and read a fund's prospectus before you invest. The prospectus is the fund's selling document and contains valuable information, such as the fund's investment objectives or goals, principal strategies for achieving those goals, principal risks of investing in the fund, fees and expenses, and past performance. The prospectus also identifies the fund's managers and advisers and describes how to purchase and redeem fund shares.

While they may seem daunting at first, mutual fund prospectuses contain a treasure trove of valuable information. The SEC requires funds to include specific categories of information in their prospectuses and to present key data (such as fees and past performance) in a standard format so that investors can more easily compare different funds.

Here's some of what you'll find in mutual fund prospectuses:

- **Date of Issue** — The date of the prospectus should appear on the front cover. Mutual funds must update their prospectuses at least once a year, so always check to make sure you're looking at the most recent version.

- **Risk/Return Bar Chart and Table** — Near the front of the prospectus, right after the fund's narrative description of its investment objectives or goals, strategies, and risks, you'll find a **bar chart** showing the fund's annual total returns for each of the last 10 years (or for the life of the fund if it is less than 10 years old). All funds that have had annual returns for at least one calendar year must include this chart.

  Except in limited circumstances, funds also must include a **table** that sets forth returns — both before and after taxes — for the past 1-, 5-, and 10-year periods. The table will also include the returns of an appropriate broad-based index for comparison purposes. Here's what the table will look like:

	1-year	5-year (or life of fund)	10-year (or life of fund)
Return before taxes	___%	___%	___%
Return after taxes on distributions	___%	___%	___%
Return after taxes on distributions and sale of fund shares	___%	___%	___%
Index (reflects no deductions for [fees, expenses, or taxes])	___%	___%	___%

- Note: Be sure to read any footnotes or accompanying explanations to make sure that you fully understand the data the fund provides in the bar chart and table. Also, bear in mind that the bar chart and table for a multiple-class fund (that offers more than one class of fund shares in the prospectus) will typically show performance data and returns for *only one* class.

- **Fee Table** — Following the performance bar chart and annual returns table, you'll find a table that describes the fund's fees and expenses. These include the shareholder fees and annual fund operating expenses described in greater detail above. The fee table includes an example that will help you compare costs among different funds by showing you the costs associated with investing a hypothetical $10,000 over a 1-, 3-, 5-, and 10-year period.

- **Financial Highlights** — This section, which generally appears towards the back of the prospectus, contains audited data concerning the fund's financial performance for each of the past 5 years. Here you'll find net asset values (for both the beginning and end of each period), total returns, and various ratios, including the ratio of expenses to average net assets, the ratio of net income to average net assets, and the portfolio turnover rate.

Profile

Some mutual funds also furnish investors with a "profile," which summarizes key information contained in the fund's prospectus, such as the fund's investment objectives, principal investment strategies, principal risks, performance, fees and expenses, after-tax returns, identity of the fund's investment adviser, investment requirements, and other information.

Statement of Additional Information ("SAI")

Also known as "Part B" of the registration statement, the SAI explains a fund's operations in greater detail than the prospectus — including the fund's financial statements and details about the history of the fund, fund policies on borrowing and concentration, the identity of officers, directors, and persons who control the fund, investment advisory and other services, brokerage commissions, tax matters, and performance such as yield and average annual total return information. If you ask, the fund must send you an SAI. The back cover of the fund's prospectus should contain information on how to obtain the SAI.

Shareholder Reports

A mutual fund also must provide shareholders with annual and semi-annual reports within 60 days after the end of the fund's fiscal year and 60 days after the fund's fiscal mid-year. These reports contain a variety of updated financial information, a list of the fund's portfolio securities, and other information. The information in the shareholder reports will be current as of the date of the particular report (that is, the last day of the fund's fiscal year for the annual report, and the last day of the fund's fiscal mid-year for the semi-annual report).

Investors can obtain all of these documents by:

●	Calling or writing to the fund (all mutual funds have toll-free telephone numbers);
●	Visiting the fund's website;
●	Contacting a broker that sells the fund's shares;
●	Searching the SEC's EDGAR database and downloading the documents for free; or
●	Accessing "How to Request Public Documents."

Past Performance

A fund's past performance is not as important as you might think. Advertisements, rankings, and ratings often emphasize how well a fund has performed in the past. But studies show that the future is often different. This year's "number one" fund can easily become next year's below average fund.

Be sure to find out how long the fund has been in existence. Newly created or small funds sometimes have excellent short-term performance records. Because these funds may invest in only a small number of stocks, a few successful stocks can have a large impact on their performance. But as these funds grow larger and increase the number of stocks they own, each stock has less impact on performance. This may make it more difficult to sustain initial results.

While past performance does not necessarily predict future returns, it can tell you how volatile (or stable) a fund has been over a period of time. Generally, the more volatile a fund, the higher the investment risk. If you'll need your money to meet a financial goal in the near-term, you probably can't afford the risk of investing in a fund with a volatile history because you will not have enough time to ride out any declines in the stock market.

Looking Beyond a Fund's Name

Don't assume that a fund called the "XYZ Stock Fund" invests only in stocks or that the "Martian High-Yield Fund" invests only in the securities of companies head-quartered on the planet Mars. The SEC requires that any mutual fund with a name suggesting that it focuses on a particular type of investment must invest at least 80% of its assets in the type of investment suggested by its name. But funds can still invest up to one-fifth of their holdings in other types of securities — including securities that you might consider too risky or perhaps not aggressive enough.

Bank Products versus Mutual Funds

Many banks now sell mutual funds, some of which carry the bank's name. But mutual funds sold in banks, including money market funds, are not bank deposits. As a result, they are not federally insured by the Federal Deposit Insurance Corporation (FDIC).

Money Market Matters

Don't confuse a "money market fund" with a "money market deposit account." The names are similar, but they are completely different:

- A money market fund is a type of mutual fund. It *is not* guaranteed or FDIC insured. When you buy shares in a money market fund, you should receive a prospectus.

- A money market deposit account is a bank deposit. It *is* guaranteed and FDIC insured. When you deposit money in a money market deposit account, you should receive a Truth in Savings form.

If You Have Problems

If you encounter a problem with your mutual fund, you can send us your complaint using our <u>online complaint form</u>. You can also reach us by regular mail at:

Securities and Exchange Commission
Office of Investor Education and Advocacy
100 F Street, N.E.
Washington, D.C. 20549-0213

For more information about investing wisely and avoiding fraud, please check out the <u>Investor Information</u> section of our website.

Glossary of Key Mutual Fund Terms

12b-1 Fees — fees paid by the fund out of fund assets to cover the costs of marketing and selling fund shares and sometimes to cover the costs of providing shareholder services. "Distribution fees" include fees to compensate brokers and others who sell fund shares and to pay for advertising, the printing and mailing of prospectuses to new investors, and the printing and mailing of sales literature. "Shareholder Service Fees" are fees paid to persons to respond to investor inquiries and provide investors with information about their investments.

Account Fee — a fee that some funds separately impose on investors for the maintenance of their accounts. For example, accounts below a specified dollar amount may have to pay an account fee.

Back-end Load — a sales charge (also known as a "deferred sales charge") investors pay when they redeem (or sell) mutual fund shares, generally used by the fund to compensate brokers.

Classes — different types of shares issued by a single fund, often referred to as Class A shares, Class B shares, and so on. Each class invests in the same "pool" (or investment portfolio) of securities and has the same investment objectives and policies. But each class has different shareholder services and/or distribution arrangements with different fees and expenses and therefore different performance results.

Closed-End Fund — a type of investment company that does not continuously offer its shares for sale but instead sells a fixed number of shares at one time (in the initial public offering) which then typically trade on a secondary market, such as the New York Stock Exchange or the Nasdaq Stock Market. Legally known as a "closed-end company."

Contingent Deferred Sales Load — a type of back-end load, the amount of which depends on the length of time the investor held his or her shares. For example, a contingent deferred sales load might be (X)% if an investor holds his or her shares for one year, (X-1)% after two years, and so on until the load reaches zero and goes away completely.

Conversion — a feature some funds offer that allows investors to automatically change from one class to another (typically with lower annual expenses) after a set period of time. The fund's prospectus or profile will state whether a class ever converts to another class.

Deferred Sales Charge — see "back-end load" (above).

Distribution Fees — fees paid out of fund assets to cover expenses for marketing and selling fund shares, including advertising costs, compensation for brokers and others who sell fund shares, and payments for printing and mailing prospectuses to new investors and sales literature prospective investors. Sometimes referred to as "12b-1 fees."

Exchange Fee — a fee that some funds impose on shareholders if they exchange (transfer) to another fund within the same fund group.

Exchange-Traded Funds — a type of an investment company (either an open-end company or UIT) whose objective is to achieve the same return as a particular market index. ETFs differ from traditional open-end companies and UITs, because, pursuant to SEC exemptive orders, shares issued by ETFs trade on a secondary market and are only redeemable from the fund itself in very large blocks (blocks of 50,000 shares for example).

Expense Ratio — the fund's total annual operating expenses (including management fees, distribution (12b-1) fees, and other expenses) expressed as a percentage of average net assets.

Front-end Load — an upfront sales charge investors pay when they purchase fund shares, generally used by the fund to compensate brokers. A front-end load reduces the amount available to purchase fund shares.

Index Fund — describes a type of mutual fund or Unit Investment Trust (UIT) whose investment objective typically is to achieve the same return as a particular market index, such as the S&P 500 Composite Stock Price Index, the Russell 2000 Index, or the Wilshire 5000 Total Market Index.

Investment Adviser — generally, a person or entity who receives compensation for giving individually tailored advice to a specific person on investing in stocks, bonds, or mutual funds. Some investment advisers also manage portfolios of securities, including mutual funds.

Investment Company — a company (corporation, business trust, partnership, or limited liability company) that issues securities and is primarily engaged in the business of investing in securities. The three basic types of investment companies are mutual funds, closed-end funds, and unit investment trusts.

Load — see "Sales Charge."

Management Fee — fee paid out of fund assets to the fund's investment adviser or its affiliates for managing the fund's portfolio, any other management fee payable to the fund's investment adviser or its affiliates, and any administrative fee payable to the investment adviser that are not included in the "Other Expenses" category. A fund's management fee appears as a category under "Annual Fund Operating Expenses" in the Fee Table.

Market Index — a measurement of the performance of a specific "basket" of stocks considered to represent a particular market or sector of the U.S. stock market or the economy. For example, the Dow Jones Industrial Average (DJIA) is an index of 30 "blue chip" U.S. stocks of industrial companies (excluding transportation and utility companies).

Mutual Fund — the common name for an open-end investment company. Like other types of investment companies, mutual funds pool money from many investors and invest the money in stocks, bonds, short-term money-market instruments, or other securities. Mutual funds issue redeemable shares that investors purchase directly from the fund (or through a broker for the fund) instead of purchasing from investors on a secondary market.

NAV (Net Asset Value) — the value of the fund's assets minus its liabilities. SEC rules require funds to calculate the NAV at least once daily. To calculate the NAV per share, simply subtract the fund's liabilities from its assets and then divide the result by the number of shares outstanding.

No-load Fund — a fund that does not charge any type of sales load. But not every type of shareholder fee is a "sales load," and a no-load fund may charge fees that are not sales loads. No-load funds also charge operating expenses.

Open-End Company — the legal name for a mutual fund. An open-end company is a type of investment company

Operating Expenses — the costs a fund incurs in connection with running the fund, including management fees, distribution (12b-1) fees, and other expenses.

Portfolio — an individual's or entity's combined holdings of stocks, bonds, or other securities and assets.

Profile — summarizes key information about a mutual fund's costs, investment objectives, risks, and performance. Although every mutual fund has a prospectus, not every mutual fund has a profile.

Prospectus — describes the mutual fund to prospective investors. Every mutual fund has a prospectus. The prospectus contains information about the mutual fund's costs, investment objectives, risks, and performance. You can get a prospectus from the mutual fund company (through its website or by phone or mail). Your financial professional or broker can also provide you with a copy.

Purchase Fee — a shareholder fee that some funds charge when investors purchase mutual fund shares. Not the same as (and may be in addition to) a front-end load.

Redemption Fee — a shareholder fee that some funds charge when investors redeem (or sell) mutual fund shares. Redemption fees (which must be paid to the fund) are not the same as (and may be in addition to) a back-end load (which is typically paid to a broker). The SEC generally limits redemption fees to 2%.

Sales Charge (or "Load") — the amount that investors pay when they purchase (front-end load) or redeem (back-end load) shares in a mutual fund, similar to a commission. The SEC's rules do not limit the size of sales load a fund may charge, but NASD rules state that mutual fund sales loads cannot exceed 8.5% and must be even lower depending on other fees and charges assessed.

Shareholder Service Fees — fees paid to persons to respond to investor inquiries and provide investors with information about their investments. See also "12b-1 fees."

Statement of Additional Information (SAI) — conveys information about an open- or closed-end fund that is not necessarily needed by investors to make an informed investment decision, but that some investors find useful. Although funds are not required to provide investors with the SAI, they must give investors the SAI upon request and without charge. Also known as "Part B" of the fund's registration statement.

Total Annual Fund Operating Expense — the total of a fund's annual fund operating expenses, expressed as a percentage of the fund's average net assets. You'll find the total in the fund's fee table in the prospectus.

Unit Investment Trust (UIT) — a type of investment company that typically makes a one-time "public offering" of only a specific, fixed number of units. A UIT will terminate and dissolve on a date established when the UIT is created (although some may terminate more than fifty years after they are created). UITs do not actively trade their investment portfolios. http://www.sec.gov/investor/pubs/inwsmf.htm

Modified: 07/02/2008

Chapter 5 - Bells and Whistles

I've learned that the best approach to mutual fund investing is based on the old saw "KISS," or "keep it simple stupid," which I repeat to myself with some frequency. After all you are hiring professional money managers to invest for growth of capital by selecting securities for capital appreciation, diversifying your investment to reduce risk and monitoring those securities, which includes making the necessary changes/adjustments required to meet changing conditions in the economy, the market and the world. That's a 24/7/365 job and it's unlikely in the extreme that someone engaged in earning a living outside the securities industry will do a better job than the professionals. It's why you pay a management fee, one of the best bargains in the marketplace today. Your job is to monitor the results on a quarterly basis, comparing them to other funds with similar objectives and making changes if your fund is not performing as expected.

That brings us to the four choices that I believe offer the best potential for growth of your investment – growth & income funds, domestic growth funds, global funds and emerging market funds. Now it's a matter of your investment "temperature" and/or your "comfort" level. If you think the United States is on its way out as a global competitor and we've lost our ability to innovate and create, then your choice is simple, buy gold, guns and butter. With those "assets" you can trade for anything when the country implodes...but don't count on that happening any time soon. On the other hand, if you understand how our economy works you'll recognize that despite market declines, corrections, adjustments or whatever else a decline in stock prices is called, the best opportunity for financial independence is a diversified portfolio of common stocks spread across the global economy.

In addition, you should understand the nature of each of these fund types before deciding on how to allocate your investment for the long term. Remember, "KISS" still applies. If your goal is long term capital appreciation/accumulation, your investment should be divided on a 50/25/25 allocation (domestic growth, global and emerging market funds). After a period of time, which will be different for everyone, you can decide to refine your allocations and adjust your three categories of funds by increasing or decreasing the percentages invested in each category and/or adding other categories. But remember, it's not required that you change your percentage allocations – it depends on your own individual comfort level – some investors are more aggressive, while others more conservative. The bottom line is the 50/25/25 allocation will work for most investors and is likely to be more successful than your current approach. The idea is to grow your investment portfolio without taking unnecessary risks or deluding yourself that income oriented investments will achieve your long term goals.

Allocating

Allocating – It all depends on your comfort level and the degree of risk you're willing to accept. Remember there's no such thing as a "riskless" investment. If you're very conservative then you might be most comfortable with a 50% allocation in the Growth & Income sector and 25% each in the Domestic and Global sectors. However, if you're willing to accept some additional risk to achieve greater growth, then you might be more comfortable with 50% in the Domestic sector with the balance split 25% each in Global and Emerging Market sectors – a possible approach for anyone _over_ 50 years of age, who still has about 10 to 15 years to retirement.

For the "aggressive" investor, those with time on their side, usually _under_ 50 years of age, who understands risk and is willing to accept it, a 50/50 split between Global and Emerging Markets sectors offers above average opportunities for growth, while a 100% Emerging Markets allocation represents the greatest degree of risk with the greatest potential for growth. But if that's your choice, you'd better have a pretty strong stomach for some of the fluctuations and gyrations you will inevitably encounter along the way. In other words, that kind of allocation is not for the faint of heart.

One of the advantages of investing in a family of mutual funds that offers a variety of funds with different objectives is the ability to exchange between and among the funds you own with one phone call. No, this is _not_ an invitation to so-called market timers who have never demonstrated a verifiable record of successful investing by "timing" the markets. And it's not for people who are spooked by the latest negative headlines. In fact, most well managed funds have strict exchange requirements that might include a fee for each exchange, limitations on the number of exchanges permitted or minimum holding periods before exchanges are permitted. Be sure to know about such restrictions *before* you commit to a long term program.

A typical case?

©*Scott Adams/Dist. By United Feature Syndicate, Inc.*

Recently a young woman who had left her job learned that her 401(k) plan had been transferred to another mutual fund organization. Without her knowledge or approval, the proceeds of her account, about $150,000, were invested in a "Target Date" fund, which is designed to allocate the investments of all shareholders between stocks and bonds, i.e., one size fits all. In this case, at 43 years of age her target date fund was called the "20/30 Fund" focused on a 20 year period to end in the year 2030. In this case it covered a 23 year period. The portfolio of that fund was 88% in stocks and 12% in bonds. Theoretically, with the passage of time, a greater percentage would be allocated to bonds while reducing the percentage of common stocks. When asked, I told her that in my opinion that was simply foolish and actually diminished the potential for significant appreciation over the 23 year period. In any case I questioned why someone 43 years of age would invest 12% of her retirement fund in bonds which percentage would increase with the passing years. Remember, the goal was capital appreciation with a 23 year time horizon. Instead, I suggested it would be more prudent for her to allocate one half of her retirement account to a domestic "500" type index fund and 25% each in a global fund and an emerging market fund. Then she can monitor the progress of her portfolio and make adjustments, i.e., after 15 years she could easily move a significant allocation of her fund to bonds if she decided that was more appropriate at that time. The point is that placing your investment on some kind of "automatic pilot" is not the solution unless you want nothing whatsoever to do with the results you hope to achieve. But hey, it's still a free country.

A Word About Allocations – Some very capable people in the industry take investment allocations to an extreme by recommending that you invest in 10, 12 and even more mutual funds. I'm not convinced that degree of diversification is either effective or necessary for two reasons. I'm reminded of a question asked of John Templeton at a shareholder meeting about buying investment specific funds, i.e., a specific industry or geographic region, etc. His response was quite simple, find a good mutual fund organization with a consistent record of above average performance and give them the ability to invest in what they feel are the best opportunities – don't limit them to one industry, market, country or geographic area, because it limits their ability to adapt to changing conditions. I believe he was right then and his answer still applies today.

However, there's another reason directly related to the concept of diversification that is sometimes overlooked. Since the Investment Company Act of 1940 was passed, regulated mutual funds are prohibited from investing more than 5% of their portfolios in a single security, excluding cash or money market instruments, or from owning more than 10% of the outstanding securities of a company. That's one of the reasons mutual funds have achieved the success they enjoy.

Remember a regulated fund cannot put more than 5% of its portfolio in one stock, which means it must own at least 20 different companies (not including cash or money market instruments). As a result, owning 8 or 10 different mutual funds means you would indirectly own a minimum of at least between 160 or 200 (possibly 300 to 500) different securities in your portfolio and be over diversified, which might result in less than desired performance results. What's best for you? What's your comfort level? Is more diversification preferred? There's no definitive answer, but owning several funds is preferable to owning just one fund or worse, one stock.

THE "NOISE"

The answers to finding and investing in a well managed fund are <u>not</u> in magazines like *Money* or *Smart Money,* or too many websites to list. Some of these sources profess to have all the answers – for a price, of course. However, there are a few things you should know about many "sources" of investment information/advice.

EQUITY FUND PERFORMANCE CHECK

©Scott Adams/Dist. By United Feature Syndicate, Inc.

Want to know how a fund has performed in different market cycles: good (bull) markets, versus bad (bear) markets? One of the best tools for this purpose is *Forbes Magazine* that uses a grading system based on bull and bear market cycles. For example, the more risky funds tend to get As and Bs in a bull market and Ds and Fs in a bear market.

Why is this of interest to you? Because depending on your investing "temperature" you'll probably be more comfortable knowing in advance how a fund is likely to perform in different market cycles. If you're risk averse, you can make a decision that you can live with as opposed to being surprised during down markets which could cause you to redeem your shares at the worst possible time.

Forbes makes it free, easy and online at www.forbes.com/finance/funds. But remember, one market cycle does not necessarily represent a definitive method of selecting a fund for a long term investment. However, it does give you a "feel" for what you might expect during different market cycles, and that does have some value. Just remember:

1. These sources exist to make money – it's important to understand that they are *not* non-profit or charitable organizations;

2. Some magazines employ informed, knowledgeable columnists who can be helpful. However, you should understand that too many financial articles are written by very nice, but very young people who often lack perspective and real life experience. Too often their "experience" might have been influenced by a college professor who may not be known for his/her investment expertise. You've heard it before – "Those who can, do. Those who can't, teach."

3. Almost invariably, these sources are selling something, a publication, newsletter, investment advice, etc.

That's not to say you can't learn something from these sources, since they can and often do provide current information on a variety of investment topics. But I believe it's a mistake to rely on them exclusively for the answers to investing for the long term. An example of some "noise" that found its way into a few publications is the "100 solution," which is supposed to solve your investment allocation decision. The solution is so simple – just subtract your age from 100 – which then means your age is the amount of your investments to be placed in income oriented funds, with the balance in common stock type funds. Voila! - problem solved.

But let's take it to its extreme. You're 30 years old so when you subtract that from 100 it tells you you're supposed to have 70% of your investment in common stock funds, which means the balance is allocated to income oriented funds. Right. Telling a 30 year old to put 30% of her investment in bonds, etc., is nothing less than a terrible disservice which can only result in missing real opportunities over the next several decades. The fact is that at 30 years old, 100% of investable dollars should be in equities to take advantage of long term growth opportunities which is surely where the best possibilities for growth abound. Well, the "100 solution" sounded good – NOT.

Another buzz term in the fund industry involves "style boxes." Rather than waste space here, if you're interested in style boxes look up *Morningstar* on the Internet. You may be impressed with their professed knowledge or you may be totally confused. Or you may be into counting stars. In either case one thing's certain – even with style boxes and star ratings no one can tell you which funds will be the best performers in the future, but it sure does help when you're selling an investment service! Nevertheless, these designations are great marketing tools for altogether too many "advisers."

> "Star ratings" – One thing Morningstar might consider is adding another designation to their star ratings – "NR," *NOT RATED*. That would be a <u>real</u> public service in that it would send a strong message to the investment manager to address a variety of deficiencies. One thing's for certain, it will definitely get the manager's attention and be of tremendous help to investors in avoiding mistakes.

<u>Full disclosure</u> - I've owned many different funds over several decades. Some did not perform well, while most did perform well on a consistent basis - call me crazy, but I never made a selection based on style boxes or stars.

The following addresses some of the things you need to know in making your mutual fund selections.

Process of Elimination

If your investment goal is growth of capital you have about 5,000 mutual funds from which to choose (see "The Numbers" on page 125), not including ETFs and closed end funds. This is another opportunity to apply the "KISS" principle whether you're doing it yourself or investing with an adviser.

At the outset it's important to accept the fact that no selection method works under all circumstances and conditions, i.e., there are exceptions to any rule. That said, I think you'll find the suggestions that follow can be helpful if not valuable in making your fund selections. First, let's address a simple fact – when I decide to buy a new car, I don't go to a supermarket or a restaurant to make that purchase. I prefer to go to a company that specializes in manufacturing and selling cars, especially if it involves serious money. The same principle applies to mutual funds, which makes the selection process a manageable task.

It's been my experience that you won't often find certain fund management companies and their products listed among the consistent above average performing funds. Those companies include brokerage houses, banks and insurance companies. (There are a number of reasons for that which could be the subject of another book.) I believe that you'll find this to be true more often than not. As a result, when searching for a new fund to add to my portfolio or to replace a fund that has not performed as anticipated, I never waste my time on funds managed by any of these three types of "advisory" organizations. In addition to less than desirable results and features, too often their focus is asset gathering and not competitive performance results. Therefore, I simply ignore the countless funds offered by banks, insurance companies and brokerage houses. I prefer to have my money managed by fund organizations whose primary, if not sole, business is mutual fund management. That's not to say that all funds managed by these three types of organizations are under performers. There are exceptions to the rule. One example is the Oppenheimer Funds which is owned by an insurance company, but appears to have retained its autonomy and original investment management culture. Full disclosure – I do not own any Oppenheimer Funds and have no relationship whatsoever with the organization.

Equity Performance Check

REALITY CHECK – Locked in?

It wasn't too long ago that if you had an account with a major securities brokerage company and invested in any of their proprietary or "house" funds, you were in for a surprise at some future date. I don't know about you, but I don't like surprises. Here's the deal – if your broker or representative left the brokerage company and moved to another firm, and you wanted to stay with him/her, i.e., transfer your mutual fund accounts to his new brokerage company – surprise! If you owned any of the "house" funds you learned that they were not eligible to be transferred to another brokerage company.

At that time Brokerage Company B could not sell/service mutual funds managed by brokerage Company A. The problem was that if you chose to follow your broker to his/her new firm your "house" funds had to remain with the original brokerage company. It was not permissible to transfer them to the new firm. That left you with two choices, remain with the original firm and deal with a new representative or sell your funds and buy different funds, usually incurring a new sales charge. That meant added expenses on top of a "taxable event," which could trigger either a taxable gain or loss that could have affected your income taxes, and that taxable event could come at an inconvenient time for you. Now you know what was one of the best kept secrets of brokerage company proprietary or "house" funds. Reportedly such restrictions are no longer enforced. However, it's always wise to inquire if any similar restrictions apply to any fund(s) or variable annuities you own. You're entitled to know because after all, that's what Full Disclosure is all about.

This is especially important for many investors in 401k Plans. If the sponsor of the plan is a bank, brokerage house or insurance company you should carefully check on the funds offered in their plans. If there's any doubt I would invest the maximum amount necessary to qualify for a company contribution to my account, with the balance of my investments in other fund organizations outside of your 401k plan. Don't believe it? Check it out – take a look at the performance comparisons of any number of these proprietary funds in either *Forbes Magazine* or *Kiplinger's Magazine* and then make your own decision.

Remember, the objective is to make the selection process more manageable and the ongoing monitoring of your investments much easier. By taking this approach you'll reduce your investment choices to perhaps 20 to 30 fund management companies, from a universe of hundreds of funds, many of which are duplicates of each other. The next step is to select and investigate about 6 of the fund managers, each of which will offer an array of different funds from which to select and allocate your investment dollars.

The Numbers

The Investment Company Institute ("ICI") is the self described "national trade association for registered investment companies, which include mutual funds, exchange-traded funds, closed-end funds, and unit investment trusts. ICI's 10,334 member funds manage $12.3 trillion in assets." In 2008, "More than 1,000 industry representatives from around the nation gathered for the ICI's 50th Annual General Membership Meeting." *(From* www.ici.org/home/08, *"Mutual Funds: Investing in America's Future.")*

As a trade association the ICI has done a great job for the investment advisers who are in the business of managing mutual funds. As a result, their congressional lobbying efforts have sometimes resulted in beneficial legislation for mutual fund shareholders. However, it's a bit of a stretch for anyone to believe that the ICI represents mutual fund shareholders, whose investments account for the $12.3 trillion in mutual fund assets (year end, 2007). In fact, it was only recently that the president of the ICI issued a public statement to emphasize the point that the ICI in fact does ***not*** represent mutual fund shareholders. It's a distinct possibility that the recent 50th Annual Meeting of the ICI had few if any mutual fund shareholders in attendance, other than those employed in the fund industry and whose firms are ICI dues* paying members.

It s important to note that under present circumstances the +90 million shareholders have no representation in industry deliberations or before congress. Instead it's assumed that those millions of shareholder's interests are represented by "independent" mutual fund directors, defined as "unaffiliated" with the investment adviser of the funds of which boards they are members. This will be further discussed in Chapter 6, "Your Fund's Independent Directors."

---

*There has always been a question about the source of those dues, the answer to which is not clear. For example, how many fund investment advisors pay their dues directly from their own revenues; how many "share" the cost of their dues with a portion paid for from fund shareholder's assets, and how many, if any, fund shareholder's assets pay the full amount of investment adviser dues? Perhaps someday the ICI will provide this statistical information in keeping with the principle of "Full Disclosure."

Nevertheless, the ICI does provide a public service by compiling and publishing statistical information that is helpful in the investment selection process. (They also provide useful literature on topics of interest for the public which is available on their website.) The ICI's "2008 Investment Fact Book," which is an overview of U.S. registered investment companies, reveals that almost 60% of mutual funds are "sponsored" (managed) by independent mutual fund investment advisors. The balance of 40% are managed by insurance companies, 10%; banks or thrifts, 11%; brokerage firms, 7%, and non-US advisers, 14%, of which an unknown number may be managed by foreign insurance companies or banks.

> Reality Check – Clearly there's a wide choice of mutual funds managed by independent mutual fund advisors from which to make your selection. Therefore, in my opinion, the average investor can eliminate those organizations, whose primary business is **_not_** managing mutual funds, i.e., brokerage firms, banks and insurance companies. It only makes sense to select your funds from those advisors whose primary, if not sole business is investment management.

Who owns mutual funds?

- Total assets of mutual funds at the end of 2007 were somewhat more than $12 trillion. According to the ICI's Fact Book:

- About one half of 401k plan and other defined contribution plans are managed by mutual funds.

- Mutual funds are held in approximately 47% of IRA plans.

- $4.4 trillion of U.S. household assets are also held in taxable fund accounts.

Where's the money?

The growth of fund investing is evident by comparing the period 1995 – 2007.

Year	Mutual Funds	Closed End Funds	ETFs*	UITs**
1995	5,761	500	2	12,979
2007	8,752	668	629	6,030
Change	+2,991	+168	+627	-6,949
	(+52%)	(+34%)	(+3,146%)	(-54%)

*ETFs, Exchange Traded Funds

**UITs, Unit Investment Trusts

$12 Trillion invested in Mutual Funds

The ICI classifies 6 different kinds of mutual funds by portfolio type.

Fund Type	Total Assets (trillions)	Number of Funds
Stock funds	$6,187	4,810
Hybrid funds*	699	478
Taxable bond funds	1,375	1,297
Municipal bond funds	380	657
Money market funds	2,947	552
Tax free money market funds	479	256
Totals	**$12,068**	**8,050**

*A mutual fund that invests in a mix of equity and fixed income securities.

For the purposes of the selection process, and to avoid unnecessary confusion, taxable bond funds, municipal bond funds and both types of money market funds are combined together as income funds, which represent a total of 2,766 funds, or 34.5% of the funds in this listing. The following funds have been omitted: Closed end funds are not considered due to the inherent disadvantages of those funds and the limited availability of ownership features; ETFs are not considered because most of them do not yet have a long term track record necessary to judge these funds over different market cycles, as well as the limited diversification of their portfolio holdings; UITs, in my opinion, were never the type of investment that could match the advantages of an open end mutual fund and, similar to closed end funds, they were and are subject to selling at a price different from their net asset value, i.e., at a discount. In fact, the declining popularity of UITs speaks for itself. This information is part of the basis of the selection process for your mutual fund portfolio.

©Scott Adams/Dist. By United Feature Syndicate, Inc.

How to Select Your Mutual Fund

The Real Deal

Comparing and monitoring fund performance ("KISS")

The most objective source for mutual fund performance results I know of is available four times a year in a supplement titled "Investing in Funds: A Quarterly Analysis," published in *The Wall Street Journal* within days of the last day of each calendar quarter. In my opinion, it's the most objective, least expensive and most authoritative source of mutual fund comparative statistics, compiled in conjunction with Lipper, Inc. a highly respected, statistical reporting firm specializing in mutual fund performance analysis for more than 30 years. This Quarterly Analysis is available for $1.50 at newsstands, which is arguably one of the best bargains for fund investors.

This information appears as a *Journal* supplement, *The Journal Report,* usually within 3-5 business days after the end of each calendar quarter. It provides an alphabetical listing by mutual fund groups, including investment objectives. The list covers 27 different classifications of stock funds by investment objectives; 10 types of taxable bond funds; 6 municipal debt funds, and 2 types of stock and bond funds, sometimes called "hybrid" funds.

> Reality Check – As a bonus, this quarterly report also includes useful and interesting articles on mutual funds, including informative interviews, as well as a table, "Mutual Fund Yardsticks," which provides the performance results for various periods for each fund category by investment objective.

The tables include the name of the fund group, its toll free number, followed by seven columns of statistics as follows:

- Individual fund name
- Investment objective
- Net asset value per share at quarter end
- Current calendar quarter performance results
- 1 year performance results (prior 12 months)

- 3 year performance results

- 5 year performance results

Quintile Rankings

The 1, 3 and 5 year performance results, plus or minus, represents the *absolute* performance results stated as a percentage, plus or minus. In addition however, each of those results is followed by a letter designation, A through E, which relates to how the fund's results for those periods compare *relative* to other funds with the same investment objective. In other words the letter designation compares the fund's performance results within the individual fund's peer group of like funds.

The A to E designations represent quintile ratings, with A indicating a fund's results are in the top 20% of funds with the same investment objective, and E representing performance results in the bottom quintile, or bottom 20% of funds with the same investment objective. What do the quintile rankings mean to you? They are the key to objective performance results comparisons. For example, your fund may have gone up 10% during a period and you might be pleased with those results as you should be. However, when reviewing the Quintile Ranking you may learn that the fund is rated "E," or in the bottom 20% of funds with the same investment objective, i.e., it performed poorly within its peer group of funds with the same investment objective. On closer examination you may find that, depending on the nature of the fund, the top 20% in the peer group delivered significantly better results than your fund. At the same time the fund's peer group overall performance results may be so close, that the difference between the top 20% and bottom 20% could conceivably be a fraction of one percent, and therefore not significant.

However, assuming the difference between the A and E quintiles is significant, is that a sign to sell your fund? No, unless you're looking at quintile ratings of "E" for each of the 1, 3 and 5 year periods, which could indicate a problem because the fund has performed poorly on a *relative* basis compared to its peer group of funds for all those periods. At that point you should begin to question if it's time to consider moving those assets to a fund with the same investment objective, but which has consistently delivered performance results that ranked in either the "A" or "B" quintile. In arriving at your decision, it's a good idea to call the fund's toll free number and review the *Journal's* performance report, including the Quintile Ranking, for an explanation of the poor *relative* performance results. If you don't hear an explanation that makes sense to *you,* that's the time to seek a replacement in a different fund group that enjoys a consistently higher Quintile Ranking.

Researching the fund group or individual fund for your portfolio selection is as simple as that. It doesn't require subscribing to an expensive advisory service or newsletter. It's the "KISS" method of selecting and monitoring your mutual fund's performance results and confirms that you're in the right fund, with the right fund manager, in order for you to achieve your investment objectives. It does not involve stars, endless raw performance percentages for isolated periods, style boxes or the "flavor of the month" performance chase. It's a review you can perform four times a year, a method I've used since Quintile Rankings were introduced – and the total cost is only $6 a year for the four *Journal** issues you need. So, you can do it yourself if you're willing to devote the small amount of time required and if you're inclined to do so. On the other hand, you can hire an investment adviser and insist that any fund recommendations made include the *Journal* and Quintile Rankings in any performance comparisons.

---

* The Journal's quarterly mutual fund performance Report usually appears about 3 days after the end of the calendar quarter and is also available online at the Journal's website. The website provides both the quarterly mutual fund performance report, as well as a monthly performance update based on month and quarter end closing prices of the funds. To access this information go to WSJMarkets.com and click on the "Mutual Funds" tab at the top of the screen. Then click on "Fund Analysis Report" from the drop down menu.

Reality Check – If you prefer another method of comparing performance results, go ahead, take the time, spend the money – knock yourself out – it's still a free country.

The Last Steps

With more than 4,000 stock funds from which to choose, where do you start? Remember, the "KISS" principle still applies by using the process of elimination.

1. Limit your selections to only those funds managed by organizations whose primary, if not sole business is money management

2. Eliminate all other mutual fund operations, i.e., those that are effectively asset gathering companies like banks, brokerage houses and insurance companies. Note: You might miss a rare winner by using this approach, but it still works.

3. Focus on known, reputable money management companies with decades of experience and a proven track record of performance as opposed to hypothetical investment results based on back testing of an investment concept, the latest example of which is ETFs.

To make the job a little easier, focus on those mutual fund organizations which are among the largest in the industry. That doesn't mean that larger is better, but it's an indication that they've been successful enough to attract significant investor attention and assets under management. The weekly publication, *Investment News,* publishes its annual "Databook" each year in mid December based on statistics at the close of the 3rd quarter of the current year. The 2008 issue listed the following mutual fund organizations as the 15 largest funds groups based on assets under management:

Fund Group	Phone Number	Website
Vanguard Group	800-997-2798	vanguard.com
American Funds Investment Co.	800-421-0180	americanfunds.com
Fidelity Investments	877-208-0098	fidelity.com
State Street Global Advisors (1)	617-786-3000	ssga.com
Barclays Global Investors (2)	415-597-2000	barclaysglobal.com
T.Rowe Price Investment Services	800-638-5660	troweprice.com
Franklin Templeton Investments	800-632-2301	franklintempleton.com
Columbia Funds Distributor Inc (6)	800-345-6611	columbiafunds.com
Legg Mason Inc. (5)	800-822-5544	leggmason.com
Dodge & Cox Inc.	800-621-3979	dodgeandcox.com
Janus Capital Group	800-525-0020	janus.com
Davis Selected Advisers	800-279-0279	davisfunds.com
Van Kampen Funds (3)	800-847-2424	vankampen.com
Oppenheimer Funds Inc. (4)	800-225-5677	oppenheimerfunds.com
Dimensional Funds Advisors	310-395-8005	dfaus.com

1) State Street Global – A bank that claims to be "the world's largest institutional money manager."

2) Barclays Global – Based in London, claims to be the originator of index funds.

3) Van Kampen – Owned by Morgan Stanley, a global financial services company.

4) Oppenheimer – Owned by an insurance company, but seems to have maintained its investment culture.

5) Legg Mason -- A brokerage house.

6) Columbia Funds – Owned by Bank America.

As mentioned, bigger is not necessarily better. There are a number of reputable mutual fund managers that, although not as big as the giants, have produced consistent above average performance results over decades, including (in alphabetical order):

Fund Group	Phone Number	Website
CGM Funds	800-345-4048	cgmfunds.com
FPA Funds	800-982-4372	fpafunds.com
Keeley Funds	888-933-5391	keeleyfunds.com
Marsico Funds	888-860-8686	marsicofunds.com
Royce Funds	800-221-4268	roycefunds.com
Third Avenue Funds	800-443-1021	thirdavenuefunds.com

In conclusion, there are other well managed funds that could fit very well in your mutual fund portfolio, but this list, while small, is a good place to start. You now have the basic information you need to begin to make intelligent decisions about your mutual fund selections. The 15 fund groups listed, including eight of the largest fund groups and seven smaller, but no less reputable, fund groups cover the spectrum of mutual funds that will help you in your quest for financial independence. All it takes is 15 phone calls or website visits and you will have the basis for setting up your own portfolio. Once you've done that, you need only check on the performance results as they appear in the *Wall Street Journal's* quarterly fund report to confirm that your funds are delivering competitive performance results and continue to do well on both an absolute and a relative basis compared to each fund's peer group. "KISS" works – take advantage of it.

Here's a simple form to record your quarterly performance results.

Performance Results/Quintile Rankings as of <u>(Calendar Quarter Ended)</u>

<u>(Your Name) Mutual Fund Portfolio</u>

	3 Month	12 Month	3 Year	5 Year
Name of Fund	% Change	% Change/ Rank	% Change/ Rank	<u>% Change/ Rank</u>

This simple form and access to *The Wall Street Journal Quarterly Mutual Fund Report* are all you need to monitor and compare your fund's performance results. Once you see rankings in the "D" and "E" quintiles, it's your warning that you need to call the fund and ask for an explanation. If that explanation doesn't make sense to you then start looking for a replacement for that fund.

401k Plans and the Rule of 72

<u>401k Plans, Absolutely Essential to your Financial Future</u>

Before discussing why you need to take advantage of a 401k Plan if offered by your employer, it might be worth knowing a little more about where you want to go and how to get there, which bring us to *The Rule of 72*. First, a Pop Quiz:

Do you really believe the day will come when...

- *Government will cut back on unnecessary spending?*

- *Industry will <u>not</u> pass cost increases on to consumers?*

- *You will demand <u>lower</u> wages and fringe benefits?*

If you answered yes to all of these questions, you have a far more serious problem than you might think. On the other hand if you're aware of and willing to accept the facts of life relative to simple economics, then you need to focus on a sensible, long term investment program. For example, you have to prepare for college funding for one or more children and/or your own financially secure retirement. This does *not* include "saving up" for a new car or an exotic vacation somewhere – those are luxuries and not related to your future financial challenges. To help better appreciate the challenge ahead it's important to understand the Rule of 72 and compound growth. It's a simple mathematical formula, a shortcut, to help estimate how money grows based on compounding (reinvesting income dividends and capital gains).

RULE OF 72

1. If you want to know how long it will take to double an investment at a specific rate of return, just divide 72 by the rate of return (72 divided by 6% = 12), which means at 6% a year your money will double in 12 years. At 8% (72 divided by 8 = 9), money doubles in 9 years. The formula works for any rate of return.

2. If you want to know the rate of return required to double your money over a specific number or years, just divide 72 by the number of years (72 divided by 10 years = 7.2) or a 7.2% rate of return a year for ten years will double your money.

The Rule of 72 is a simple tool which demonstrates the importance of putting time on your side in achieving your financial goals – the more time you have, the greater your chances of achieving successful investment results. In addition, it also emphasizes that a "small" 1% change in the rate of return can make a huge difference in investment results. Remember, rates of return change; they fluctuate, while time is a constant factor that can't be replaced, adjusted or changed. Therefore, putting time to work in your investment program is one of the most important factors to consider.

Why you must invest in your 401k Plan

There's no need to guess when the answers to estimating your retirement income requirements are readily available to you. Simply access FINRA's (Financial Industry Regulatory Authority) website www.finra.org, and take advantage of their "Retirement Calculator" on the site. This calculator is convenient to use and there's no charge for the service. If you do nothing else, at least you'll have an unbiased estimate of what you can expect during your retirement years. How does a 401k Plan fit into your financial future? Suppose you were able to make an investment that automatically increased by 50% of the amount you invested? Or suppose that you made an investment that declined in value by 33% and your invested dollars are not affected? That's what 401k Plans are in plain English. Remember those Four Letter Words? Well "Dumb" is the perfect word for anyone who does not take advantage of a 401k Plan investment – especially if your employer matches your contribution (usually up to one half the amounts you invest up to a maximum of 3%, one half of the first 6% you invest). Figure it out. Let's say your salary is $50,000 a year and you contribute 6%, or $3,000 of your salary. Your company can match that contribution with another 3%, or $1,500 of your salary. That means your total investment automatically increases by 50%! When was the last time you were that lucky? On the other hand let's assume stock prices go down and your fund(s) go down by as much as $1,500, or 33%, you're still even – your $3,000 is still worth $3,000!

If for no other reasons these factors are so compelling that you have to be "Dumb" *not* to start and continue to make the maximum contribution to a 401k Plan if your employer offers it to you. But you have to avoid a couple of mistakes. First, if the plan allows you to invest in your company's stock, be sure to limit your company stock investment to no more than 10% of your contribution – and that's a maximum. No matter how loyal you feel to your employer there are not too many "Googles" out there while they are outnumbered by the Enrons, WorldComs etc. No one should run the risk of losing their entire accumulated 401k investment because they were too "loyal" to their employer.

In addition, altogether too many plan participants have either all or too great a percentage of their investment in money market funds. Why would anyone do that? Think about the lost opportunity of a 50% gain in your contribution or wasting the loss of protection against a 33% drop in stock prices. The best investment in these types of plans is still equity mutual funds and never, as in <u>NOT EVER,</u> in any kinds of annuities.

Borrowing from your 401k Plan

What about "borrowing" from your 401k Plan? The simple answer is <u>DON'T</u>, i.e., as in *never,* do it in almost every case. While there are exceptions to not borrowing from your Plan, there could be rare occasions when it might be the only choice, i.e., un-reimbursed medical expenses or rent or mortgage payments to avoid eviction or foreclosure. However, borrowing for any other of the few permitted expenses almost never makes any sense, especially for college expenses – that's why public colleges and universities exist and why it's a good idea for a college student to have a part time job for pocket money and a full time summer job to help defray all other college related expenses.

Above all, remember that borrowing money from your plan could involve consequences that can be painful if the amount borrowed is not timely repaid, including current taxation of the amount borrowed plus a 10% tax penalty. ***Don't do it.***

NOTE:

There is a move afoot to grant approval to a method of utilizing 401k plan assets for loans by use of an approved debit card or check writing privileges available only to employees who are pre-approved by their employer. This possible approach, which is subject to regulatory approvals and adoption, might make sense for some 401k plan participants. It's still in the review process so remain alert for its possible approval and availability. However, assuming it is approved in some form, wise investors will proceed with caution and make every effort to avoid using plan assets for temporary purposes, which can only diminish the eventual value of your plan assets at retirement.

Photo "Album"

Oppenheimer Original Sales Team l to r: Dan Calabria, Dick Samartin, Stan Egener

Oppenheimer National Sales Team l to r:
Dan Calabria, Stan Egener, Don Spiro, President, Ed Smith, Dick Samartin

Axe Castle, Tarrytown, NY
Why some funds didn't make it

John Templeton and Dan Calabria
It was another good year

Templeton Funds Annual Shareholder Meeting

Templeton Funds Annual Shareholder Meeting
Shareholders attend meetings

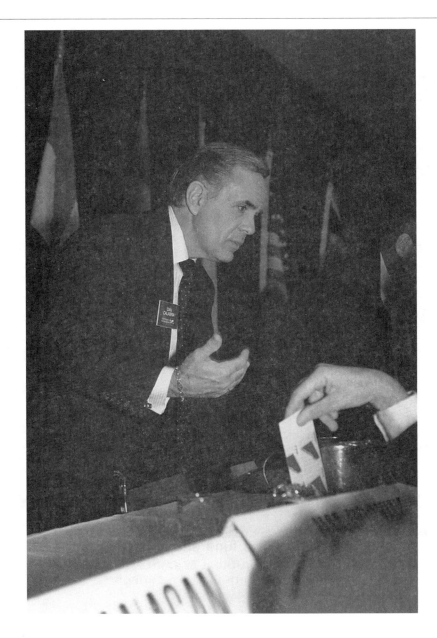

**Templeton Funds Annual Shareholder Meeting
Answering questions**

Part III –
Wading Into the Future

Chapter 6 -
Your Fund's Board of Directors

Independent Directors

(In this chapter all references are to *independent* directors, unless otherwise stated.)

Publicly offered mutual funds must have a board of directors 75% of whom have no affiliation of any kind with the investment advisor to the fund. When the Investment Company Act of 1940 was passed it required that only 40% of the board be unaffiliated with the advisor. However, over the decades since passage of the Act the regulatory environment and conditions have changed, which led to a super majority of unaffiliated ("independent") directors to represent the interests of the owners of a mutual fund - its shareholders. Make no mistake: the owners of a fund are its shareholders, not the investment advisor or anyone else. But how can these owners be sure that their corporation is being managed properly? Of course if they're not happy with its performance results, they can sell their shares, but that may trigger a taxable event and incur additional expenses in reinvesting the proceeds elsewhere.

The basis for requiring independent directors on every publicly owned mutual fund board is to oversee the manager and represent the interests of the mutual fund's owners/shareholders with a *"Duty of Care and Loyalty."* It's important to understand that in addition to their role as "watchdogs" on behalf of fund shareholders, directors are also subject to state law fiduciary duties of care and loyalty. It's widely recognized that the *duty of care* generally requires that directors act in good faith and with that degree of diligence, care and skill that a person of ordinary prudence would exercise under similar circumstances in a like position. The *duty of loyalty* generally requires that directors exercise their powers in the interests of the fund and not in the directors' own interests or the interests of another person or organization.

However, the question has often been asked whether the term "independent director" is nothing more than an oxymoron, i.e., do these directors in fact represent the interests of the shareholders they are paid to serve? There has been much criticism of independent directors, some of which is justifiable and some of which is based on ignorance, often voiced by those with an ax to grind.

Are there legitimate criticisms of directors? Without question - here are a couple of examples of justifiable criticism of directors not adequately exercising their oversight responsibilities on behalf of shareholders.

<u>How long should it take for a shareholder to receive a required report from a fund?</u>   The current requirement in place for decades provides that shareholder reports (Annual and Semi-Annual Reports) must be mailed no later than 60 days after the end of the six or twelve month reporting periods. But there's nothing that prevents a fund from mailing the reports prior to expiration of the 60 day period. To offset this criticism, some mutual fund advisers make this information available on a much more timely basis on their websites where interested shareholders can register for automatic notification of online availability of the reports. However, some fund companies seem to be stuck in a time warp when information was manually typed, hand delivered to a printer followed by an exchange of proof copies and corrections. But that was then and we've made light years of progress in our communication systems where documents can be created, corrected, changed and delivered by computer in blinding speed. In fact there's no reason, much less any justification, for the delayed delivery of information to shareholders – they're paying for it and it should be available to them on a timely basis. Unfortunately, directors seem not to care when important, required shareholder information is received by their shareholders or if it's timely delivered.

Shame on the Fund industry

Based on antiquated regulations most mutual funds do a terrible job of keeping their shareholders informed. In our hi-tech environment, where information can be transmitted within seconds there's no longer any reason for the funds to be so casual about communicating important information. After all, open end funds are corporations that close their books every day. In fact, it might be the only business to run a "balance sheet" and income statement every day. That's why the price to purchase or sell shares is calculated daily and the reason these transactions are processed at the close of the markets each business day. However, one would think that these documents are still set in "hot" type and proofs carried by hand between the fund and its printer. We all know that it doesn't work that way anymore.

We also know that performance results for thousands of funds are calculated and published within days, if not hours, of the end of a reporting period. However, there is an exception with respect to required Audited Financial Statements, which can take up to a couple of weeks – for well managed mutual fund organizations.

Here's the problem. The following table lists 7 different mutual funds I currently own. It provides the date of the report, the type of report and the date it was received, including the number of calendar days elapsed from the date of the reporting period and the date of receipt.

Date	Report Type	Date Received	Elapsed Days
12/31/07	Annual Report	3/22/08	82
12/31/07	Annual Report	3/21/08	81
12/31/07	Annual Report	3/14/08	74
12/31/07	Semi-Annual Report	3/17/08	77
12/31/07	Annual Report	3/19/08	79
11/30/07	Annual Report	2/10/08	72
10/31/07	Annual Report	1/16/08	77

Based on this information, and the widely accepted practice throughout the industry, you would think that the computer, internet and instant communications had not yet been invented. And yet most funds brag about being on the cutting edge of research information and development. Apparently the same standard of care and concern doesn't extend to keeping shareholders informed in a timely manner.

Could there be anything worse? Well, yes. The fund reports for 11/30/07 and 10/31/07 were *80 pages long, covering 7 different funds* and *122 pages covering 14 different funds,* respectively. Think about that - you own one fund in the group and you're required to wade through multiple pages of printed information that is of no use or value to you. Why is that so? It would be interesting to know how many directors actually directly own shares of the funds they oversee and their reaction when they receive a report in the mail about 10 weeks *after* the end of the reporting period at which time the information is stale and outdated, providing little of value to the shareholder. And for this shareholders are paying significant operating expenses while the directors are "monitoring" – what? Is this a way to save money for shareholders, when the information received is so badly outdated or in a format that makes it decidedly unfriendly to read? Whatever money is saved is not worth it and not in the best interests of the shareholders. There are far more effective ways to lower operating expenses than shortchanging shareholders on information that's important to them.

Does it get worse than that? Again, yes. I know of a self-described low-load variable life insurance product that offers a total of 65 different mutual funds managed by 18 different fund organizations. The prospectus required to be delivered to shareholders comes in two volumes, comprising about 500 pages, printed on both sides! It boggles the mind to conceive that any organization willingly distributes its prospectus in the form of a 2 volume "paper dump." But it appears to be legal since it's filed with the SEC. However, it begs the question of directors reviewing and approving the two volume paper dump and concluding that it's in the best interest of the shareholder.

Some will argue that the practice is perfectly legal and in compliance with regulations, which is probably true. But that does not mean that any independent directors can delude themselves into thinking that it's in the best interest of the shareholders to do so.

A recent fund advertisement

Another example of questionable if nonexistent oversight is an advertisement that appeared in *The Wall Street Journal* early in 2008. The following is the verbatim text of that advertisement. The explanatory text appeared below a performance chart in a 2 column format that measured 6-1/2 by 6-1/2 inches that described the chart, which measured 6-1/2 by 3-1/2 inches.

Past performance is no guarantee of future results. The performance quoted represents past performance and current performance may be lower or higher. Investment return and principal of an investment will fluctuate so that the investors' shares, when redeemed may be worth more or less than their original cost. To obtain performance information current to the most recent month-end, please go to (website address). Returns referred to as Class A reflect a deduction of the maximum sales charges. Performance at NAV does not include the effect of sales charges.

Performance includes the reinvestment of income dividends and capital gain distributions. Historical performance for Class A prior to 10/3/2002 is based on the performance of Class III of the fund's predecessor fund, (name of predecessor fund). Prior to 10/3/2002; returns have been adjusted downward to reflect the (name) fund's higher direct fund operating expenses including 12b-1 fees in effect at its inception. These fees were 1.06% for Class A. 12b-1 fees are 0.30% for Class A. Class III of the predecessor fund did not pay a 12b-1 fee. The advisor is reimbursing a portion of the 12b-1 fee for Class A. Had the fee not been reimbursed, returns for Class A would have been lower. Returns reflect expense limits previously in effect for all classes, without which returns would have been lower. The expense ratios include the fund's direct operating expenses as of 12/31/2006 and the indirect expenses of the underlying funds in which the fund was invested for the period ended 12/31/2006. The indirect expenses were estimated to be 0.48%.

*Prior to 5/1/07, GMO Global Balanced Index, the fund's benchmark consisted of 48.75% S&P, 16.25% MSCI All World ex-U.S., 35% Lehman Brothers Aggregate Bond. Effective 5/01/07, the fund benchmark consists of 65% MSCI All Country World, 35% Lehman Brothers Aggregate Bond. It is not possible to invest directly in an index.

Because the fund invests in other mutual funds, the fund will incur fees and expenses indirectly as a shareholder of the underlying funds. For more information regarding the expenses of the underlying funds, see the fund's prospectus.

An investor should carefully consider a fund's investment objectives, risks, charges and expenses. This and other important information can be found in the fund prospectus. To obtain a prospectus, contact your financial advisor or visit (website). Read the prospectus thoroughly before investing or sending money.

The return of principal is not guaranteed due to fluctuation in the NAV of the fund caused by changes in the price of the individual bonds held by the underlying funds and the buying and selling of bonds by the underlying funds. Bond funds have the same inflation, interest rate and credit risks that are associated with the individual bonds held by the underlying funds. Generally, the value of bond funds rises when prevailing interest rates fall and falls when interest rates rise. Foreign investments may contain more risk due to the inherent risks associated with changing political climates, foreign market instability and foreign currency fluctuation. Risks of international investing are magnified in emerging or developing markets. The stocks of smaller companies may be more volatile than those of larger companies due to the higher risk of failure. Derivatives involve additional risks, including interest rate risk, credit risk, the risk of improper valuation and the risk of non-correlation to the relevant instruments they are designed to hedge or to closely track.

(name of investment adviser) followed by: **NOT FDIC INSURED. NOT BANK GUARANTEED. MAY LOSE VALUE.** (name of fund distributor)

Presumably this ad was written to elicit the interest of and inquiries from potential investors. Among the many responsibilities of independent directors is the review (but not approval) of sales and marketing materials. After reading this ad, you have to wonder if the directors ever saw the ad prior to publication, if at all.

Worse, you have to wonder if any director could explain what the ad says or means. After more than 4 decades in the fund industry, I'm still baffled with what this ad attempted to describe and how it serves the interests of the current shareholders, *who may have paid for the ad with 12b-1 fees deducted from total assets of the fund, i.e., how did shareholders benefit from paying for the cost of this ad?*

The point is that directors are handsomely rewarded for serving as directors. Their compensation is paid from total assets of the fund(s) on the basis that they will serve the best interests of their fund's shareholders in an oversight role, i.e., as a "watchdog." These are just two very small examples that raise questions about how some directors are performing their roles in representing their shareholder's interests with the standard of loyalty and care required of them.

The Future for Mutual Funds

With 94 million shareholders, the mutual fund industry is in the enviable position of continuing to grow and has the potential to serve its shareholders far more effectively simply based on continuing increases in advisory fee revenues, which are directly related to an increase in total fund assets. But there are major challenges that need to be addressed. In a worst case scenario another investment vehicle could be created that is at least as effective for investors and available to them at a lower cost. I believe that's a real possibility which could result in a dramatic decline in the number of mutual fund investors and total assets under management. How likely is such a possibility? There's an investment alternative already available to 401k Plan investors that might give the fund industry a run for its money and if nothing else force the industry to reconsider its management fee structure. That alternative is known as Collective Investment Funds ("CIFs"), which was the subject of a recent article that appeared in *The Wall Street Journal*. There's no reason for the industry to relinquish its leadership as the investment of choice for average Americans provided that industry leaders and the independent directors step up and confront that possibility.

The Mutual Fund Landscape

Despite how difficult it might be for shareholders to obtain timely information, written in plain English, as opposed to boiler plate legalese, shareholders are better informed than they were just 10 or 20 years ago. Nevertheless, this factor is one of the reasons why CIFs for 401k Plans have attracted attention and grown in number and availability. *The Wall Street Journal* story highlighted CIFs as "substantially cheaper" than mutual funds primarily because they're not subject to the same SEC regulations and they're not available for investment outside of qualified retirement plans. The article points out that the Fidelity and Vanguard groups and Charles Schwab now offer them in their plans. Current statistics should be of concern for the fund industry based on a study by a consulting firm that revealed that large defined contribution plans using mutual funds in their 401k plans declined to 58% in 2007, down from 65% in 2003, while plans using CIFs increased from 33% to 39% over a two year period, according to the article.

This has occurred despite the fact that CIF prices are not listed in newspapers or on financial websites and they often value their plan holdings monthly or quarterly. Based on the manner in which the fund industry distributes its reports, there is no significant difference for fund shareholders. And as 401k plan participants continue to grow and more workers learn about their options, this is the time for fund companies and directors to recognize that there is some real competition in the marketplace. Finally, there were an additional 151 new CIFs offered in 2007 compared to 2006. It's possible that a trend may well be underway, which the fund industry ignores at its own peril.

That's just one of the reasons why fund managers and directors need to refocus their joint efforts to learn how they might offer a better, less expensive, more competitive product in the retirement plan field. That market continues to grow as more workers learn of the benefits of partial matching contributions by their employers, the tax deduction and current tax shelter on earnings in their plans and the importance of ensuring that their plans are not subject to excessive fees for management, administration, etc., which serve to reduce the return on their invested contributions. Simply, it's a growing market that cannot be ignored.

"IEDs"

The challenges facing the fund industry are real and could be described as IEDs – Investor Explosive Devices, which are bound to be ignited as shareholders learn more about what they own and how some boards function. As that occurs, the 94 million fund shareholders will realize that they own their mutual fund and they are paying directors to represent them and perform as watchdogs on their behalf. They will also learn that they have the power and ability to change things because they also have the right to vote for their congressional representatives. And eventually those politicians will realize that fund shareholders can vote in their own self interest to offset the powerful lobbying forces that have been so effective in the political arena. In other words, Congress will eventually realize that in order to own a mutual fund one has to be 18 years old, which is exactly the age when they become eligible to vote for their representatives.

If the challenges facing the industry are addressed those in control might realize that there's an opportunity to take advantage of the "less is more" approach to marketing, i.e., lower costs equal greater sales, market share and revenues. It remains to be seen how many fund organizations will take advantage of this opening as three industry stalwarts seem to have already awakened to the potential of CIFs. This could be a harbinger of the future for directors who have willingly cooperated with investment advisers in the creation/approval of the alphabet soup of fund share classes. Those classes were presumably designed to lower acquisition costs for investors by the use of 12b-1 fees that subsidize the advisor's marketing costs. The precedent has thus been established for boards to use their considerable influence to convince investment advisors that management fees based on "breakpoints" need to be revisited with the objective of reducing fees for certain classes of investors, i.e., retirement plans of all types, as well as charitable and non-profit organizations, etc.

New Role of Independent Directors

While it's a given that directors do not manage or control investment advisors, nevertheless, in their role as the shareholder's representative, they can be a powerful voice in attempting to convince the fund's advisor that more can and should be done for the shareholders. There's no doubt that we are entering a new era for mutual funds and their directors. Securities markets are still in a difficult environment, credit markets appear to be besieged by problems of a magnitude never before confronted and we just ended a nine year period where securities prices closed lower than they were nine years ago. (The Dow Jones Industrial Average closed at 11,947 on December 31,

1999 and stood at 8,776 on December 31, 2008.) Of course, most func shareholders who had their money invested during this entire period would have preferred better results on their investments, but despite the fact that the Dow declined during the period, it's unlikely that every single mutual fund investor lost money in their mutual fund. Meanwhile total fund assets declined by about 30% by the end of 2008, which still represents a very attractive target and source of new sales and commissions for competitors. It's quite possible that we may be embarking on an era that will focus on asset retention as opposed to increasing market share.

Directors have two choices – ignore the realities of the market place and competition or recognize that they have an opportunity to make a great, proven investment concept even better by improving it with changes that cry out for adoption, including revision of 12b-1 Plan schemes, advisory fee breakpoints, improving the current selection process and qualifications of board members, discontinuing the practice of unilateral control over their compensation and holding annual meetings and election of directors so that shareholders can begin to understand what their funds are all about, who manages them and why they should be long term investors. Let's look at each issue.

12b-1 Fees -
The Multi Billion Dollar Boondoggle

Up until very recently fund shareholders were paying billions of dollars annually, *every year*, for "services" they may not need, want, or be aware of. These billions of dollars are paid every year for a variety of expenses, almost all of which result in virtually no discernible benefit to shareholders. The dirty little secret here is that the real beneficiaries of these fees are the investment advisors who use those revenues for purposes that primarily benefit the advisors. Part of these fees are paid to registered representatives, financial planners, advisers, etc., and there's no reason those payments should be discontinued. Remember, most shareholders paid some form of acquisition costs when they made their investments and they also bear all of the operating costs of the funds. Rather, 12b-1 fees should be paid for by the investment advisor since they are the primary beneficiaries of the billions of dollars of 12b-1 revenues expended each year.

SEC cost/benefit study

In 2004 the SEC invited comments on a "Proposed Rule: Prohibition on the use of Brokerage Commissions to Finance Distribution." One of the comment letters submitted was from Ms. Lori Walsh, Financial

Economist, Office of Economic Analysis, United States Securities & Exchange Commission. That 29 page letter dated June 26, 2004, provided the history and background of the 12b-1 Rule, including extensive tables in support of the conclusions of the paper. The letter began with an "Executive Summary," which is reproduced below:

Executive Summary

Rule 12b-1, promulgated pursuant to the Investment Company Act of 1940, allows mutual fund advisers to make payments from fund assets for the costs of marketing and distribution of fund shares under the auspices of 12b-1 plans. The original justification for the plans, as put forth by the mutual fund industry in the 1970s, was that such fees help attract new shareholders into funds through advertising and by providing incentives for brokers to market the fund. Arguably, asset growth from any means benefits shareholders through economies of scale in management expenses and lower flow volatility, which decreases liquidity costs for the fund. If, through 12b-1 plans, funds are able to increase the rate at which their assets grow, then shareholders may be able to attain these cost reductions sooner than by investing in a fund with no 12b-1 plan. However, the costs must decrease sufficiently to cover the cost of the plan, and the benefits of the cost reductions must be passed onto shareholders, or shareholders will not be better off.

Opponents of the rule argue that there is no evidence that 12b-1 plans are successful at growing funds or that shareholders benefit from such plans. Furthermore, they argue that there is a conflict of interest from allowing fund advisers to use fund assets to pay for attracting new investors, since fund advisers earn fees based on assets under management.

This paper addresses whether 12b-1 plans are successful in leading to faster asset growth and whether the shareholders that pay for 12b-1 plans receive any net benefits from the plans. The paper finds that while funds with 12b-1 plans do, in fact, grow faster than funds without them, shareholders are not obtaining benefits in the form of lower average expenses or lower flow volatility. Fund shareholders are paying the costs to grow the fund, while the fund adviser is the primary beneficiary of the fund's growth.

The letter reviewed the history of the 12b-1 Rule and how over time it morphed into something never contemplated when the Rule was adopted in 1980. The "Conclusions" arrived at (reproduced below) speaks for itself, in that they directly address the critical issues that call into question the current use of 12b-1 Plan revenues. It also raises serious questions about the specious reasons offered for continuing to spend shareholder's money for purposes that are a direct benefit to the investment advisor and are of no discernible benefit to fund shareholders. Unfortunately, Ms. Walsh's letter may have gotten lost in the barrage of letters submitted by those who are the beneficiaries of 12b-1 payments. The following are the conclusions of Ms. Walsh's letter.

VI. Conclusions

> If 12b-1 plans constitute a net benefit to investors, the amount of the annual fee should be recovered through higher net returns. Higher net returns could derive from either lower expense ratios due to economies of scale or higher gross returns due to the enhanced capacity of funds to either invest in assets with higher yields or reduce transactions costs. Overall, the results are inconsistent with this hypothesis. 12b-1 plans do seem to be successful in growing fund assets, but with no apparent benefits accruing to the shareholders of the fund. Although it is hypothetically possible for most types of funds to generate sufficient scale economies to offset the 12b-1 fee, it is not an efficient use of shareholder assets. No shareholder will be better off investing in a small 12b-1 fund in hopes of helping the fund grow to attain these scale economies.
>
> Furthermore, these higher expenses do not translate into higher gross returns. Indeed, fund flows may be more volatile and gross returns may be lower for funds with 12b-1 plans. These results highlight the significance of the conflict of interest that 12b-1 plans create. Fund advisers use shareholder money to pay for asset growth from which the adviser is the primary beneficiary through the collection of higher fees.

To repeat the last sentence of the "Conclusions":

"Fund advisers use shareholder money to pay for asset growth from which the adviser is the primary beneficiary through the collection of higher fees." (Emphasis added)

To the best of my knowledge, I'm not aware of any individual or organization that attempted to refute or challenge Ms. Walsh's letter. However, others did submit letters in an attempt to support retention of the use of 12b-1 fee revenues as a subsidy to very profitable and successful investment advisory organizations and selling organizations.

(A copy of Ms. Walsh's letter is available on the SEC's website (www. sec.gov) by accessing the "Search" page and typing "lwalsh042604. pdf" in the search box on the right hand side of the screen.)

The Director's Role –
The Phantom SEC Rule Amendment

Each year directors are required to approve their 12b-1 Plans and it's not an easy call. Assuming they receive the required detailed report of Plan expenditures, and despite the fact that any number of such expenditures may be open to question, they are in an unenviable position. The fact is that mutual fund shareholders and their directors are effectively held hostage to 12b-1 plans because of the real risk of discontinuing such plans which is twofold:

1. new sales are likely to grind to a halt, and

2. redemptions could virtually cause fund assets to disappear since they will be moved to other funds that continue 12b-1 payments.

This amounts to a double whammy in that discontinuance of the fee payments are an open invitation to sales representatives to move client funds to another fund group that pays 12b-1 fees, thus insuring continuance of the annual revenues to the sales organizations *and* the representative collects another commission on assets moved to a different fund. And in the process shareholders could find themselves with an unplanned for taxable event.

That's the quandary faced by fund directors, but there is a solution which thus far regulators appear to be reluctant to consider. It's a given than any such change has to be universal to maintain a level playing field for fund boards and shareholders. That means new regulations are required to avoid disadvantaging shareholders or punishing them because their directors did the right thing. As a result, the only sensible way to address this problem is to amend the Rule requiring that the investment advisor assume responsibility for the payment of the fees simply because they are the primary beneficiaries of those fees. If any adviser believes that current advisory fees are inadequate to cover these costs, they can simply propose that its advisory fee be increased to the extent of the current 12b-1 fees charged against total fund assets, which requires both director and shareholder approval. Since there is no effective change in the cost to the shareholders it's likely to be approved and then shareholders will understand what it is they're paying for, and directors would no longer be responsible for annual approval of these charges. Two benefits will result:

1. Such fees will be readily discernible and fully disclosed to investors/shareholders.

2. Shareholders will finally have the opportunity to accept and approve this annual charge, removing the burden of annual review and approval by the directors.

It's important to stress that the conditions under which the 12b-1 Rule was adopted have dramatically changed. Today the strength, profitability and viability of investment advisory organizations is indisputable compared to market conditions and the state that the fund industry was in back in 1980 when the Rule was originally adopted. The number of funds, total assets, and number of shareholders are at record highs and investment advisors are enjoying record revenues, due in part to the fact that multi billions of dollars a year in sales, marketing and distribution expenses have been shifted to shareholders with little if any discernible benefit to them.

Should sales organizations and representatives be paid ongoing fees for their efforts? Why not? They should be paid, *but by the ultimate beneficiaries of the payments, the investment advisory firms.* There are countless honest, conscientious sales representatives, financial planners and advisers who do great work on behalf of their clients. *But there are untold numbers of shareholders who pay 12b-1 fees and get little if anything in return.*

There are some in the industry who try to justify these costs to shareholders because they might get a consolidated account statement that reflects all of their investment holdings versus a separate statement from each fund they own. That might be a consideration if it was valid. But, are stockholders charged a similar fee by General Motors, GE or Procter & Gamble, etc., for owning shares of those companies, which fees in turn would pay for advertising those products or compensating the representative who sold the stock to his/her client? Every year? Unless the proponents of the current system can explain why a fee of this nature is justified, but applies *only* to mutual funds then serious consideration must be given to assessing 12b-1 fees on *all* publicly offered securities, *every year*, or discontinuing this questionable use of shareholder assets.

"SIFMA" and "Omnibus Accounts"

The Phantom SEC Rule

(SIFMA describes itself as representing the interests of "more than 650 securities firms, banks and asset managers," whose mission is "to promote policies and practices that work to expand and perfect markets, foster the development of new products and services and create efficiencies of member firms, while preserving and enhancing the public's trust and confidence in the markets and the industry.")

In 2007 the Securities Industry and Financial Markets Association* ("SIFMA") issued a "White Paper" dated June 13, in which it attempted to justify continuance of 12b-1 fees. Anyone familiar with the nature and history of SEC Rule 12b-1 would find it difficult to reconcile the arguments made by SIFMA and the spirit, letter and intent of the Rule adopted in 1980 – look it up. No amount of historical revisionism can change the clear, plain language of the Rule. This White Paper might be described in many ways, none of which include an objective treatment of the subject. To its credit, in the "Executive Summary," the Summary freely acknowledges about the only indisputable statement in its contents –*"The SEC adopted Rule 12b-1 at a time of moribund fund sales and high loads."* It also states, *"It might be appropriate to improve disclosures for the benefit of investors and fund boards, but it would be a major mistake for the SEC to withdraw or substantially curtail Rule 12b-1, or otherwise to restrict the fee arrangements that have fostered innovation, flexibility and investor choice."* However, nowhere in the document is there any discussion of how to improve disclosure for the primary beneficiaries of those purported benefits, who pay for them, or who is the ultimate beneficiary of these additional annual costs to shareholders.

For example, the Paper states that *"many funds have chosen to delegate most of their traditional responsibilities, such as recordkeeping, to the broker-dealer,"* which putting it mildly, has no relationship to the facts. The fact is that it was the major selling organizations that created an environment where they "proposed" to the funds that they would assume all recordkeeping functions for their clients with the funds *paying them* a portion of transfer fees for those activities. This led to the now famous *"omnibus accounts"* where shareholder identification is kept secret from the funds and purchases and redemptions are "bundled" each day with only one transaction forwarded to the fund, either a purchase or sale, while client accounts are adjusted by the selling organizations. The fact is that these are the types of accounts that were often involved in the market timing and late trading scandals just a few years ago. For anyone to think that these accounts were conceived as a benefit to fund shareholders is a real stretch. The fact is they were designed as an additional source of revenues for the selling organizations and in order to keep secret the identities of individual investors from the funds.

Among one of the most self-serving statements in this document is: *"Mutual fund boards should be able to approve and evaluate 12b-1 plans in circumstances involving expanding investor choice and offering innovation. Fund boards should not fear "second guessing," provided that the fees serve the needs of investors,"* which is contrary to the reason why directors are responsible for looking after shareholders' interests. The real question is how do those shareholders realize any benefits that could be considered any different from shareholders not involved in such marketing schemes? The answer is more than just obvious. Unfortunately, the Paper seriously misled readers with the following statement: *"Rarely is the basic load less than 7.5 percent of the total price that the investor pays and it has not exceeded 9 percent. An 8.5 percent sales load is most common."* This claim is embarrassing because it's based on their footnote, which identifies the source of their assertion as an SEC report to Congress that was issued on *December 2, 1966,* **more than 41 years ago(!)** and simply does not reflect the current sales charge structure that exists today.

This so-called "White Paper" deserves a full, factual rebuttal, which won't come from the ICI and has not been offered by mutual fund directors, and begs the question: Just who is representing the best interests of fund shareholders? If SIFMA really believes the contents of this Paper they should back it up by having their members provide for full, prominent disclosure of these fees, the amounts involved, how the money is spent and finally, how shareholders who are unknowingly charged the fees realize any discernible benefits from them, or if shareholders believe they are worth the cost.

In summary, this self-serving White Paper was designed to justify 12b-1 expenditures, the revenues for which come from each shareholder's account, but pointedly omits describing anything even remotely beneficial to shareholders who pay for "services" they may not need or want, and which are not required. Perhaps someday shareholders will be asked directly if they approve of paying for "services" they don't need or want. The truth of the matter is that in reading the entire report it's clear that it is devoid of any serious attempt to demonstrate any real value, much less justify, the cost to shareholders of 12b-1 charges assessed on them each year, every year.

12b-1 Plans – Annual Approval – The Phantom SEC Rule

Perhaps one of the reasons why these plans require only director approval and not shareholder approval annually is that one type of the 12b-1 plan is called a "Compensation Plan,"* wherein all revenues from the plan go directly to the investment advisor/distributor who uses those revenues in any way it deems appropriate. For example, can anyone imagine two different funds, Fund A and Fund B in the same fund group, where 12b-1 fees are assessed on both funds, but spent only on sales/marketing efforts for Fund A? Or if any of the 12b-1 fees from one fund are deducted and, for any reason, expended on another fund in the same fund group? Is it conceivable that shareholders of one fund would knowingly have any part of their assets diverted to promote a fund they don't own and from which they realize no benefit whatsoever? Where does the prospectus disclose that one fund is subsidizing another fund? That's the net effect of a so called 12b-1 "Compensation Plan" and it's difficult in the extreme to imagine fund shareholders voting to approve such a plan. And that's a major reason why shareholders should have the right to vote for or against such plans, every year. It also calls into question the rationale used by some directors who approve those plans – every year.

---

*In some cases mutual fund boards have adopted these "Compensation Plans" based on a proposed amendment to SEC Rule 17D-3. That proposed amendment could be interpreted as permitting the use of shareholder assets without any restrictions, specific reporting or full disclosure requirements. There's only one problem, the proposed amendment to Rule 17D -3 was NEVER (as in not ever) adopted by the SEC and therefore cannot be relied upon to justify so-called "Compensation Plans," i.e., the phantom amendment does not exist! The question then becomes how this scheme is permitted to exist and why regulators seem to have ignored this blatant use of a non-existent provision of 12b-1 plans? Perhaps someday a member of the legal profession will take the time to research this and "persuade" those funds that have compensation plans based on this phantom amendment to rescind those plans and return all such monies expended to their shareholders.

(Fact: The proposed amendment to Rule 17D-3 was never approved or adopted by the SEC and was finally withdrawn on January 23, 1995.)

Of note, fund directors have their own "independent" counsel who probably assured directors that their votes for these plans somehow satisfy their standard of care and loyalty to their employers, the fund's shareholders. How does that work?

While attempts may be made to rationalize such schemes, the fact is that directors are held hostage to this practice because of the likely results of voting to put an end to the current use of fund assets, which was never conceived or contemplated when Rule12b-1 was adopted in 1980. Look it up.

©Scott Adams/Dist. By United Feature Syndicate, Inc.

The ICI and 12b-1 Fees

What would you guess is the position of the ICI and its affiliated organization, the Independent Directors Council ("IDC"), on this subject? Both groups filed their own comment letters with the SEC on this subject, on the same date, June 19, 2007.

In their letters the ICI and the IDC describe themselves in part as follows:

ICI –

"ICI members include 8,766 open end investment companies (mutual funds), 670 closed-end investment companies, 440 exchange-traded funds, and 4 sponsors of unit investment trusts. Mutual fund members of the ICI have total assets of approximately $11,242 trillion (representing 98 percent of all assets in US mutual funds); these funds serve approximately 93.9 million shareholders in more than 53.4 million households."

IDC –

"IDC serves the independent director community and provides a venue to advance the education, communication and policy positions of fund independent directors."

We know that the ICI is the trade, lobbying organization for investment advisors and they have made quite clear that it does *not* represent fund shareholders. And we know that IDC membership is comprised of independent directors of the funds sponsored by ICI members. It's important to note that all mutual funds are formed as separate, distinct corporations which are owned by their shareholders. Equally important is the fact that according to the 2007 ICI Annual Report, the ICI Board of Governors is comprised of 44 officers/employees of investment advisory firms and *8 independent mutual fund directors*. Perhaps someday we'll learn how that translates into 8,766 mutual funds as "members" of the ICI. It's interesting to note that the former name of the ICI was the National Association of Investment Companies. Did something happen when the name of the organization changed?

We also know that at the present time there exists no viable, organized entity that represents mutual fund shareholders. We know the nature of the ICI and where its primary interest lies so there's no reason to devote any time to how they arrived at the conclusions in their letter, which pointedly avoided any reference to the burden of these ongoing, never ending 12b-1 fees assessed on shareholders. However, this does raise the question about ICI dues being paid for fully or partially from a fund's total assets, i.e., those shareholders pay to support an organization whose objective is to represent investment advisors and *not* mutual fund shareholders.

Of interest, however, is the IDC comment letter, purportedly representing the views of their independent director members, whose sole clients are the shareholders they represent. It's a cleverly crafted letter written by attorneys who have no obligation to represent fund shareholders' views on the subject, and which pretty much tracked the ICI's position. The IDC letter does include a stunning paragraph in the section titled "Modernization of Board Oversight":

"The current fund distribution system is very different from the one that existed when Rule 12b-1 was adopted. While distribution systems and the uses of 12b-1 fees have evolved significantly over the past 27 years, the process that fund directors must follow under Rule 12b-1 in considering and approving the 12b-1 fees has not. Some directors and their counsel read 12b-1 as currently written to require that directors engage in fairly detailed review of their funds' distribution arrangements. Such a review is at odds with the role of directors as general overseers of the interests of shareholders."
(Emphasis added)

Hello? The Rule as written is quite clear and describes the duties of the directors clearly, without equivocation. You have to wonder how many directors are willing to testify before the SEC on this specific subject. As concerns their view as "… at odds with the role of fund directors as general overseers of the interest of shareholders," since when is it not the director's responsibility to review/oversee expenses borne by the fund's shareholders? In fact, such oversight is one of the primary responsibilities of directors. It almost appears that the IDC, an affiliate of the ICI, prefers that directors simply rubber stamp that which the investment advisor puts before them. It's possible that the attorney who authored this letter is either unaware of or prefers to ignore the following specific requirement imbedded in Rule 12b-1:

"..any person authorized to direct the disposition of monies paid or payable by such company pursuant to the plan or any related agreement shall provide the company's board of directors, and the directors shall review, at least quarterly, a written report of the amounts so expended and the purposes for which such expenditures were made;"

What is it about that language that's not clear? Are directors getting these quarterly reports, reviewing and approving them as required? Do they know the identity of "… *any person authorized* to direct disposition…?" When was the last time a board authorized an audit of a year-end 12b-1 report presented to them? Of course, clever lawyers can craft all kinds of rationale to support an opinion contrary to a rule or regulation. Another alternative could be a proposal for the elimination of fund directors as unnecessary under any circumstances. Why not? It's not as if that idea hasn't already been floated - but quickly denied by the ICI. By eliminating the review/approval requirement, Rule 12b-1 would quickly become the honey pot some desire and result in open season on shareholder assets for any purpose. Would that be considered "at odds" with the role of fund directors as general overseers of mutual funds? An interesting question.

The effects of the "recommendations" of both the ICI and IDC comment letters is based on false logic, which has never worked. It's obvious that neither of these organizations represents the interests of fund shareholders and should not be relied upon for their opinions on how and for what purposes fund shareholder assets should be used. To give them credence on this issue is simply inappropriate and contrary to shareholders' best interests.

Finally, *Reuters* carried a story on September 14, 2007 on its website (www.today.reuters.com/misc) under the headline "Mutual fund group defends distribution fees." The article described the president of the ICI, Paul Stevens, as having "acknowledged that some changes may be needed, such as renaming 12b-1 fees and disclosing their purpose to investors." Aside from using a new label to make the scheme more palatable, that is a damning admission of the absence of full disclosure of what 12b-1 fees have become and for what purpose they are used. It takes more than just a long stretch to conceive that the ICI has any interest whatsoever with respect to the best interests of fund shareholders, except by happenstance.

The Mutual Fund Directors Forum

MFDF describes itself as follows:

"The Mutual Fund Directors Forum, a nonprofit organization for investment company directors, promotes vigilant, dedicated, and well informed independent directors and serves as their voice and advocate on important policy matters."

MFDF has never tried to hide its purpose, which is to serve and act as an advocate for <u>independent</u> mutual fund directors. Full disclosure: I was honored to serve on the MFDF Advisory Board for approximately 5 years and can attest to the integrity and the independence of the organization and its work in providing real, objective guidance to directors relative to their responsibilities and duties in compliance with applicable law, rules and regulations.

As evidence of their work, interested readers should access their website, www.mfdf.com, and read their May 2007 publication, "Best Practices and Practical Guidance for Directors under Rule 12b-1." That document provides all anyone needs to know about Rule 12b-1 in a fair, concise and objective plain English description of the Rule and the issues faced by directors and in turn by investors in today's marketplace. To its further credit MFDF recently announced its involvement with several other respected entities in creating a permanent organization comprised of a number of key independent fund directors. The group would function as a venue for independent fund chairpersons and lead directors who are independent of a fund's advisor in order to share their experiences and face the challenges confronted by the industry.

Unfortunately, MFDF has not yet achieved the recognition it has earned and deserves. When it does, the industry, the regulators, and by extension the shareholders, will be better served. If you're a fund shareholder drop a note to the chairperson of the board of your fund and inquire if the board is member of MFDF - and if not, why not?

Another Related Issue

> In addition to the multitude of issues surrounding the validity of 12b-1 plan fee payments, the July 9, 2007 edition of Investment News highlighted another issue about 12b-1 fees that deserves attention. An article titled "12b-1 fees come under attack again" described an SEC sponsored roundtable discussion which included the following statement made by Barbara Roper, director of investor protection for the Consumer Federation of America.
>
> "Using such fees to pay for continuing advice for clients as the mutual fund and brokerage industries claim to do, could run afoul of the Investment Advisers Act of 1940," which provides that "brokers are prohibited from receiving 'special compensation' for investment advice."

It's obvious that there are many serious questions about current practices relative to 12b-1 plan payments, all of which are payments borne by fund shareholders, that need to be fully discussed and resolved.

A Director's "To-Do" List for the Future

In addition to regulatory requirements, the mandate for directors should be to do their utmost to ensure that shareholders' interests are served; to make every effort to inform and educate shareholders with complete, full disclosure of all factors relative to their investment; to help shareholders more fully understand what their funds are all about, and why they should own them as long term investors. In doing so they must keep the advisor's "feet to the fire," by acting as the proverbial watchdog on behalf of those who pay them handsome compensation in the form of directors' fees. Anything less is not good enough. However, based on the manner in which some issues are handled you have to wonder if every director understands his/her mandate. They're not there to "go along to get along." Rather they're there to negotiate with the advisor on behalf of shareholders in order to achieve maximum benefit for the shareholder. The following is a list of proposals that should be given the most serious consideration by directors and which they should adopt to fulfill their obligations in acting with a duty of care and loyalty to their employers, the shareholders of the funds they serve.

Chief Compliance Officer

©Scott Adams/Dist. By United Feature Syndicate, Inc.

Everyone knows that the mutual fund industry is <u>not *over regulated.*</u> Rather it is over-lawyered. One of the most important reforms adopted as a result of the market timing, late trading scandals of a few years ago was the creation of the office of CCO, a change much needed and long overdue. However, the change has not been properly implemented. There's only one way a CCO can do the job and that is with complete autonomy and independence from the investment advisor. That means the position should be compensated directly by the fund(s) they represent, i.e., the CCO should be an <u>employee</u> of the fund(s) and function as a direct report to the board of directors. The mechanics of this arrangement are easily managed by a competent board of directors and should be implemented immediately.

The reason for reporting directly to the boards is self-evident – the CCO cannot serve two masters, which clearly makes for a conflict of interest. The position was created to provide directors with direct, unvarnished, legal/compliance guidance in fulfilling their roles as watchdogs on behalf of shareholders. However, it's simply impossible for one individual to do what the job requires. That's why the CCO should have as his/her direct reports an Internal Audit Staff ("IAS"), responsible for direct oversight of daily fund operations based on an "Operations and Compliance Manual" distributed to all fund employees, from the CEO to the newest hire, *including all independent directors*. That manual should be the "bible" for the advisor and related affiliates to be used by the IAS in performing periodic tests of systems, policies and procedures. All such results would be reviewed by the CCO and presented as available to directors as a regular agenda item.

Of course some who should know better will whine and react with alarm about additional staff and costs for the function. The answer to these "concerns" is simple: have the CCO and the IAS replace the independent counsel for the directors which costs between $200,000 and $500,000 or more per year. This simple change will cover most if not all of the costs of "internalization" of this function. If the directors feel it's absolutely essential to engage independent counsel they can have one available at a modest retainer and have their services available on request. The result will be that the board and shareholders will not be subject to someone focusing on a billing meter to ensure a pre-determined income for overstaffed law firms specializing in make-work projects and boilerplate legal "stuff."   As an aside, it would be interesting to see how many current independent counsels will jump at the job of a CCO for a whole host of reasons, not the least of which is to maintain their own self respect. The point is that when the CCO/IAS do their jobs there will be limited if any need for independent counsel, which reduces costs for shareholders. The end result is that both directors and shareholders will be more than adequately served and at a lower net cost to the fund.

What needs to be emphasized is that directors and shareholders have a true identity of interests, which is quite unique. Anything favorable to either should be beneficial to both. Who doesn't "get that?" And if there are any investment industry lawyers who have a problem with that "concept" or find it strange, they should start looking for a different line of work. The combination of a CCO and IAS is the only way this relatively new change can be effective – it serves both the directors and the shareholders and is likely to reduce net expenses for the fund. To assume that the "cost" of a CCO can be "shared" by the investment advisor and the fund is nothing less than naïve and self defeating.

The time has come to adopt this sensible, cost effective approach to ensure that a CCO can do the job required to be done.

Director Reforms, Compensation

Over Worked or Over Paid?

(Overheard at a meeting of the independent directors of the <u>Exotica Mutual Funds.</u>)

Chairman: As you know, this has been a difficult period for us. Our funds have underperformed the markets; sales were down and we're in net redemptions, assets have declined and our operating expenses have risen again. It's been a very stressful year. Of course it does no good to cry over spilt milk or circumstances beyond our control. Our Compensation Committee, which is comprised of all independent members of the board, has recommended that our annual director fees be increased effective immediately. Your unanimous approval has been duly noted and let the minutes reflect that we will continue to closely monitor director's compensation.

Unfortunately, that's the perception that some observers have of mutual fund directors since they set their own compensation without requiring shareholder approval.

Over Worked or Over Paid?

Directors should <u>*not*</u> determine their own compensation. This longstanding practice should be discontinued simply because they are the employees of the fund's shareholders and not an autonomous group without any responsibility to its "employers." This is a fact that seems to have escaped some in the industry who should know better. The obvious failure of the current approach to director compensation is the method most often used in determining director fees. That method is based on either the total amount of assets under management or the number of funds in a fund complex. Here's the problem in each case. Directors have absolutely nothing to do with the amount of assets in a fund complex. They do not select portfolio securities, cause securities prices to go up or in any way engage in portfolio management, the primary reason for good performance that causes total assets to increase. In addition, directors have absolutely nothing to do with the sales/marketing program implemented by the investment advisor or its affiliated distributor. Everyone knows that with the exception of merging two funds the only ways fund assets grow is by having good performance and/or good sales, neither of which is dependent on the involvement of fund directors. The fact is that since directors do not select portfolio securities or develop or implement sales/marketing programs any increase in total assets under management should not be a factor in director compensation.

Anyone who thinks the current approach makes sense should also support a *decrease* in compensation when assets decline due to negative performance or net redemptions.

Directors do not recommend or create new funds for addition to a complex of funds. Newly created funds are another possible source of increased total assets in a fund complex. However, that's in the province of the investment advisor and subject to approval of the directors. But that's the extent of their involvement in the process, which includes reviewing boiler plate documents, a job easily managed by the CCO who is qualified to do that job and present the proposal to the directors for their approval.

Too often directors' compensation is reviewed by comparing the compensation paid to other fund boards based on their total assets or the number of funds in a complex as justification for increasing compensation to those levels. Why? Is there any basis for believing that a director from one fund board will be induced to leave and join another fund board because of the level of compensation? Has that ever occurred? If so, it's rare indeed. In addition, any director who serves on the basis of director's fees is not the kind of director that should have the job.

Reality Check – The January 2009 issue of *Fund Directions* carried an article titled "Director Pay expected to stay flat in 2009..." While that should not come as a surprise in light of what happened to net asset values in 2008, the article did contain a stunner: "*One independent director has kept track of all the hours she's spent in committee meetings and on fund related things. 'At my billable rate – I'm a bargain!' she said. 'Shareholders are getting their damn money's worth!'* " Hopefully that's *not* the attitude of the overwhelming majority of independent, but it could be an indication of how some of them approach their responsibilities. This particular director is the perfect poster person for annual election of directors where her sentiments might be shared with the shareholders of the fund board(s) on which she serves. The real question is why her own board allows her to continue to serve and not be removed immediately.

Over worked or over paid?

Solution

The only sensible way to resolve this issue and bring the shareholders into the equation is to give the job of evaluation and recommendation to an independent third party who can objectively perform the analysis required. The goal is to arrive at a reasonable level of compensation based on the time involved and the nature of the director's duties. In this regard, the issue of director liability is a red herring since directors determine the level of "D&O-E&O" insurance they carry and which they determine to be adequate and is paid for by the fund. Directors, who feel they should receive additional compensation for any real or imagined risk they undertake, can resolve any such concerns simply by resigning. The independent, objective, third party consultant is the only acceptable way to determine compensation and avoid the inevitable criticism that exists otherwise.

Advisory Fee Breakpoints

Over the last 15-20 years the growth of mutual fund assets under management ("AUM") has been nothing less than spectacular. In most cases it was well deserved and earned on the basis of investment performance and the services enjoyed by shareholders. It's a given that any advisor that undertakes the major challenges of entering the mutual fund business, investing considerable money and time, should be entitled to recover that investment and be rewarded accordingly. In addition, under our capitalist, free enterprise system there should be no limit on profits earned by any company except with the possible exception of some forms of essential goods or services. As a result, there are no statutory limits on the amount of the advisory fees that can be charged to a mutual fund. However, those fees are subject to annual review and approval by the independent directors.

The question has been raised about investment fees which are often scaled down based on total AUM. For example, the base advisory fee on AUM may be 60 basis points ("bps"), or three fifths of one percent of AUM from zero to one billion dollars; 55 bps over one billion to $1.249 billion, etc. The principle is quite simple: as assets increase higher levels of assets are assessed lower advisory fee rates based on "economies of scale." However, despite the lip service paid to this subject, the reality is that in many, if not most cases, any such reduction in fees realized at higher levels of AUM are negligible for fund shareholders. In fact, "sharing" of breakpoint reductions are so small for shareholders that they go unnoticed. This was highlighted in the March 2008 Bulletin issued by *Management Practice,* which is a market-focused strategic consulting firm, serving financial, industrial, service, and consumer organizations. The March Bulletin featured an article, "Highlights from Discussions on Mutual Fund Profitability and Economies of Scale," that included an illustration at a certain breakpoint and concluded in the example that *"Sharing economies of scale is 4% to shareholders and 96% to the advisor."* (A copy of the Bulletin is available at www.MFGovern.com.) This example demonstrates that any such economies of scale are tilted overwhelmingly in favor of the advisor and offer little benefit to shareholders.

Suggested Action

This is an area in which directors can really earn their fees simply by negotiating a more meaningful reduction in fees at higher levels of assets. For example, the level of fee breakpoints could be significantly lower to ensure that any such reductions have a positive effect on shareholder's investments. In this regard, such reductions have a direct, positive effect on investment performance, which is good for both the advisor and the shareholders, i.e., "less is more." By taking a proactive role in negotiating lower breakpoint levels, directors can demonstrate their value to shareholders in their role as their representatives. Simply rubber stamping breakpoint fee levels is contrary to good governance practices. In addition, the resulting positive publicity could be very effective in motivating additional investments from shareholders, as well as attracting new shareholders, as more and more attention is focused on operating expenses in the fund selection process.

The mandate for fund directors is clear and as AUM increase it is an established fact that the advisor's costs of operations do not increase at anywhere near the same rate, if at all. The mutual fund business is not dependent on bricks and mortar or changing production designs. The advisor's mandate is also clear – to provide consistent above average performance results for the shareholders. When they do, AUM increase, advisory revenues increase and both the advisor and shareholders enjoy the benefits of improved performance results and cost savings.

Directors are wise to take this proactive approach if for no other reason than that it's their duty - and to justify their annual compensation.

Selection and "Election" of Directors

The November 29, 1999 issue of *Forbes Magazine* included an article titled: "Nice work if you can get it," in which it described a mutual fund director's job as "nice pay for a part time job – six figures at some families." It also ran the photos and annual fees paid to a number of then sitting mutual fund directors, including: Nancy Kissinger, wife of Henry Kissinger, Lowell Weicker Jr., ex-U.S. senator, Wendy Gramm, wife of then U.S. Senator Phil Gramm, Warren Rudman, ex-U.S. senator, Jack Fields, ex-U.S. representative, Elizabeth Moynihan, wife of then U.S. Senator Patrick Moynihan, Edwin Garn, ex-U.S. Senator, Walter Mondale, ex-Vice President. Remember that was in 1999 and with more than 8,000 funds today it's a major undertaking to search the names of all fund directors. In fairness, many if not all of those listed may no longer serve on any fund boards.

But that's not the point. At that time the role of the independent director was quite different from what is required today. That doesn't mean that there was ever a time when mutual funds should have directors with little if any investment knowledge or experience. Have things changed since then? Maybe, but it appears that a former Hollywood actor and a retired football player currently serve as independent directors of two different fund complexes.

Meanwhile the February 11, 2008 edition of *Investment News* carried a story about fund directors possibly delegating some of their duties subject to SEC approval included the following comments by Laura Pavlenko Lutton, a senior fund analyst at Morningstar, Inc.: "If the question is how do we make the board more efficient, I'd come back to who's sitting on the board, what's their background." She continued, "I'd look at, 'Could we get the board a little muscle by recruiting folks who understand the issues?'"

<u>Fact: *Directors are not elected for life and do not enjoy tenured positions.*</u> However, you wouldn't know it based on how the current system works. Where is it written that once elected to a board, shareholders no longer have the right to re-elect those same directors or opt for different directors? There is no such provision in the Investment Act of 1940, or in any securities rules or regulations.

Some years ago I participated in a panel of directors, the discussion topic of which was recruiting and selecting new directors. As the last speaker, I made the point that the solution was really self-evident. All we had to do was to place a "Help wanted" ad in the business/financial press as follows:

> "Seeking an individual with knowledge of financial matters, accounting issues, Federal securities laws and good business judgment. No experience required."

Of course this was said tongue-in-cheek as intended and everyone got the point. We have to change the attributes and requirements for future directors. Two important requirements would be: Director candidates must serve as "apprentice" directors, for a two year period without voting privileges, with compensation during the two year period at one half the rate of experienced, elected directors. This would go a long way toward board "diversification," with the emphasis on knowledge and competence from day one.

This would completely change the complexion of fund boards so that all voting directors would have a working knowledge of fundamental fund issues, operations and compliance. The effect is to have all newly elected or appointed directors hit the ground running before casting their first vote. Is that too great a burden in light of directors' responsibilities? Shouldn't those charged with "watchdog" responsibilities have a working knowledge of those issues that come before them? Or is this a position for a "trainee?" To ignore this important issue is nothing less than irresponsible and flies in the face of the fiduciary obligations of fund directors.

The principle is the same as hiring anyone for a position in which they have no directly related experience and giving them decision making authority. How does that work? And how many readers have been hired for any job on that basis? The least shareholders should expect is that those who are being handsomely rewarded for their service should have at least the same knowledge and familiarity with mutual funds as they have. Who would argue otherwise?

Continuing Education Programs

Finally, the industry has to adopt minimal standards for directors unrelated to any current rules or regulations. A first step in that regard is establishing and requiring a Continuing Education Program that must be satisfied by every fund director. I have attended more industry programs and conferences than I can remember. But one thing I have always noticed is that despite the fact that there are approximately 3,000 directors it's rare that industry conferences are attended by more than several hundred directors and extremely rare for attendance to approach 500 directors. Even with 500 directors in attendance it means that about 84% of directors are *not* in attendance, and points to a real problem that needs to be addressed and remedied. If any director is unable to satisfy Continuing Education Program requirements, they should be removed from the boards – without any exceptions.

Annual Shareholder Meetings

Much has been said about the expense of holding annual shareholder meetings. However, any such related expenses pale in significance compared to the *multi billions of dollars* spent each year for 12b-1 fees, which are paid for by shareholders. In addition, there is a legitimate concern relative to poor or low attendance at such meetings. This can be resolved by including the following agenda items for annual meetings:

1. Fund update by the president of the fund.

2. Report on performance and portfolio holdings by the chief investment officer or portfolio manager(s).

3. Election of and mandatory presence of all directors.

Proxy statements for the meeting should require a brief, personally written statement from each director up for election or re-election to the board. This should also include a written statement by the board chairman reporting on issues confronted and addressed by the board since the previous meeting. In other words, the directors should provide the basis for their election/re-election to the board in their own words.

Adequate notice of the meeting should be provided and meetings held in a geographic area based on the greatest concentration of shareholders. The notice should include a real proposed agenda, which will go a long way toward motivating shareholder attendance and overcome apathy on their part. This notice should be sent by mail and by email, the preferred, optional method of communication of many shareholders. Part of this approach involves holding the meeting in a centrally located venue during evening hours or on a Saturday. That's not too great a burden to improve shareholder relations/communications, build shareholder loyalty and confidence while encouraging additional investments, i.e., there's no downside, it's a win/win for everyone.

In this regard, no special regulatory exemptions or approvals or boiler legal opinions are required. It simply requires that directors demonstrate a real interest in their employers – the shareholders. And they might finally meet a real, live shareholder.

Look, directors are handsomely rewarded and in some case excessively rewarded. Some directors seem to feel that their responsibility simply involves attending several meetings each year, approve the Minutes of the prior meeting and vote yes on any and all proposals put before them. That is simply unacceptable and must be changed. The fact is that some directors never contribute to meetings, while others consider them a social event and a good source of additional income without any concern for the duties and obligations they have to fund shareholders. Any directors who fit that description should be removed from fund boards – now.

Glacial "Speed"

A final note and some "inside baseball." It was ten (10) years ago that *Fund Directions ("The Trusted Voice of Fund Trustees")* organized a "Roundtable" discussion that included five independent directors in which I was a participant. The transcript of that discussion was published as a "Supplement" to their regular monthly issue in May 1998. While the Supplement never made any "best seller" list, nevertheless it reveals how little progress has been made on key governance issues since that time.

As you read through the following eight pages you'll recognize several issues that remain topics of discussion today, including: Fair value pricing; Profile prospectuses; 12b-1 fees; 401k plans, and director compensation. Here we are ten years later having survived the year 2000 "crisis," the dot com bubble, the market timing, late trading scandals and we're deeply immersed in the current investment banking, no-low interest home financing and a myriad of derivative securities issues, all of which are certain to reveal more than we could imagine, and a number of the issues raised in 1998 remain a "work in progress."

What will it take for the industry, Congress and the regulators to address and resolve these longstanding issues as well as others that require attention? Where are the "Masters of the Universe" when we need them? On second thought, strike that question.

The 1998 Roundtable Supplement follows.

Fund Directions: Director's Roundtable, 1998 Reprint

Reprinted with permission of Fund Directions. Published by Institutional Investor.

FUND DIRECTIONS
THE TRUSTED VOICE OF FUND TRUSTEES

A PUBLICATION OF INSTITUTIONAL INVESTOR

VOL. 7 NO. 5   MAY 1998

SPECIAL SUPPLEMENT: DIRECTORS' ROUNDTABLE

Dan Calabria: Trustee, the **Florida Tax-Free Funds**, the **ASM 30 Index Fund** and the **Idex Series Fund**.

Issue: Should the **Securities and Exchange Commission** revisit rule 12b-1 to provide an incentive to reward positive sales as opposed to compensation being paid even when a fund is in steady net redemption?

Bob Spies: Trustee, **First American Funds**.

Issue: Managing the growth that we're going through due to acquisition. Right now we're at $23 billion. **Piper Jaffrey** has about $6.5 billion in assets, so when the acquisition closes, we will be at $30 billion. We are going to expand our board from seven to nine trustees.

Ed Beach: Trustee, **Prudential Mutual Funds**.

Issue: We were concerned with board consolidation. We had 37 directors. But we were spending a lot of time duplicating. So we're now down to about 21 trustees with four clusters. We have increased board efficiency and productivity.

Ken Domingues: Formerly affiliated director and cfo at **Franklin Resources**.

Issue: There are now six director groups with five or more directors at Franklin/Templeton. The board would like to improve efficiency in the director process to minimize work load and enhance performance.

Gordon Shillinglaw: Trustee, **AARP Funds**, former **Scudder Funds** trustee.

Issue: Because of the demographics of our shareholders, we have to maintain a board that has greater diversity. Beyond that, we may decide to shrink the size of the board. The challenge will be to maintain a balance among backgrounds we want to have on the board.

As the **Securities and Exchange Commission** puts renewed emphasis on the importance of fund boards in protecting the interests of shareholders, trustees, now more than ever, are taking a step back to examine their fiduciary roles. As a result, many boards are paying particularly close attention to the way they set up procedures to monitor general compliance, valuation, 12b-1 fees, expenses and other fund issues.

The editors of *Fund Directions* recently brought together five directors to discuss and exchange ideas on the concerns that are making the agenda in their boardrooms. In addition to sharing their thoughts on pertinent issues, the directors also offered a glimpse of some of the policies and procedures that they have put in place to monitor those concerns.

An edited version of the directors' roundtable follows this page.

FUND DIRECTIONS

May 1998
Directors' Roundtable Supplement

Q: *Has your board implemented mandatory share guidelines?*

Ed Beach: Yes, we've asked that it be done. And it has. The SEC says you're supposed to be totally independent, if you're an independent director. Well, now let's say you have a substantial portion of your net worth tied up in mutual funds, you might not be independent as far as I'm concerned. As an accountant, I could never have stock in a firm that I did the audit for.

Gordon Shillinglaw: I have just the opposite feeling. For a long time, I've had shares in every fund in which I serve. I do that to identify my interests with those of the shareholders.

" A *t a shareholders meeting, you have two people show up, and one of the questions is, 'why don't the directors [hold shares]?' "*

—*Ed Beach, independent trustee, Prudential Mutual Funds*

Bob Spies: In February, First American adopted a policy where the directors have to have enough investments in the funds to equal their annual compensation.

Beach: That's what we have. And it's investments in all the funds that count.

Spies: I actually did move a substantial amount of money in my retirement program into our funds. I personally believe if you're going to be on the board, you should have a stake in the fund. It's just loyalty.

Shillinglaw: I even had shares in the gold fund. I sold them after I went off the board.

Dan Calabria: There are two points that I'd like to make: I think every director and every portfolio manager should have at least a nominal investment [in a fund], even if it's only $1,000. If nothing else, it will make [directors] aware of what shareholders receive and when it's received.

Shillinglaw: Good point.

Calabria: Beyond that, at Idex, they've done something that I thought is terrific. Very beneficial and easily solves this

problem. They have a deferred compensation program where you can take a percentage of your fees and have it invested in the funds of your choice, in any proportion you want. A portion of directors' fees becomes tax deferred and tax sheltered until some point in the future when you pay the tax.

Shillinglaw: Are these actual shares ...?

Management Share Ownership
Calabria: These are phantom shares. Management does the allocation and reporting and the bookkeeping for it, but what difference does it make? It doesn't show up as share ownership, you're right. But it certainly does give you an identity of interest with the investors in that, you know, your money is there and it's an advantage to do that. So I think it's great. Now I'm going off on a bit of a tangent. I always felt very strongly that directors should own shares of the fund in which they serve.

I'll go a step further and, this is a hot-button item today, we don't have enough portfolio managers who own shares of the same fund they manage. And there are investment advisers who don't own, corporately, shares of the fund. It's difficult to understand these portfolio managers who are up on everything in the world except personal ownership of funds. And I think every prospectus should have a page in chart format that says these are our officers, directors and our portfolio managers. These are the funds they work with and these are the number of shares they own.

Shillinglaw: But you do have one problem with that.

Calabria: What's that?

Shillinglaw: That is a portfolio manager trading in shares, his own product. He gets some information about something that's going to go on and sells shares, or buys shares, before these actions take effect. And I know that the Scudder ethics code, for example, includes the portfolio managers. They have to get clearance on any purchases or sales of shares in their own funds.

Beach: We have the same requirements.

Calabria: Well, I think that's eminently more acceptable than their trading individual securities where they can do some serious front running. Is it worth the trouble? Is it worth the effort? And if you're a long-term investor, that's going to pop up on the screen in no time and it's going to be embarrassing for you. On the other hand, they can do front running on individual stocks and, you know, you may never know about it.

Code of ethics

Shillinglaw: But the code of ethics is supposed to [prevent front-running].

Calabria: I agree with it, and I wish I could say I have confidence that the code of ethics is enforced uniformly and religiously. I don't believe that.

Beach: We started to get a report from the ethics committee every quarter. If there's any violations of any magnitude, it's picked up between the quarters and reported immediately.

Calabria: Ed, but that's after the fact, okay?

Shillinglaw: Here's the real point. A mutual fund is the classic, fiduciary responsibility of relationships with the investors.

Beach: We fire major violators [front-runners].

Shillinglaw: Okay. You should fire them.

Beach: We do just that.

Shillinglaw: Monitoring these things after the fact, in my opinion, doesn't cut it. Now we have the ability and the machinery and the wherewithal to make sure all of this is done properly.

Beach: We put in the safeguards that we can. They [managers] can't have a brokerage account with another brokerage firm without our permission. And if they want to do any trading, we know what their account is with Prudential. And if they start with somebody else...there's a problem then, at that point.

Spies: Our portfolio managers, or any of our officers of **U.S. Bancorp** who are knowledgeable of the investment side of the business, cannot make a trade for their own portfolio without clearing it ahead of time. And then everybody, including our directors, sign a statement of any trades they made other than governments or mutual funds, on a monthly basis.

Calabria: That's as it should be, and I think most mutual funds operate under the same criteria. My point is that we shouldn't even allow the possibility of anything going wrong, deliberately or inadvertently, under any circumstances, because if it ever surfaces, it's going to be extremely damaging to the fund and the shareholders and the industry. And we shouldn't take that risk.

Q: *How do you set up the system whereby you report someone's done front-running?*

Calabria: I suggest that the rule be that if the portfolio manager likes a stock and it's in the fund, buy the fund. And if you don't want to buy the fund, then stay out of the market.

Q: *Meaning that if we catch you afterwards, you're fired?*

Spies: If we're tracking a stock, the portfolio manager, not just in our fund, but our managed accounts, cannot buy that stock without clearing it first.

Q: *Do you have a special committee set up to monitor this?*

Calabria: Oh, yes.

Spies: No. We don't.

Shillinglaw: The mechanism is there, but still people can get around it.

Spies: You still can get around it.

Attendance requirements

Q: *What has your board done about enforcing attendance requirements?*

Beach: Years ago, the meetings were not scheduled well enough ahead of time, but several years ago, we started scheduling meetings a year ahead of time. They were circulated and said if this is a conflict, you let us know now. And then we set the schedule up and we didn't change them, particularly. Now, with those provisions, I think attendance is just almost mandatory.

Shillinglaw: I agree with that.

Beach: And I'm not talking about hooking in on the

3

FUND DIRECTIONS
May 1998
Directors' Roundtable Supplement

telephone. So our rule now is that the attendance that counts as far as we're concerned, is actually being present physically. And I think...I mean, we get paid pretty good to work.

Q: *You actually have a policy where they have to be there?*

Beach: Yes. If they miss two in a row, they could have a problem.

Shillinglaw: For a lot of resolutions, a telephone vote does not count.

Beach: And in some cases, it has to be a majority of the outside directors.

We have never had any problem with attendance. We have one trustee who has every year a conflict on the date with another board meeting. But if you're not careful, you reduce everyone to the lowest level. And you don't want to do that. But you've got to get people to understand that they have to be there.

Fair value pricing

Spies: We've got to define what we mean by fair value pricing before we discuss it.

What you're defining as fair value is for securities for which we do not have any quoted market prices of some kind or another. You have to have a procedure. We have a standing procedure that states when there's a crisis in the sense that this stock is not traded for one day, two days, or whatever reason, you have to have an answer for what are you going to do about that. And you have to establish a price. And that will be fair value pricing.

Also, if your fund has warrants or securities that are linked to other, heaven forbid, even a derivative or two, how do you deal with that? There's got to be a policy, a formula that is approved by the directors.

We have a procedure to follow for shares that are not, in effect, being traded in the local market. We also have a valuation committee that meets periodically to examine whether the formula or the amount is still appropriate. We meet at least quarterly and ask ourselves, Do we still think we should value this at a certain price? Do we still think that we should use the capital asset pricing model that our guru in the firm thinks is appropriate? That's one side of fair value. The other side of fair value is the Fidelity issue.

Calabria: There's one indisputable fact in this business, and that's that you have to price that portfolio every day. With that knowledge, why in the world, how in the world, does a portfolio manager ever get himself into the situation, with some rare exceptions, where he's going to buy a stock where there's no market. Okay? And presto, how do we price it? Why did you buy it; how did you buy it; and how are we going to prevent that in the future?

Spies: It depends on your fund. There are many kinds of securities, private placements, for example, that may be very, very good investments, and there's no way of pricing them daily because they're not traded. And there may be restrictions about when you can sell them and so on and so forth. But you don't want to let that be a major portion of the portfolio.

Calabria: I understand, but if you have to price the fund and came up with an net asset value every day, it presumes you're going to have a liquid market there and a ready market. The worst-case scenario is if everybody stepped up to the plate and said, "Sell my shares." What do you do?

Shillinglaw: But an international fund, by definition, has some potential problems to identify. Whether you're dealing in Latin America, South America or in the Asiatic rim, the Pacific Basin.

Calabria: I was with **Templeton** for seven years, and we priced the fund every day in St. Petersburg and, yes, there were days when it was difficult to know the price, but they did their best to come up with a price. There was no such thing as fair value pricing at that time. The portfolio manager, who was responsible for repurchasing the stock, had an integral role in the process.

> ### Board Diversity
> I'm a person who spent 32 years in the mutual fund industry. The one thing that I'm amazed at is the rarity of retired mutual fund people who serve on boards other than those who remain on the board of the fund for which they worked. And I'm curious, there are theories that say well, you want to get a diversity on your board and you want an academician, you want an attorney, you want a corporate businessman, you want a financial man, et cetera. And, with all due respect, I would suggest that there's nobody who knows how the industry works and should work, than those who've lived it. And yet we see so very, very few on boards. And I wonder why? In other words, why wouldn't a **Merrill Lynch** board bring in a retired executive from **Dean Witter** or **Prudential** or something like that.
> — **Dan Calabria**, independent trustee

FUND DIRECTIONS
May 1998
Directors' Roundtable Supplement

Shillinglaw: Well, I think in all fairness we ought to say that the SEC focused on the fair value issue, including Fidelity's, and it said that the practice was acceptable.

Calabria: They've been wrong before.

Shillinglaw: I think Dan has said we've got two issues. The first issue is whether any traded, open-end mutual fund should have illiquid investments. That's one. Then if you were to take the position, yes, they can have them within limits, then you have to have some procedure for fair value pricing. And the procedure has to be followed and has to be monitored by the board.

Q: *Does anyone want to talk about a process that they've put in place?*

Calabria: I think you lead the process by speaking with the adviser and the portfolio managers and the traders, too. You get a feel for the market conditions, circumstances and make a judgment. How much of this involves risk? Kind of back into it.

Shillinglaw: But sometimes you get things like derivatives for which there really is no market. You have to do it by formula.

"*The result of that exercise was sending the message to the portfolio manager that if you're going to deal in these kinds of stocks, we're going to zero you out.*"

——**Bob Spies**, *independent trustee*, **First American Funds.**

Spies: We experienced a problem in Asia. We had one issue that was in our international index fund, a $70,000 issue. We have a pricing committee headed by a director, portfolio manager and administration. And they got together very quickly and determined we cannot price this issue. So they priced it at zero. It affected two-tenths of 1% of the net asset value. They immediately said at the time of the Asian issue, that we no longer will lend securities to Japanese banks, nor will we deal with the **Bank of Tokyo**. We're comfortable with that. We don't deal a lot with derivatives. Derivatives have earned a bad name, but there's a hundred different kinds of derivatives. A lot of them are very good.

Calabria: The example you cited is a perfect case. A $70,000 issue which had no value and that's what you priced it at.

Shillinglaw: But you don't know right away. They didn't know whether it had any value, so they gave it back. I think there's a problem in doing that. If it had been carried at a value before that and you said, okay for this period, we'll use zero. And when we get more evidence, we will go up to a value again. For the people who buy and sell shares during that interval, that may be a problem.

Spies: We didn't think there was any value to it. So based on the fact that we didn't think there was any value...[we valued it at zero].

Shillinglaw: Fine. Okay. If you make an appraisal and you say as far as we can tell this security now has zero value and it's down at zero. On the basis of whatever the best information you have, you have to do that.

Spies: By zeroing them out, any portfolio manager worth his salt, is going to say, I don't want to get too many of these. And unless the board can formulate policies to have those kinds of messages ready and able to shoot out to these fellows, it's very difficult to keep them on track because they're dealing in an entirely different world when they're trading a portfolio. They're not thinking about what the directors are thinking. A very different perspective.

Shillinglaw: Our procedure is at every board meeting, we get a report on which issues have been fair valued, in your sense of the term, during the previous quarter. What happened to them? When was the position open? When was it closed? What difference did that make to the price per share? And usually, you find that it didn't make much difference at all. Once in a while, there's one in which the formula was wrong. Sometimes it's wrong up. Sometimes it's wrong down. But in general, it's been very good.

Spies: It's not a perfect world. We're back to Dan's observation about the fair value pricing on the Asian

5

FUND DIRECTIONS

May 1998
Directors' Roundtable Supplement

security. The SEC also, in its examination, did find the smaller fund groups didn't have the deliberative process that you're talking about. And apparently, the SEC found that the reason that happened was because the smaller fund groups just don't have the organizational skills or backup to do the expensive review that the larger groups do.

Calabria: Then why are they being paid a management fee?

Spies: I don't know. That's an issue. But clearly in that instance, you had some who were using a market price, however suspect.

Q: *How has the profile prospectus affected the boards' responsibility?*

Shillinglaw: I'm not sure it's my responsibility as a board member to micromanage that process. You've got fund counsel, marketing people, distributors and portfolio managers to do that. I think the board needs to monitor that process and make certain that the simplification is readable but still adequately exposes the risk.

Spies: Yes, we need to make sure that we are protected, and one way we are protected is that we have our own independent counsel. And they lead it from a legal point of view.

Calabria: The board should act as a catalyst. They should oversee the whole process but motivate the management company to move forward on this.

Shillinglaw: Absolutely. Absolutely.

Q: *How can you motivate management to go forward?*

Calabria: Just by raising it at the board meetings and asking for a progress report and not letting it slip off the agenda.

Spies: It's like our Year 2000 issue that we, as trustees, have been working with the adviser [to] tell us what their plan is, and asking for a timetable, schedule and quarterly status reports. It's very important to the board.

Q: *What advice would you give to the smaller funds that don't have independent counsel?*

Shillinglaw: I would say to the small groups, if they don't have the resources, just make sure it's in plain English. They have enough resources to do that.

Q: *What about an issue like Year 2000?*

Calabria: A simplified prospectus is one thing. But if that fund's audit's managers were not prepared for the Year 2000, the first thing I would do is let the adviser know I was seriously considering resigning from that board.

Shillinglaw: Depends on what you get paid for as a director. It's your responsibility to make sure that this thing isn't going to fall apart.

Calabria: But in addition, they have the right to engage outside counsel any time. And if they don't do it, then it's their problem.

12b-1 fees

Shillinglaw: I think the directors have to evaluate that or someone has got to determine the process and determine if it's cost effective and if it's in the shareholders' best interest to permit this to happen.

> "We have no 12b-1 plans, and we will not have 12b-1 plans—not while I'm on the board."
>
> —*Gordon Shillinglaw, independent trustee, **AARP Funds**.*

Calabria: I think the concept is sound, and I was always a big supporter of the 12b-1s. But as it evolved, I think it might be wise for the industry to look back and recognize—I'm coming out from way in left field on this—if 12b-1 fees are paid, then from my perspective as a director and a shareholder, it should be for net sales. However, this should come from the SEC revisiting the concept of 12b-1 compensation and the reality as it exists today.

I'd like to take that one step further. I haven't seen any evidence that says once a fund gets above a certain threshold site, and I don't know what that threshold is, that there really are any economies of scale that would justify using shareholder money to pay for sales or marketing.

Shillinglaw: Good point.

Spies: The big barrier that I see between funds is the big funds with big accounts have lower expense ratios than the funds with small accounts. They do go up with the size of the fund to some extent. But eventually the industry has got to address that issue. We're getting bigger and bigger, and I think our profile is growing. Are we so enthralled with the sales and the assets that we've lost sight of some of the basic responsibilities?

Calabria: It's one of the most difficult things to explain, particularly to an existing shareholder. I think if you can track the source of the 12b-1 shares, and you should be able to, you can evaluate whether the 12b-1 fees are worth it or not. But the tough part is to try to analyze that because this has been a period of recordbreaking sales in an extended bull market.

Shillinglaw: It seems to me the only justification for a 12b-1 plan is that you either get more money in there or you get a larger account size so you can reduce that expense ratio by enough to offset the 12b-1 plan. And I've never seen any evidence that that happens.

Calabria: Well, one of the issues is, and I've experienced this, where a broker actually wakes up on January 1 every year and looks at over $100,000 in income from 12b-1 trailers. There are reps today who have, and others who are in the process of getting their wives and/or children registered so that when they pass on, the 12b-1 fees continue. But what about services or new sales?

Beach: And that actually happens now?

Calabria: Oh, yes. If I were a broker today, I'd do it. It only makes sense for them. However, as independent trustees, it is an issue that needs to be considered.

401(k) issues
Calabria: I think every managing company selling 401(k) plans has the major responsibility—every 401(k) account that opens should carry with it notice that says a couple of things. One, you can lose money. Two, you should not be investing unless it's for a minimum of five years and hopefully 10 years or more. And three, don't be concerned about the market going down because it will. These things need to be said for many 401(k) investors who are relatively unsophisticated, with little understanding of how the securities markets work.

Shillinglaw: I think you're right. The investors need to know that it's long-term money because the tax benefits are lost if they take the money too soon. But you know, I have the sense that the 401(k) investors come a little bit more aware of what's going on in the market than we might guess because...there are all kinds of exchanging going on. They can't take it out of the plan, but they move it in and out of equity funds and into money funds.

Calabria: Is that a sign of knowledge or lack of knowledge?

Shillinglaw: Perhaps lack of knowledge.

Calabria : If people get a quarterly report and see that their fund went down 8% or 9%, they say, "I'm out of here."

Shillinglaw: Oh, I agree.

Calabria: But the truth is very, very few people read a prospectus, including us. That's why it's important to move ahead with simplified prospectus in plain English.

"There is a varying amount of performance information being made available to retirement plan shareholders."

—**Ken Domingues**, *former affiliated director,* **Franklin Resources**.

Spies: We don't have a lot of experience with individuals, but we have substantial 401(k) trust assets in our funds. There are real fiduciary responsibilities for the 401(k) participant. The investor has the right to change the allocation. So in each and every case, we go out to that company and we have training and fully try to explain and make certain that they understand the risks of the markets. I'm comfortable with our process.

Ken Domingues: I was on the accounting/treasurers committee of the **Investment Company Institute**. We informally discussed 401(k) plans, systems and shareholder communication. I believe that the retirement plan investor doesn't really have access to knowing what his plan balance is until quarterly or monthly, in some cases. But that's not true for all of them. Some of the shareholders don't even get prospectuses on how many different funds they're in, in some cases. There's a

FUND DIRECTIONS
May 1998
Directors' Roundtable Supplement

weakness there that I think needs to be addressed. Unequal information makes these people second class investors.

Q: *What type of process have you put in place to review the board's compensation, if any? And how do you go about formulating one?*

Shillinglaw: Well, I can tell you what we did at the AARP funds. We had not changed our basic structure in 14 years. It was time we did. We had inflation. Instead of the six or seven funds that we started with, we now suddenly have 15 funds. We had some trustees who were on all funds. Some who were only on some funds. So there was a great disparity in the amount of compensation per trustee. Now, I was the highest paid, because I was on the greatest number of funds. So we set up a process in which we asked for certain kinds of data from the adviser. Got the data. And our criteria were that we wanted to adjust the 1984 compensation fee rates to adjust for increased responsibility and inflation but to wind up with a fee structure that either maintained or decreased the trustee cost per fund. And we were able to do that because all of sudden we had a lot more funds. In effect, we're saying more responsibility but not proportionately more responsibility. We also have a number of our members who feel that service on the board is partially pro bono, so they would be very reluctant to see anything that even gets close to the median compensation of fund complexes of our size. So our compensation is now about $35,000 for 15 funds.

Calabria: I don't serve on any board where I get to hear that. That is very modest compared to the responsibility involved.

Shillinglaw: I agree. Compensation has something to do with our ability to maintain a strong board. We want to be able to attract people who are highly successful in their own fields. And I think that may be difficult if the compensation level isn't high enough.

Calabria: Our board is pretty much anonymous. The average investor has no idea who we are. But you're right in one sense. The risk that I think you're running is whether or not there's a happy medium out there. I don't know where it is. If the board is overpaid, you can be accused of being too closely allied with the managing company. Boards that receive very modest fees may feel that the management company doesn't place much value on their role, and if a director doesn't like it, he or she can leave.

Beach: We do director compensation review once a year for all the funds. Compared with these reports that concern us, we're a little on the high side. If you don't pay, you're not going to get the people you want.

Shillinglaw: Do you have disparity of fee levels among your various trustees depending on how many funds they're on?

Beach: Sure. Yes. But if you and I are on the same board, we're going to get the same fee.

Shillinglaw: For that board?

Beach: For that board, that's right.

Calabria: Providing you have a per meeting attendance component.

Beach: Yes. But we do not have any per meeting attendance. Which I don't like there. I think you ought to have a per meeting. If you don't show, you don't get paid.

Spies: At **First American**, we have a board development committee. It searches out potential board members and also recommends any changes in compensation to the board. We just went through that process. Our goals remain below our peer group average. But it hadn't been looked at since assets were at $7 million, and now they're approaching $30 billion, from 20 funds to 32 funds and will be 39 funds shortly. They're definitely a more diverse group of funds. What we did was we get some **Lipper Analytical** and ICI data and analyzed it. It was only part of the process, but we came up with a different compensation package than we had. We recognized the more complex funds that we were dealing with. The asset growth side had nothing to do with compensation. There are a lot of different responsibilities and a lot of different things the board does with the funds. We went to our investment managers and our administrators and we said, "Tell us how effective you think this board is?" And they came back and they said we're consistently prepared at the meetings, knowledgeable, and are good at communication. They're thorough. The questions they ask are good. They felt that they had a board that was very well prepared.

Calabria: And the fact that you approved the contract every year. (Laughter).

Chapter 7 -
The Future of Mutual Funds

Everyone understands that friends are those on whom we can rely; whose judgment we trust and who are interested in our welfare. And then there are other "friends" who – well you know.

The mutual fund industry may be the largest repository of investor savings and hope for the future. The number of people employed in the fund industry, directly, and indirectly, is enormous. The fact is that mutual funds have an impact on our economy that goes beyond anyone simply investing a few thousand to a few million dollars in a fund. Perhaps that's why the fund industry is unique in that it operates under a federal law, the Investment Act of 1940 ("'40 Act"). However, it seems that some feel that the '40 Act is "outdated" and has outlived its usefulness, which is more than strange. The fact is that over the last decade or two mutual funds have achieved a level of growth that is nothing less than remarkable despite the fact that some influential players think that the current system is "outdated." This has caused many industry observers to ask, "If it ain't broke, why fix it?"

A few years ago, on the heels of the market timing and late trading scandals, the SEC proposed that the chairman of a mutual fund board be an independent director. Until then most fund board chairmen were executives of the investment advisor. Let's agree that there's nothing inherently wrong with an executive employed by the fund's advisor serving as the chairman of a fund board. However, it's possible that this was an attempt to send a message to the industry that this symbolic role can be important if only for the perception it conveys to the investing public, some of whom were more than a little uncomfortable with what had occurred. Let's also agree that this symbolic change was nothing but cosmetic in nature since a chairman does not control or dictate policy to the board regardless of whether the chair is an independent director or an advisory company executive. In fact, any suggestion, proposal or resolution from the chair requires the majority approval of board members. That said it's more than a little surprising that some people reacted as if the proverbial barbarians were at the gate.

One group in particular, the US Chamber of Commerce ("CC"), rose in high dudgeon, took the SEC to court and succeeded in overturning the SEC's requirement for independent board chairs. Despite that court decision today the great majority of fund board chairs are independent directors. I guess this proves that the CC was right, provided you have a warped view of reality. Let's look at how the CC describes itself on its website, including its mission statement.

US Chamber of Commerce

"Whether you own a business, represent one, lead a corporate office, or manage an association, the Chamber of Commerce of the United States of America® provides you with a voice of experience and influence in Washington, D.C., and around the globe. Our core mission is to fight for business and free enterprise before Congress, the White House, regulatory agencies, the courts, the court of public opinion, and governments around the world."

Mission Statement

"To advance human progress through an economic, political and social system based on individual freedom, incentive, initiative, opportunity, and responsibility."

Programs and Affiliates

"The National Chamber Litigation Center - our law firm that defends business interests and sues government agencies."

This is interesting simply because almost all publicly offered mutual funds are corporations, which begs the question: How many of the +8,000 mutual funds, with a total of 94 million shareholders, are members of the CC? Are any of these *incorporated* mutual funds dues paying members of the CC? You have to wonder if the CC would have filed their lawsuit if they had 8,000 mutual funds as members. As a result, the real reason for the CC's lawsuit remains a mystery.

It's also interesting to note that the website identifies "The National Chamber Litigation Center" as one of its affiliates. Research indicates that this "Litigation Center" is autonomous since in response to an inquiry it was learned that the voting members of the CC were never asked, and therefore did not approve the lawsuit against the SEC. This raises the question if any member of the CC had any knowledge of this lawsuit before they read about it in the press. It also raises a question about whether this is an appropriate use of member dues paid by countless small business members, many of which might be mutual fund investors. The answers to those questions could be illuminating, to say the least.

American Enterprise Institute

Then there's another influential organization, the American Enterprise Institute ("AEI"), which has undertaken a campaign to completely change the structure, operation and regulation of mutual funds. The AEI website describes its organization and purposes in part as follows:

AEI's Organization and Purposes

"Competition of ideas is fundamental to a free society.

The American Enterprise Institute for Public Policy Research is a private, nonpartisan, not-for-profit institution dedicated to research and education on issues of government, politics, economics, and social welfare. Founded in 1943, AEI is home to some of America's most accomplished public policy experts--from economics, law, political science, defense and foreign policy studies, ethics, theology, medicine, and other fields. The Institute sponsors research and conferences and publishes books, monographs, and periodicals. Its website, www.aei.org, posts its publications, videos and transcripts of its conferences, biographies of its scholars and fellows, and schedules of upcoming events.

AEI's purposes are to defend the principles and improve the institutions of American freedom and democratic capitalism--limited government, private enterprise, individual liberty and responsibility, vigilant and effective defense and foreign policies, political accountability, and open debate. Its work is addressed to government officials and legislators, teachers and students, business executives, professionals, journalists, and all citizens interested in a serious understanding of government policy, the economy, and important social and political developments."

Those purposes are commendable and interesting in light of what appears to be a full court press to supersede the requirements of the '40 Act. AEI has held meetings, issued press releases and distributes a book, "Competitive Equity," which makes the case for what they believe is a much preferred restructuring of the SEC's role, as well as challenging the continued need for the '40 Act. However, other than proclaiming that European mutual funds operate under a better system, they have yet to convince anyone that their research supports their theory. In fact their assertions have been repeatedly challenged, but the campaign continues. In searching their website, www.aei.org, just insert the words "mutual funds" in their search box and you'll find a long list of topics related to mutual funds which are interesting, but often misguided. Has it occurred to AEI that with more than 8,000 mutual funds available to the public, that fact embodies their stated purpose, *"Competition of ideas is fundamental to a free society?"* Despite that fact, AEI issued a press release on April 5, 2007 one part of which deserves comment.

<u>"Helping Mutual Fund Investors Get Lower Fees Through Price Competition"</u>

"By pointing to the rate-setting process as the cause of the huge expense ratio disparity among mutual funds, the authors challenge the long-standing policy of the Securities and Exchange Commission, which believes that the problem with mutual fund pricing stems from a "conflict of interest" between the advisor and the fund's shareholders, and as a result has sought to increase the proportion of independent directors on fund boards and encouraging these boards to press advisers for reduced fees and expenses. Wallison and Litan contend that this effort has been misdirected for forty years, and that it has only made the problem worse. The authors remind us that in every industry in which rate deregulation has occurred and companies have been allowed to set their rates competitively – including airlines, telecommunications, trucking, and securities brokerage – competition has increased and consumer prices have declined. There is ample reason, they argue, to believe the same would happen in the mutual fund industry once advisers are free to compete on the basis of fees."

After reading this excerpt the reaction is – Wow! I think it's important to understand the facts. There most assuredly is a form of "conflict of interest" in the relationship between the investment advisor and the fund's shareholders. It's the same "conflict of interest" that exists between vendor/service providers and their customers. The vendor/service provider seeks the highest possible price for its services and the customer seeks the lowest price for it dollars. It's customarily known as a free market economy. To the best of my knowledge, this was not the basis for the SEC's position for increasing independent members on fund boards. Is it conceivable that the authors of this piece are not aware of the market timing and late trading scandals of just a few years ago?

It never ceases to amaze me when critics focus attention on what they perceive to be wrong with the industry while completely ignoring the fact that the objects of their criticism are quite likely to be the cause of the phenomenal success of the fund industry. In referring to "… the rate setting process as the cause of the huge expense disparity among mutual funds…" it's impossible to understand what they mean. What "rate setting process?" There is no rate setting process. Investment advisors determine the advisory fee they will charge when they register a fund with the SEC and that rate is approved by an appointed board of directors, which board is then subject to shareholder approval. The fact of the matter is that any fund investment advisor can set its advisory fee as low as it wishes, including charging no fees whatsoever. There is nothing to prevent an advisor from permanently or temporarily lowering its advisory fees. Yes, they are also free to waive any or all advisory fees at any time. And they don't need the approval of the board to do so. If some industry critics are sincerely interested in lowering fund expenses why not focus their attention on 12b-1 fees which are significant when compared to advisory fees. For example, a fund with a 1.50% advisory fee plus the standard 12b-1 fee of one quarter of one percent has effectively increased fees to shareholders by sixteen percent (16%). A fund with an advisory fee of 1% with the standard 12b-1 fee has effectively increased fees by twenty-five percent (25%)! But somehow the AEI press release completely (conveniently) ignores the huge comparative costs of 12b-1 fees, the "benefits" of which to shareholders are highly suspect, to say the least.

Perhaps both the CC and the AEI would enjoy significantly greater credibility if they revealed the basis on which both of them have embarked on a crusade to change the legal and regulatory system that has worked fairly well for more than 60 years. Maybe they've been overwhelmed with requests from their membership and mutual fund shareholders to take the actions in which they're engaged – but for what purpose? And while at it, why not disclose and share with the public the identity of their members who "requested" that they get involved with mutual fund governance? After all, isn't the principle of full disclosure one that every organization should follow?

While the AEI may have supporters for their campaign let's hope that they are more familiar with the subject than as reported in the April 2008 edition of *Fund Directions.* That edition included an article on the "2008 Mutual Funds and Investment Management Conference," hosted by the ICI and the Federal Bar Association in Scottsdale, Arizona. A discussion on fund board structure that referenced the AEI book included several comments from Paul Roye, senior vice president of Capital Research and Management (The American Group of Funds).

Prior to joining Cap Research, Paul was arguably one of the best informed and knowledgeable Directors of the SEC's Division on Investment Management, where he was known for his informed judgment, candor and knowledge of the industry *and* the '40 Act. Prior to joining the SEC Paul was with a major '40 Act law firm in Washington DC, where I met him when he was outside counsel to the Templeton Funds. No one questions Paul Roye's qualifications or credentials.

Paul has never hidden his opinion that Rule 12b-1 should be revised for a host of reasons, not the least of which is to remove it from the oversight/approval requirements on fund directors. He has voiced his support of the current fund director system, but suggests that while the role of the director should remain an oversight function, he also feels certain changes are necessary to dramatically improve disclosure requirements, which would include a unified management fee so investors will know and understand what it is they are paying for. Paul Roye's career is an example of how an investment advisor can work with independent directors in resolving any number of issues confronting the industry. The industry needs more people like Paul Roye, as well as informed critics.

Perhaps one of the most interesting questions surrounding the involvement of the CC and the AEI in mutual fund governance issues is where were they when the market timing and late trading scandals occurred a few years ago. Did they file any lawsuits against the SEC or any mutual fund advisors? Did they offer any recommendations for preventing such abuses in the future? In addition, has either organization made any public pronouncements or recommendations relative to the current serious issues involving mortgage backed securities or the Fannie Mae and Freddie Mac debacles? What were their respective positions when the Glass Steagall Act was repealed in 1999? Have they made any effort to connect the dots relative to the effects of that repeal, which removed the wall that separated banking and investment/securities activities? Is it possible that their litigators and authors were too busy occupied with more pressing issues? Perhaps someday we'll learn the answers to those questions.

For the record I believe in and support the Chamber of Commerce and the work of the American Enterprise Institute. But I respectfully disagree with their actions and involvement in an industry that has achieved the remarkable degree of success enjoyed by the mutual fund industry. At best I think their respective actions are woefully misguided. Instead I believe their time and members' dues would be better invested in investigating the mortgage securities meltdown and the Fannie Mae, Freddie Mac disaster, the ripple effects of which will be felt for many years.

Critics, We Have Critics

In 2008 the book, "The Investor's Dilemma," written by Louis Lowenstein, was published. It included a laundry list of criticisms and misinformation about the mutual fund industry. To address each of the issues raised would require a separate book. In fairness, however, there are several valid criticisms that do have merit and they speak for themselves. But let's focus on one example of unfounded criticism.

It's a well established fact that investment advisory organizations are legal entities that exist to make a profit. In addition, there is no legal limit to the profits an investment advisor is permitted to earn. The same of course is true of any legal for-profit business – including law firms. However, the book takes to task one investment advisor, the T. Rowe Price organization, and singles it out for quite severe criticism. Why? Because they operate a profitable business - nothing illegal or immoral, just that they are a very profitable business. This caught my attention because I happen to own some T. Rowe Price funds. For the record, I have no relationship with any individual in the T. Rowe Price organization and have never had any personal business relationship with them. I own some of their funds because, in my opinion, they are a reputable, professional investment management organization, which is why I was surprised at the criticism aimed at them.

In the chapter titled "Greed is Good," the author comes down hard on T. Rowe because it happens to be a successful and very profitable investment advisor. My first reaction was - since when is that illegal or immoral? I'm still baffled at the reason for this severe criticism. In fairness, the book was written well before T. Rowe sent out the Spring 2008 Edition of their "T. Rowe Price Report" to shareholders, which included a reference to the subprime mortgage crisis that has had a significant "ripple effect" on securities markets.

Permission was granted by T. Rowe Price to reproduce the text of their commentary relative to the subprime mortgage crisis, which follows.

Subprime Mortgage Sleuth Sees Problems Continuing

Susan Troll earned her nickname the "Duchess of Doom," by being ahead of the pack. Her story illustrates the importance of T. Rowe Price's reliance on its own credit analysts when assessing fixed-income securities.

Ms. Troll, a credit analyst for the firm for 10 years, began issuing warnings about potential trouble in the subprime mortgage markets early 2006. So the firm virtually eliminated its exposure to such securities by early 2007 – months before that market blew up.

She says there were many warning signs in the subprime market – particularly the rapid growth in demand for collateralized debt obligations (CDOs), an investment-grade security backed by a pool of bonds, loans, and other assets.

"Many managers really didn't understand the risks of the underlying securities they were buying to put into their CDOs," she recalls.

"The tremendous amount of demand for these structured products drove originators of subprime home loans to loosen their underwriting standards to levels that were just ridiculous.

"We saw a large growth in affordability products – loans designed to help borrowers purchase more home than they could actually afford. We also saw a lot of speculation. The most concerning thing was an increase in the layered risks in loans.

"The most toxic formula was little or no income documentation from the borrower plus a second 'piggyback' loan to cover the down payment. Finally, there were increased amounts of fraud: The no-doc and low-doc loans became known as 'liar loans.'"

In keeping with her nickname, Ms. Troll predicts further fallout from the subprime meltdown, "There's not really a near-term solution. Home prices are still declining, and we probably haven't seen the bottom yet.

"As a result, rating agencies are going to continue downgrading these mortgage bonds, which will lead to further downgrades in the CDOs that own them and ultimately to further write-downs for the banks or whoever holds those CDO positions.

> "This will plague the market for the rest of this year and probably into the next."
>
> As for the Federal Reserve's recent bail-out plan to lend $220 billion in exchange for troubled mortgage-backed securities, Ms. Troll says it likely will "restore some degree of liquidity to the markets, but it won't get to the root of the problem: the need to stop home prices from falling further."

No doubt others in the industry have voiced similar opinions, but it's important to note that in this particular case, it's quite possible that T. Rowe Price fund shareholders did avoid these securities and the losses attributable to them. So the question then becomes whether T. Rowe Price is entitled to be as profitable as they are. I doubt that many fund investors are complaining. While it's too early to know how many fund managers, including T. Rowe Price, will escape the fallout from the Freddie Mac/Fannie Mae meltdown, critics should be more careful of broadside criticisms which are based on personal opinion as opposed to actual facts. Unfortunately, there's altogether more than enough criticism of the fund industry from sources whose motive is not readily discernible. Investors would be wise to try to determine if claims made by some critics square with the facts, including critics who initiate lawsuits.

An Informed "Critic"

Interestingly there is a "critic" of mutual fund governance who seems to have done his homework. Alan Palmiter, Professor of Law at Wake Forest University, makes a good case that most of the failings or weaknesses in the fund business can be attributable to less than attentive fund directors. Professor Palmiter wrote his paper, *"The Mutual Fund Board: A Failed Experiment in Regulatory Outsourcing,"* in 2006. (This paper appears in its entirety in Appendix A.) In 2007, he sent copies of the paper to about 50 mutual fund chairmen asking for comments. He is reported to have received a total of two (2) responses, the nature of which is not known. Several months ago, *Fund Directions,* the fund industry newsletter, carried an article about the paper which seemed to indicate that Professor Palmiter's work was received with something less than enthusiasm by the fund director community. Unlike the work product of other critics it's clear that Palmiter's paper raised a number of valid issues and concerns deserving of consideration by fund directors.

In his paper Professor Palmiter argues that fund boards have not lived up to the expectations of the '40 Act. The following describes some of the issues raised relative to the failures of boards in fulfilling their mandate as "watchdogs."

- Ineffective negotiation by fund boards in availing benefits for shareholders based on improved technologies and substantive benefits from economies of scale.

- "Poor performance" in negotiating lower management fees.

- Inadequate supervision of investment advisers and their affiliates.

- "There are no qualification standards for fund directors."

- "Ultimately, the fund board *insulates* the management firm from direct regulatory oversight." (Emphasis added)

- "… the board is at most a bureaucratic compliance office."

- While assets have grown expense ratios have often risen.

- "Even worse than their performance on negotiating management fees, boards have achieved nothing for their investors by approving loads – especially 12b-1 fees."

- "… there is no impetus for fundamental reform."

Clearly Professor Palmiter presents some justifiable criticisms. Rather than be ignored they should be explored and discussed by industry leaders, fund directors and the SEC. Unfortunately, some in the industry seem to have adopted a "shoot the messenger" approach to fund governance, which is a mistake.

It would be wrong to simply dismiss the paper in its entirety since it does offer several alternatives to the current regime worthy of further study, including:

- Creation of a new Self Regulatory Organization that would act in a supporting role to an overworked SEC.

- Creation of an industry oversight board to establish uniform, minimum fund governance standards.

- Focus on new "expert" directors not unlike a certified financial analyst to provide independent guidance to the board relative to any number of issues related to portfolio holdings.

- Promote some form of motivation for the courts to give serious consideration to deficiencies in governance practices that arise periodically.

- A dramatic overhaul of shareholder/investor disclosure documents that would best serve investors in arriving at an informed investment decision.

There's much to be gained from Professor Palmiter's analysis. However, not everything in the paper is on target. For example, while the idea of adopting the European system of fund regulation and governance may have some appeal, a closer look reveals any number of flaws that would not pass muster in the US. It's hard to believe that many of us would take any comfort from having the banking industry acting as a form of "middle man" in serving shareholder needs, much less governance requirements. The first question that arises is: Who is overseeing the banks? On what basis should shareholders look to them for good governance practices? It also raises the issue of looking to a socialist form of government that depends on much greater government control and regulation. Since when was that a solution to any of our problems?

The fact is that this paper could provide the impetus for a long overdue review and analysis of our current approach to fund governance. In his conclusion, Professor Palmiter drives home the point –

"A lackadaisical watchdog may be worse than no watchdog at all."

What's Next?

The issues facing mutual fund governance are too important to our economy, fund investors and the securities industry to ignore. Throwing out the proverbial "baby" with the bath water is not the answer. Rather, the time has come for the industry to step up with all the players contributing to making a great investment concept even better by improving on a system that may need more than just tweaking. The SEC can't do it alone. And we should try to avoid politicians meddling in an area with which they have demonstrated little expertise. No amount of lobbying by the ICI and others will result in the needed reforms. What then?

I believe that the Mutual Fund Directors Forum with its membership limited to independent directors is uniquely positioned to undertake this task. The Forum is not controlled by the advisor community and enjoys an excellent relationship with the SEC.

Provided that they are not subjected to undercutting by certain industry factions, or subject to a lawsuit by a Chamber of Commerce affiliate, it has an excellent chance to make a real contribution in arriving at the kinds of answers that cry out for consideration and implementation.

Let's bring together the Forum, the SEC, industry experts (not lobbyists), the Chamber of Commerce (not its litigation arm) and the American Enterprise Institute so that fund shareholders might look forward to a long overdue resolution of a number of "sticky" problems.

New Voices

The Coalition of Mutual Fund Investors

In addition, fund shareholders can also participate by exercising their considerable muscle and urging their directors to begin to live up to their mandate and more effectively represent their interests. I know of only one fledgling organization that can play a part on behalf of fund shareholders to make improved governance a reality, the Coalition of Mutual Fund Investors ("CMFI").

Interestingly CMFI was formed after the market timing and late trading abuses were uncovered in the fund industry some years ago. Subsequently it was learned that the companies involved in these abuses appeared to have violated prospectus disclosures made in filings with the U.S. Securities and Exchange Commission.

As a result of regulatory actions, more than twenty-five (25) enforcement proceedings that included $3.3 billion in fines and penalties have been collected from the defendants in these cases. The SEC is still in the process of returning this money back to the investors who were harmed by these abuses.

As a result of the mutual fund scandals, the SEC has proposed and implemented more than fifteen new regulations in an attempt to improve the financial services industry and to protect the interests of individual investors.

The Formation of CMFI

The Coalition of Mutual Fund Investors was founded by Niels Holch, a lawyer/lobbyist and amateur investor, and functions as an Internet-based fund, shareholder advocacy organization located in Washington DC. Holch has been interested in mutual funds for more than twenty years and his experience and insight enables the Coalition to act as a credible advocate for mutual fund shareholders. As a hobby he developed a unique framework for investing in funds that evaluates the performance and skill of the individual managers of a fund, rather than relying on the institutional performance of each fund.

The Coalition's mission statement includes four goals:

(1) To advocate full disclosure of all mutual fund activities to investors;

(2) To improve regulatory protections and industry "best practices" for the benefit of long-term mutual fund investors;

(3) To facilitate education opportunities for mutual fund investors, and

(4) To communicate public policy issues to mutual fund investors.

CMFI has been an active participant in the regulatory changes that have been implemented since the scandals occurred. The Coalition has presented testimony before Congress and has submitted comment letters to the SEC on many of its proposals for regulatory reform. CMFI is an excellent resource for individual investors seeking to learn more about the mutual fund regulatory process. It provides coverage of all mutual fund policy issues in Washington and provides email alerts to investors interested in following these issues. CMFI encourages investors to get involved in the public policy process and provides information on its website (www.investorscoalition.com), to help individual investors contact the SEC or their Congressional representatives about mutual fund issues.

CMFI's Advocacy on Behalf of Individual Investors

While the SEC has improved the mutual fund regulatory rules over the past five years, more work remains to be done. CMFI believes that the SEC and the Congress need to address the following issues which remain after the fund scandals:

More Transparent Disclosure of Fund Expenses.

The "expense ratio" used by mutual funds to help investors evaluate fund costs must be updated. Under the current rules, this ratio does not include the actual brokerage commissions paid by a fund for portfolio transactions. Even though these commissions may be a very significant expense, portfolio transaction costs are only disclosed annually in a document called the Statement of Additional Information (SAI). To help improve comparability across funds, CMFI has recommended that brokerage commissions be converted to a percentage of a fund's assets and either included in a fund's expense ratio or disclosed as a separate transaction cost ratio. Brokerage commissions should not be buried in an SEC disclosure document; instead this information should be fully disclosed to investors in a manner which is uniform across all funds for purposes of comparison.

CMFI also is an advocate for disclosing the dollar amount of a fund's operating expenses that each investor incurs on a yearly basis. Current rules rely on hypothetical expense disclosures which are meaningless to many investors. A better model is to require disclosure of an estimate of an investor's portion of these annual operating expenses. These dollar amounts should be disclosed at least annually on shareholder statements.

More Disclosure of Third Party Payments.

Many investors use third party intermediaries, including brokers, financial advisers and retirement plans to purchase and sell shares.

It's a common practice for mutual fund advisors/distributors to make compensatory payments to these intermediaries for selling fund shares. These payments are generally not disclosed, nor are the activities for which the payments are used disclosed. In addition to providing incentives to distribute or market a fund's shares, these payments are made for record-keeping and other administrative activities. CMFI believes that investors should know about these payments and what they are being used for. The Coalition seeks disclosure of all payments by and to all parties involved in the sale or distribution of mutual fund shares. Only with full disclosure of these third-party payments will investors be in a position to evaluate both the existence and the cost of these arrangements.

More Disclosure of Transactions within Omnibus Accounts.

Many financial intermediaries, including brokers and retirement plans, use omnibus account transactions in mutual fund shares for their customers. Under this practice, the intermediary consolidates all of the orders for its customers into one aggregated order, instead of disclosing the individual transactions occurring at the investor level.

The use of this accounting "system" prevents a mutual fund from knowing about frequent trading activities and other abuses occurring within these omnibus accounts. And the absence of disclosure of this information is an obstacle to a mutual fund's ability to enforce its policies and procedures in a uniform manner across shareholder classes. CMFI has been a strong advocate for full transparency within these accounts, so that market timing and other problems can be uncovered and addressed in a timely manner.

Many of the abuses uncovered by state and federal regulators occurred in omnibus accounts and new SEC rules do not go far enough to fix the problem.

CMFI is an advocate for requiring that each financial intermediary, including brokers and retirement plans, disclose investor identity and transaction information on a daily basis, so that a mutual fund can enforce its policies and procedures in a uniform manner. In this regard, it's not necessary for the intermediary to disclose a client's name, address, etc. Instead it should be mandatory that all transactions disclose the tax identification number (usually the Social Security number) of the shareholder, which is required for securities transactions throughout the securities industry. There is no reason or justification for any intermediary to withhold or conceal this information.

Mutual fund shareholders would be wise to look into the Coalition of Mutual Fund Investors as a means of supporting the kind of advocacy organization that seems rare indeed in the mutual fund industry today.

****

Our Obligation

The mutual fund industry has a real obligation to continue to maintain its position as the best choice for investors. It has a golden opportunity to be the premier choice of investors and avoid what has happened to other financial "franchises" in the past. But it won't happen automatically. It's going to take a concerted effort to ensure that investors can rely on a fair and honest compensation arrangement while avoiding self-dealing by overreaching investment advisor organizations.

That means that economies of scale must be implemented with real savings for shareholders. It means that directors have to accept their role and responsibility as overseers of the shareholders interests. No more lip service or rubber stamping. That doesn't mean adopting an adversarial position, but a good business relationship, the kind that exists in virtually all business relationships.

****

Stay current on important events and changes that affect you as a mutual fund investor. Bookmark www.mutualfundsbureau.com for periodic updates and commentary about mutual funds.

Appendix

A. "The Mutual Fund Board: A Failed Experiment in Regulatory Outsourcing" Alan R. Palmiter, Professor of Law, Wake Forest University.

B. Glossary of Commonly Used Mutual Fund Terms

C. Fund Investor's Information Sources

Appendix A

THE MUTUAL FUND BOARD: A FAILED
EXPERIMENT IN REGULATORY OUTSOURCING

Alan R. Palmiter[*]

There is no there there.[1]

Mutual fund boards are a curious institution. Mandated by the Investment Company Act of 1940, they are tasked as "watchdog" supervisors of the management firms that organize, administer and market mutual funds.[2] The fund board and its "independent" directors approve fund transactions with the management firm and ensure compliance with the 1940 Act and implementing SEC rules. Fund directors thus function as outsourced regulators, with their selection and compensation in the hands of the management firm they supervise.

This essay argues that the outsourcing to mutual fund boards of key regulatory functions—principally the review and approval of management contracts—has not lived up to the hopes of the 1940 Act. Fund boards have been weak and even feckless protectors of fund investors, their deficiencies exacerbated as mutual funds have grown into the leading investment vehicle for private retirement savings in the United States.

Gauged by the important metric of management fees—whose negotiation is delegated to fund boards—the experiment in regulatory outsourcing has failed. As the mutual fund industry has grown in size and scope, the fund board has shown itself to be mostly ineffective in negotiating on behalf of fund investors to realize the value from improved information technologies and growing economies of scale. Study after study finds fund expense ratios *growing* over a period when fund assets have exploded.

Just as significant as their poor performance in negotiating lower management fees, fund boards have also failed in their supervision of fund design and marketing. Fund boards, charged with the approval of fund mergers and dissolutions, have acquiesced in the strategy of many fund groups of creating a stable of "above average" funds by merging losers into winners. Fund groups then heavily market the resulting winners (also an activity subject to board supervision) by appealing to the "past is prologue" mentality of many fund investors. Fund boards have failed to respond to the "cognitive biases" of fund investors, a problem aggravated by the shift of retirement savings from employer-managed defined-benefit plans to employee-managed defined-contribution plans.

* Professor of Law, Wake Forest University. My thanks to Jim Fanto and Ahmed Taha for commenting on an earlier draft, and to Jeff Wolfe and Min He for their research help.

---

1   GERTRUDE STEIN, EVERYBODY'S AUTOBIOGRAPHY 298–300 (1937) (describing how, after returning to California from a lecture tour, Stein sought to visit her childhood home in Oakland, but could not find the house).

2   *See* **Burks v. Lasker, 441 U.S. 471, 484 (1979).**

Why has the fund board failed? The structure of the board has hobbled its ability to function as originally envisioned. "Independent directors" are selected and nominated by the management firm, subject to a perfunctory "rubber stamp" by fund investors. The fund board is composed of parttimers who rely on the fund's management firm for information, direction and compensation. Even if they wanted to, the fund directors cannot realistically threaten to take the fund's business elsewhere. Negotiation on behalf of fund investors is understandably an empty ritual.

More deeply, the fund board operates without meaningful oversight. Each overseer envisioned by the 1940 Act—the SEC, federal courts and state courts—has deferred to fund directors on the hopeful assumption that oversight will come from elsewhere. Despite regular and continuing attempts by the SEC to strengthen board independence, the agency has failed to create true board independence or to give the board clear guidance. Federal courts, though called on to oversee the board's setting of management fees, have refused to become mired in valuing management services. State courts accept the bedrock principles of the business judgment rule, thus presuming that fund directors act on an informed basis with a rational basis, in good faith, and without a conflicting personal interest.

Director professionalism, part of a relatively recent "best practices" movement in the mutual fund industry, offers some promise—but at most can only be aspirational. It does not correct the structural impediments of the fund board or create mechanisms that would oversee fund directors.

Although fund directors have become more aware of their functions and responsibilities, they continue to be diffident, highly-paid actors in the face of a fund management culture that focuses on building market share, asset size, and profits. Against these odds, director professionalism has little chance.

Ultimately, the mutual fund regulatory regime places its faith in the fund investor market—despite the animating premise of the 1940 Act that disclosure-based market protection is inadequate. Recent studies make clear that fund investors continue to be inept consumers, plagued by informational and cognitive biases. Fund investors are largely ignorant of fund expenses, the relationship of expenses to fund performance, and the mixed relevance of past performance to future returns. They respond only weakly to no-load funds and low fees, and even less to changes in fees and fund risk. The dysfunctional investor market is fueled by fund marketing (approved by fund boards) that shapes and reinforces investor biases.

This essay first reviews the creation and development of mutual fund boards, examining their composition and their intended regulatory role. It considers the institutions charged with overseeing fund boards (the SEC and courts) and the deference they have shown to fund boards. The essay then presents empirical data on the performance of fund boards drawn largely from the finance literature, data that uniformly suggest that fund boards have failed to adequately supervise fund management firms. Finally, the essay considers various proposed reforms to mutual fund governance and offers a comparison to foreign mutual funds, whose regulatory systems operate without fund boards. Imagine!

I. MUTUAL FUND BOARDS—OUTSOURCED SUPERVISOR

The board of directors is a defining feature of the corporate structure that was adopted by the U.S. mutual fund industry at its inception. The Investment Company Act of 1940 built on this edifice, giving special gatekeeper functions to the board and its "independent directors." Over time, the SEC has delegated additional responsibilities to the fund board.

Under the resulting board-centric structure, the fund board (in theory) supervises the activities of the mutual fund management firm.[3] The fund board carries out its supervisory functions with minimal oversight.

A. CORPORATE STRUCTURE: FROM THE BEGINNING

Investment companies in the United States are a relatively recent phenomenon. The first was organized as a corporation in 1924. U.S. investors were more comfortable with the corporate form, with its supervisory board of directors, compared to the British model of investment trusts that had developed in the late nineteenth century.[4] The corporation, unlike the trust, offered an internal supervisory mechanism to oversee the discretion of the portfolio manager. In the late 1920s investment companies flourished.

Besides supplying a supervisory board of directors, the corporate form offered other advantages. It permitted the investment company to issue various classes of securities—common and preferred stock, debentures, and mortgage bonds. This facilitated leverage for equity investors, promising them above-market returns in a booming market.[5]

In addition, corporate law (unlike the more rigid law of trusts) permitted a wide range of self-dealing transactions—if approved by the corporation's disinterested board of directors. The sponsor, typically a financial services firm that had brought the investment company into existence, could manage the investment portfolio and receive fees. Sponsoring investment banks could sell securities to their investment companies, often securities the banks themselves brought to market. Sponsoring securities firms could sell brokerage services, while commercial banks could lend money, to their captive investment companies.

---

3   **Wallace Wen Yeu Wang,** *Corporate Versus Contractual Mutual Funds: An Evaluation of Structure and Governance*, **69 WASH. L. REV. 927, 956–58 (1994) (evaluating the comparative merits of the structure and governance of the two dominant forms of mutual funds).**

4   **The trust permitted investors to buy an interest in a portfolio of securities deposited with a trust company. The trust company committed itself to rules regarding the kinds of securities to be purchased, holding periods, and management of the investment portfolio. JOHN KENNETH GALBRAITH, THE GREAT CRASH 1929, at 47–48 (1988).**

5   **The 1940 Act prohibits leverage by open-end mutual funds, both for investors and in the fund's portfolio. *See* 15 U.S.C. § 80a-18(f) (2000) (prohibiting open-end funds from issuing senior (debt) securities to investors); *Id.* § 80a-18(f), (g) (prohibiting open-end funds from borrowing money except temporarily, but not in excess of 5% of the total fund assets, or from a bank unless subject to a 300% asset-coverage condition).**

In 1940 when Congress got around to regulating investment companies, it grafted its regulatory scheme onto the existing corporate structure and placed its faith in the fund board as a substitute for investor self-reliance.[6] Congress noted that disclosure under the Securities Act of 1933 and the Securities Exchange Act of 1934 had not deterred "the continuous abuses in the organization and operation of investment companies."[7] Generally these acts provide only for publicity, but "the record is clear that publicity alone is insufficient to eliminate malpractices in investment companies."[8]

Having found supervision by fund boards inadequate in the 1920s, Congress oddly chose to strengthen the hand of the board. For many abuses identified by Congress—such as preferential trading by insiders, dilutive pricing of portfolio shares, exorbitant selling charges, undisclosed and unapproved changes in investment policies, unauthorized transfers to new management firms, self-dealing sales of worthless securities, borrowings by insiders without repayment, and lack of transparency on fund finances—the solution was greater board supervision.[8]

Although the 1940 Act does not require the corporate form, the regulatory regime effectively assumes that mutual funds will be organized as (or along the lines of) a corporation. There must be a board of directors (or its equivalent) to oversee fund operations and approve contractual arrangements with the fund's service providers.[9] There must be shareholder voting to elect board members and approve fundamental changes.[10] These requirements apply whether the fund is structured as a corporation or another form such as a business trust.

Outsourcing to the fund board of a supervisory/regulatory function was consistent with the general approach of the securities laws. The Securities Act of 1933 delegated supervision of public securities offerings to nongovernmental watchdogs—namely, the directors and officers of the issuer, the underwriter and the financial auditor. The Securities Exchange Act of 1934 delegated supervision of trading in public markets to self-regulated stock exchanges and the National Association of Securities Dealers. In each case, the SEC and the courts retained a significant oversight role.

Oversight of the fund board, however, is lacking in the 1940 Act. There was—and still is—no self-regulatory oversight body. The SEC is not tasked with reviewing the fund board's ongoing approval of the fund's management contracts and marketing arrangements. The courts, though later assigned a role to oversee management fees, have shunned the responsibility. For

---

6   *See generally* **Alfred Jaretzki, Jr.**, *The Investment Company Act of 1940*, **26 WASH. U. L.Q.** 303 (1941); **Walter P. North**, *A Brief History of Federal Investment Company Legislation*, **44 NOTRE DAME L. REV.** 677 (1969); **Comment,** *Investment Company Act of 1940*, **50 YALE L.J.** 440 (1941).

7   **INVESTMENT TRUST STUDY, INVESTMENT COMPANY ACT OF 1940 AND INVESTMENT ADVISERS ACT OF 1940, H.R. REP. NO. 76-2639,** at 10 (3d Sess. 1940).

8   **Paul F. Roye, Div. of Inv. Mgmt., U.S. Sec. & Exch. Comm'n, Remarks Before the Am. Law Inst./Am. Bar Ass'n Inv. Co. Regulation and Compliance Conference, The Exciting World of Inv. Co. Regulation (June 14, 2001),** *reprinted in* **Tamar Frankel & Clifford E. Kirsch, INVESTMENT MANAGEMENT REGULATION,** at 32–33 (3d ed. 2005).

9   *Investment Company Act of 1940, in* **6-83 SECURITIES LAW TECHNIQUES** § 83.01 (Matthew Bender 2006).

10   **Mutual funds must adopt fundamental policies as to key investment activities—capital structure, permissible investments, investment strategies, risk-reward profile of securities issued by the fund—which can then be changed only by shareholder vote.** *See* **15 U.S.C. §§ 80a-8(b), 80a-13(a) (2000).**

both the SEC and the courts, more daunting than the volume of fund transactions has been the problem of valuation of management services. The federal securities regime assiduously avoids delegating questions of value to the SEC or the courts, instead leaving them to markets. In the case of mutual funds, given the doubts about the efficiency of the investor market, the question of value was left to private negotiations between the fund board and the management firm. It was a desperate (and overly hopeful) delegation.

B. FUND BOARDS: COMPOSITION AND SELECTION

The 1940 Act regulates the composition and election of fund directors. A centerpiece of the 1940 Act is the requirement that at least 40 percent of the board be independent of the management firm.[11] Beyond the statutory requirement, current SEC rules condition the use of the more important exemptions on a board composed of a majority of independent directors—creating a de facto regulatory minimum.[12] A proposed rule, still in limbo, would increase the proportion to 75 percent and require an independent board chair.[13]

The 1940 Act dictates that shareholders elect fund directors, but only for the initial board and to fill vacancies if less than a majority of the board is shareholder-elected.[14] Thus, funds operate without annual board elections.[15] Independent directors must be nominated by a majority of independent directors and elected by shareholders, though vacancies can be filled by the board in the case of the death, disqualification, or bona fide resignation of an independent director where there remain sufficient shareholder-elected directors.[16]

These rules have not, however, created an independent institution of fund supervisors. The definition of "interested person" makes it relatively easy to seat outside directors sympathetic

---

11   *Id.* § 80a-10(a) (providing that at least 40% of board of directors of registered investment company must consist of individuals who are not "interested persons").

12   Role of Independent Directors of Investment Companies, Investment Company Act Release No. 24,816, 66 Fed. Reg. 3734 (Jan. 2, 2001).

13   *See* Investment Company Governance, Investment Company Act Release No. 26,520, 69 Fed. Reg. 46,378, 46,381 (July 27, 2004). In June 2005, the D.C. Circuit found that the SEC had acted within its authority in adopting the governance rules, but had violated the Administrative Procedures Act by not adequately considering (1) the costs of complying with the governance rules and (2) disclosure requirements as an alternative. Chamber of Commerce v. SEC, 412 F.3d 133, 136 (D.C. Cir. 2005). After compiling a more developed record of the costs of the new rule, the SEC re-adopted it. *See* Commission Response to Remand by Court of Appeals, Investment Company Act Release No. 26,985, 70 Fed. Reg. 39,390 (June 30, 2005). In April 2006, the D.C. Circuit vacated the rule on the ground that the Commission had not adequately considered its cost, but withheld the issuance of the mandate for ninety days to afford the Commission an opportunity to reopen the record for comment. Chamber of Commerce v. SEC, 443 F.3d 890, 909 (D.C. Cir. 2006).

14   U.S.C. § 80a-16(a) (2000) (permitting board vacancies to be filled by the board so long as at least two-thirds of the board remains shareholder-elected). The SEC has taken the position that, beyond the election of the initial board and the filling of vacancies when required by the statute, the requirement of annual meetings is generally a matter of state law. JOHN NUVEEN & CO. INC., *SEC No-Action Letter* [1986-1987 Transfer Binder] Fed. Sec. L. Rep. (CCH) ¶ 78,383 (Nov. 18, 1986).

15   The fund must be organized in a state that does not require an annual shareholders meeting—a dispensation offered by states looking to attract mutual fund incorporation. DEL. CODE ANN. tit. 12, § 3806 (2006) (generally permitting voting practices that comply with federal rules); MD. CODE ANN., CORPS & ASS'NS § 2-501(b)(1) (2006) (same).

16   15 U.S.C. § 80a-16(b).

to management firm interests. [17]Independent directors are typically securities industry executives and professionals whose firms provide direct or indirect services to mutual funds. There are no qualification standards for fund directors.[18]

Compensation for service on mutual fund boards, particularly for larger mutual fund families, is typically much higher than for service on boards of operating companies.[19] Moreover, the rules on director tenure discourage new blood on the board.[20] Thus, most fund boards are composed of industry-friendly, highly paid, long-serving directors. The lack of independence of mutual fund directors, even those who carry the label "not interested," has long been an open secret.[21]

When the election of directors does occur, the process is "largely ritualistic."[22] The management firm selects the initial board, and new directors (including independent directors) are vetted by the management firm.[23] In the 60 years of mutual fund regulation in the United States, no director nominees have ever been presented to oppose the management slate. Fund shareholders have little choice (if they bother to vote) but to rubber stamp nominees proffered by the management firm.[24] There is no incentive to undertake the expense of a proxy fight. Any fund shareholder dissatisfied with the management firm's directors would have sold long before.

C. FUND BOARD: SUPERVISORY FUNCTIONS

---

17   For example, executives of brokerage firms are considered "not interested," so long as their firm has not executed trades for the mutual fund group in the previous six months. *See* U.S.C.A. § 80a-2(a)(19)(A)(v), (B)(v) (West 2006). The same six-month waiting period applies to executives of banks and other lenders to the mutual fund group. *See id.* § 80a-2(a)(19)(A)(vi), (B)(vi). In addition, former officials or business associates of the management firm are considered independent after a two-year waiting period. *See id.* § 80a-2(a)(19)(A)(vii), (B)(vii) (permitting SEC by order to determine that executives who had a "material business or professional relationship" with the mutual fund group lack independence, but only if the relationship arose in the prior two years). *See generally* **Larry D. Barnett,** *When is a Mutual Fund Director Independent? The Unexplored Role of Professional Relationships under Section 2(a)(19) of the Investment Company Act,* **4 DEPAUL BUS. & COMM. L.J. 155 (2006).**

18   **Chris Tobe,** *Mutual Fund Directors: Governance Changes Proposed for Independent Directors in the U.S.,* **8 CORP. GOVERNANCE 25, 28 (2000) (pointing out that fund experience is not a prerequisite to board service).**

19   **For example, the compensation of the seven independent directors of T. Rowe Price was increased for 2005 from $150,000 per year to $190,000 per year (the independent chair from $215,000 to $290,000).** *See* **T. Rowe Price Family of Funds 17 (Feb. 28, 2006),** *available at* **http://sec.gov/Archives/edgar/data/75170/000087183906000015/finalproxy06.htm.**

20   **Since shareholders must elect new directors only when the number of shareholder-elected directors falls below two-thirds of the board, there is a premium on long-serving incumbents and a penalty against installing new directors.** *See supra* **note 15 and accompanying text.**

21   **Robert H. Mundheim & William J. Nutt,** *The Independent Directors of Mutual Funds,* **WHARTON Q., Spring 1972, at 8, 8.**

22   **Richard M. Phillips,** *Deregulation under the Investment Company Act—A Reevaluation of the Corporate Paraphernalia of Shareholder Voting and Boards of Directors,* **37 BUS. LAW. 903, 908 (1981).**

23   **William J. Nutt,** *A Study of Mutual Fund Independent Directors,* **120 U. PA. L. REV. 179, 215–16 (1971).**

24   **As the SEC has noted, passivity of fund shareholders is the norm. Mutual funds often find it difficult to obtain a quorum for shareholder meeting, and the voting outcome is almost always consistent with the wishes of the management firm. DIV. OF INV. MGMT., SEC, PROTECTING INVESTORS: A HALF CENTURY OF INVESTMENT COMPANY REGULATION 272 n.82 (1992) [hereinafter SEC Staff Report Protecting Investors].**

The fund board has two essential functions: (1) negotiating and approving the contract with the management firm (thus setting the terms and price of the asset management and marketing services provided fund investors) and (2) supervising the compliance of the management firm and other service providers with the legal requirements of the 1940 Act regulatory scheme.[25]

In each area, independent directors have a critical monitoring role. As explained in a recent report by the SEC staff on the virtues of an independent board:

> [R]eliance is placed on the independent directors, rather than the Commission, to oversee any conflicts of interest in the transactions permitted by the rules and to protect the interests of fund investors.[26]

Ultimately, the fund board insulates the management firm from direct regulatory oversight.[27] The fund board relieves the SEC (or another oversight body) from responsibility for supervising the management firm and reviewing its fee arrangements with the fund. The board legitimates the management firm as a profit-seeking business.

1. Contract Negotiation and Approval

The 1940 Act requires that the fund board annually approve the investment advisory and underwriting agreements between the fund and the management firm.[28] This board is responsible for negotiating and setting the advisory fees and responsibilities of the management firm, the arrangements for buying and selling portfolio investments, and the fund's marketing approach.

The regulatory scheme places the fee-setting responsibility on the board—rather than fund investors, the SEC or the courts. Given the "ponderous task" of evaluating fees and other costs,

---

25   **26. James H. Cheek, III,** *Report of the American Bar Association Task Force on Corporate Responsibility*, **59 BUS. LAW. 145, 150–54 (2003)** (identifying board responsibilities with respect to investment advisory arrangements, distributions arrangements, and other statutory and regulatory responsibilities).

26   *See* **U.S. Sec. & Exch. Comm'n,** *Exemptive Rule Amendments of 2004: The Independent Chair Condition, A Report in Accordance with the consolidated Appropriations Act* **16 (Unpublished Working Paper, April 2005),** *available at* **http://sec.gov/news/studies/indchair.pdf [hereinafter SEC Staff Report on Independent Chair]. This reliance on independent directors reflects the policy decision in the 1940 Act to subject conflicts transactions in the mutual fund not to "fairness" review by an external decision-maker, such as the SEC or the courts, but rather to oversight by the relatively untested institution of outside directors.** *Id.* **at 9–11.**

27   **The fund board also insulates the management firm from investor litigation. Under state corporate law, shareholder derivative suits can be commenced only after the shareholder makes a demand for board action or pleads the futility of demand. Thus, the board serves as a gatekeeper for investor litigation. If an investor challenges illegal conduct by the management firm, the board (or a committee of independent directors) can conduct an investigation and make a business judgment as to the merits of the claim.** *See* **Donald C. Langevoort,** *Private Litigation to Enforce Fiduciary Duties in Mutual Funds: Derivative Suits, Disinterested Directors and the Ideology of Investor Sovereignty*, **83 WASH. U. L.Q. 1017, 1026–28 (2005).**

28   *See* **15 U.S.C. § 80a-15(a)(2), (b)(1) (2000) (requiring annual approval of multi-year agreements by either the board of directors or majority vote of the shareholders). The investment advisory agreement must also be approved initially by a majority of voting shares.** *See id.* **§ 80a-15(a).**

the regulatory scheme assumes that fund investors are incapable of valuing fund management services and the task would overwhelm the SEC.[29] Over time, fund fees have become increasingly complex, with different kinds of sales charges (front-end, contingent deferred, and 12b-1 fees) and expense ratios.[30]

Fee setting by the fund board involves a negotiation ritual that begins with the management firm proposing fees that the board (sometimes) suggests be lowered. The management firm then accepts whatever marginally lower fees it concludes the market can bear. Take the recent fee negotiation at AIM, a large mutual fund group targeted in the market trading scandals that came to light in 2003. To resolve charges that the fund group had allowed favored clients to skim profits from long-term investors through rapid trading in and out of funds, AIM (and its affiliated Invesco group) agreed to reduce fees charged to investors by $75 million over 5 years.[31] In 2005, management proposed a fee reduction of $17 million. When independent directors demanded further cuts of $3 million, management "winced" and agreed.[32] These amounts, however, pale in comparison to the $742 million in annual revenues for the fund group on $64 billion in assets under management.[33]

The fund board's cabined role is not for lack of formal authority. Delegation to the management firm does not strip the board of its authority under state law to "manage and direct" the business and affairs of the fund.[34] Nonetheless, the board is ill equipped and ill situated to do more. It has no independent staff to advise it on matters of investment policy, fund operations, or fund design. It has no realistic option (or threat) to hire a new investment adviser or management firm. And the regulatory structure of the 1940 Act prevents the board from undertaking radical reforms like changing the fee structure from asset-based fees to performance-based fees.[35]

---

29   *See* **Wang,** *supra* **note 3, at 988.**

30   **There are two primary visible fees: sales charges and expense ratios. Sales charges are paid by the investor when shares are purchased (front-end load) or when shares are redeemed (contingent deferred sales load). Beyond the load, funds can charge for marketing and advertising expenses through "12b-1" distribution fees.** *See* **Payment of Asset-Based Sales Loads by Registered Open-End Management Investment Companies, Investment Company Act Release No. 16,431, 41 SEC Docket 207 (June 13, 1988) (describing legislative and administrative history leading to adoption of Rule 12b-1). The expense ratio covers the operational services provided by the management firm— namely, investment management, administration (record-keeping and transaction services to fund investors), and operating expenses (custodial fees, taxes, legal and auditing expenses, and directors' fees).** *See* **JOHN C. BOGLE, BOGLE ON MUTUAL FUNDS 197–201 (1994). In addition, funds pay for trading costs (brokerage fees) that are charged against fund assets.** *See* **U.S. GEN. ACCOUNTING OFFICE, GAO-03-551T, MUTUAL FUNDS: INFORMATION ON TRENDS IN FEES AND THEIR RELATED DISCLOSURE 1 (2003) [hereinafter GAO Mutual Fund Fee Report].**

31   **Tom Lauricella,** *Independent Directors Strike Back,* **WALL ST. J., July 5, 2006, at R4.**

32   *Id.*

33   *Id.*

34   *See* **DEL. CODE ANN. tit. 8, § 141(a) (2006).**

35   *See generally* **John C. Bogle, Founder and Former Chairman of the Vanguard Group, Remarks to the Boston College Law School, Re-Mutualizing the Mutual Fund Industry—The Alpha & The Omega (Jan. 21, 2004),** *available at* **http://www.vanguard.com/ bogle_site/sp20040121.html (discussing fund directors' refusal to change the fee structure).**

2. Compliance Office

The fund board also functions as a compliance office, a role outlined in the 1940 Act and enlarged significantly by SEC rules.[36] The board is tasked with reviewing and approving specified fund practices to regulate conflicts between the fund and the management firm, and to ensure the management firm is in regulatory compliance.[37] By the SEC's count, the fund board is called on under the 1940 Act and its rules to review and approve fund transactions in 27 different situations, some of which are delegated to the full board, while others are delegated only to independent directors.

Some compliance functions delegated to the full board include:[38]

- valuation of portfolio securities that do not have a readily-ascertainable market price

- setting the time of day when net asset value is determined

- approval of custody contracts (annually) with members of national securities exchanges, clearing agencies, book-entry systems, and foreign custodians

- approval of the fund's code of ethics, which must be designed to prevent fraudulent, deceptive, or manipulative practices by management firm insiders in connection with personal securities transactions.

Other compliance functions are delegated only to independent directors, on whom the SEC has "relied extensively" to exempt funds from prohibitions under the 1940 Act:[39]

- approval of 12b-1 fees (marketing fees paid from fund assets, as opposed to loads paid by fund investors when buying and selling shares)[40]

---

36   *See* **Wang**, *supra* **note 3, at 996–1001. Interestingly, the shift of regulatory oversight from the SEC to fund boards arose mostly from 1975–2000, a period characterized by SEC rule-making that exempted management firms from conflict-of-interest prohibitions of the 1940 Act on the condition of approval by independent directors.** *See* **Tamar Frankel**, *The Scope and Jurisprudence of the Investment Management Regulation*, **83 WASH. U. L.Q. 939, 946 (2005) [hereinafter Frankel,** *Jurisprudence of Regulation*] **(providing detailed list).**

37   *See* **Paul G. Mahoney**, *Manager-Investor Conflicts in Mutual Funds*, **18 J. OF ECON. PERSP. 161, 162 (2004) (describing cash flow in mutual funds and the resulting incentives facing fund managers, brokers, and other third parties and the associated conflicts of interest).**

38   **Wang**, *supra* **note 3, at 994.**

39   **SEC Staff Report on Independent Chair,** *supra* **note 27, at 16.**

40   **In adopting Rule 12b-1 (which permits use of fund assets to defray marketing expenses), the SEC commented that "the more capable the disinterested directors are of overseeing the kinds of activities of investment companies which are of regulatory significance, the more the Commission will be willing to reduce the regulatory restrictions." Bearing of Distribution Expenses by Mutual Funds, Securities Act Release No. 6254, Investment Company Act Release No. 11,414, 21 SEC Docket 324 (Oct. 28, 1980).**

- approval of the fund's auditor (which must be an independent public accountant)

- approval of securities transactions with the management firm (or its affiliates) as permitted by various SEC rules

- determination (annually) whether participation in joint liability insurance policies is in the best interests of the fund

- review and approval of fidelity bonds.

The compliance function is largely ministerial, with the board checking off items on the SEC-provided checklist. Recognizing the emptiness of the compliance function, the SEC has tried to relieve boards of some of the tedium, replacing annual review in a number of areas with board action "only when necessary."[41]

Compliance outsourcing to the board and independent directors, however, is not all encompassing. Certain conflict transactions cannot be approved by the board or its independent directors, but instead require SEC approval. For example, transactions with the management firm beyond those specified in the advisory agreement are prohibited unless they receive prior approval from the SEC.[42] Authorization by the board is not enough.

In performing its compliance function, the board is under no obligation to set up internal controls and rarely acts as an investigator of management firm compliance.[43] Not surprisingly, fund directors rarely discover compliance lapses.[44] Instead, illegality is typically uncovered by the auditor or government regulator with the help of a whistle-blower in the management firm.[45] For example, fund boards were largely absent in identifying or moving to correct the late-trading and market-timing scandals that shook the mutual fund industry in 2003.[46] It was the New York

---

[1]   *See* **Frankel**, *Jurisprudence of Regulation, supra* **note 37, at 986 (summarizing the 1993 change, which was "intended to enhance the effectiveness of investment company boards by substituting more meaningful requirements for an annual review requirement" such as requiring "that directors make and approve changes only when necessary").**

[2]   *See* **15 U.S.C. § 80a-17(a), (b) (2000). Under § 17(a), the management firm cannot "knowingly" sell or purchase securities to or from the mutual fund, except when the fund is redeeming its own shares or selling them to its investors. Similar restrictions apply to borrowing from and lending to the mutual fund.** *Id.* **Under § 17(b), however, the management firm can apply to the SEC for an order exempting a proposed transaction. By statute, the SEC is to consider whether the proposed terms are reasonable and fair and do not involve overreaching, and whether the proposed transaction is consistent with the mutual fund's investment policies.** *Id.*

[3]   **Some have speculated that board passivity is a product of the mind-numbing compliance functions entrusted to it.** *See,* **e.g., Tamar Frankel**, *Money Market Funds,* **14 REV. SEC. REG. 913, 915 n.18 (1981) (suggesting that increased compliance tasks and fees paid by fund advisors causes directors to become more susceptible to control by the management firm).**

[4]   *See* **Victor Brudney**, *The Independent Director—Heavenly City or Potemkin Village?,* **95 HARV. L. REV. 597, 617–19 (1982) (discussing court cases where independent directors failed to challenge management self-dealing).**

[5]   *See* **Paul E. Kanjorski, Congressman, Remarks during House Hearing, Mutual Funds: Who's Looking Out for Investors? 109, 127 (Nov. 6, 2003),** *available at* **http://commdocs.house. gov/committees/bank/hba92982.000/hba92982_1.htm ("[W]e really do not have inside capacity to understand what these organizations are doing until a whistleblower comes forward or until an extreme situation occurs where we focus a great deal of light on the subject.").**

[6]   **Mercer E. Bullard**, *Comments on Martin Lybecker's Enhanced Corporate Governance,* **83 WASH. U. L.Q. 1095, 1098–1101 (2005) [hereinafter Bullard,** *Comments on Corporate Governance*]. **"[M]utual fund scandal was the best evidence that in practice [independent directors] are not effective watchdogs."** *Id.* **at 1102–03.**

Attorney General, followed by the SEC, who investigated and exposed most of the illegal and fraudulent practices.[47]

The attitude of management firms toward the compliance function is captured by a vignette told by Professor Tamar Frankel:

> It was rumored that Securities and Exchange Commission's examiners would form monitoring groups. These groups would sit at the offices of large mutual fund Managers, and supervise their operations, the way FDIC agents sit at large bank offices. Asked for a reaction to this action, I was told in confidence how a senior Manager in one large fund complex reacted. He said something like: "That is sheer waste of money. No one would speak to these monitors and they will be put in a box and forgotten." I was astounded. Here was a golden opportunity to gain the best guarantee of honesty at no cost. It was an opportunity to show the world and the regulators that this fund complex had nothing to hide. I expected the Managers to receive the government monitors with open arms, show them around, and offer them a comfortable office from which to supervise and hopefully report and advertise the fund complex's compliance with the law. This Manager did not expect the investors to value trust.[48]

The SEC has implicitly acknowledged the inadequacies of the fund board in its compliance function. In the rules responding to the late-trading and market-timing scandals of 2003, the SEC required management firms to appoint a compliance officer with significant authority and direct access to the fund board.[49] The SEC stated the hope that these internal compliance officers would serve as whistle-blowers and alert the SEC to noncompliance by recalcitrant management firms. The implicit doubts about the fund board could not have been more obvious.

D. DIRECTORS' DUTIES: EXTERNAL OVERSIGHT

The fund board performs its supervisory and compliance functions with only minimal external oversight. The 1940 Act gives the SEC only limited authority, and fund investors even less, to challenge fund directors in federal court. Federal courts, consistent with the apparent intent of the legislation, have shunned meaningful review of board activities, particularly with respect to the setting of management fees. Instead, the 1940 Act assumes that directors will be accountable as a matter of state fiduciary law and directorial professionalism. State courts have deferred to fund boards under the business judgment rule and state procedural rules on pre-suit demand. A fledgling movement for more professionalism on fund boards offers some hope, but is constrained by the structural weaknesses of the fund board—and ultimately carries no legal weight.

---

47   **Mercer Bullard,** *The Mutual Fund as a Firm: Frequent Trading, Fund Arbitrage, and the SEC's Response to the Mutual Fund Scandal,* **42 HOUS. L. REV. 1271, 1272 (2006) (noting that the scandals resulted in dozens of civil and criminal prosecutions and billions in monetary sanctions). Mutual fund scandals revolved around fund practices that allowed favored institutional traders to engage in fund arbitrage, which involves buying fund shares at a discount and redeeming them once the price has been corrected, with profits coming from other fund shareholders.** *Id.* **at 1285.**

48   **Frankel,** *Jurisprudence of Regulation, supra* **note 37, at 956.**

49   **Compliance Programs of Investment Companies and Investment Advisers, Investors Company Act Release 26,299, 68 Fed. Reg. 74,714 (Dec. 24, 2003).**

1. SEC Oversight

The SEC has been diffident in its oversight of the fund board.[50] Besides regular (mostly hollow) calls for greater board independence and authority, the SEC has done little to make fund governance more responsive to investor needs. The SEC has not armed directors with the information and other resources to effectively bargain on behalf of fund investors.[51] The SEC has not brought enforcement actions against fund directors for nonfeasance in negotiating fund fees or controlling excesses in fund marketing.[52] The SEC has neither sued management firms to challenge their fees nor filed amicus briefs in support of investor litigation making such charges.[53] In short, the SEC has stood by the design of the 1940 Act regime to outsource regulatory supervision of the management firm to the fund board.

The SEC's recent efforts to increase board independence,[54] far from introducing major reforms in board governance, largely codify existing industry practices:

> The rule [mandating a majority of independent directors] will accomplish little. The board majority requirement is nothing but a warmed-over rehash of an SEC Investment Management Division proposal advanced eight years ago. Worse it is beside the point. Today, many, if not most, funds have a majority of directors who are supposed to be independent of the external advisor to keep fees and expenses in line. In many cases, funds' independent directors already populate funds' nominating committees [since funds with Rule 12b-1 plans must have self-nominating independent directors].[55]

---

50   Tobe, *supra* note 19, at 27 ("'[F]und directors have done an outstanding job.'" (quoting SEC Commissioner Steven Wallman)).

51   For example, the SEC does not require that management firms disclose their profits to their fund boards. *See* John P. Freeman & Stewart L. Brown, *Mutual Fund Advisory Fees: the Cost of Conflicts of Interest*, 26 J. CORP. L. 609, 656–58 (2001) (itemizing SEC inaction).

52   Under § 36(a) of the 1940 Act, the SEC has (limited) authority to seek injunctive action against fund directors for the "breach of fiduciary duty involving personal misconduct." 15 U.S.C. § 80a-35(a) (2000) (originally enacted as Act of Aug. 22, 1940, ch. 686, Title I, § 36) (action in federal court against any person who "serves or acts" for a registered investment company). Section 36 of the 1940 Act is hereinafter cited as 15 U.S.C. § 80a-35. Under § 36(b) of the 1940 Act, the SEC (along with fund investors) can also sue fund directors and the management firm "for breach of fiduciary duty in respect of [management] compensation." *Id.* § 80a-35(b). In addition, the SEC could also sue fund directors to enjoin the "violation of any provision of this title, or of any rule, regulation, or order hereunder." *Id.* § 80a-41(d) (Supp. II 2002).

53   Freeman & Brown, *supra* note 52, at 656.

54   In 2001 the SEC conditioned its ten most commonly used exemptive rules on a board composed of a majority of outside directors. Role of Independent Directors of Investment Companies, Securities Act No. 7932, Exchange Act Release No. 43,786, Investment Company Act Release No. 24,816, 66 Fed. Reg. 3734 (Jan. 16, 2001). The rule also required that funds disclose the fund shares held by directors, including independent directors. In 2004 the SEC sought to increase the proportion of disinterested directors to 75% and add a requirement that the board chair be a disinterested director. Investment Company Governance, Investment Company Act Release No. 26,520, 69 Fed. Reg. 46,378 (July 27, 2004). The rule also would enable disinterested directors to hire their own staff and lawyers, and to caucus among themselves.

55   Freeman & Brown, *supra* note 52, at 657–58. In addition, the use of outside counsel is widespread, given the encouragement of the practice by federal courts. *See* Tannenbaum v. Zeller, 552 F.2d 402, 428 (2d Cir. 1977) (recommending that independent directors receive advice from independent counsel, rather than counsel for the management firm).

The SEC has also turned its attention to improving disclosure to fund investors. Since 1988, the SEC has required that mutual fund prospectuses include a fee table showing fund fees and charges as a percentage of net assets.[56] In 2004, the SEC required that funds disclose in tabular form (in their semi-annual and annual reports) the cost in dollars of an investment of $1,000 that earned the fund's actual return and incurred the fund's actual expenses during that fiscal period.[57] Funds must also explain the types of costs charged to the fund, not just provide an operating expense ratio— though the SEC does not require a break-down of different fees and operating expenses.

The SEC, however, has rejected individualized disclosure in account statements of actual expenses paid by investors—disclosure strongly recommended in a 2004 GAO report on fee transparency.[58] The GAO asserted "seeing the specific dollar amount paid on shares owned could be the incentive that some investors need to take action to compare their fund's expenses to those of other funds and make more informed investment decisions on this basis."[59] The SEC concluded such disclosure would not show fees at comparable funds and was concerned about costs for assembling the information when investor accounts are held by financial intermediaries, such as brokers and financial advisers.[60]

While the SEC showed concern about costs, absent from its releases on enhanced fee disclosure is "how investors can, in light of the newly disclosed information, proceed to the next step . . . whether their interests are best served by doing some comparative shopping."[61] Without "processable" information that can be understood and used, the benefits of disclosure are wasted. As Professors Cox and Payne argue:

> Learning that your expense ratio is 1.29% is helpful but more so if this number can easily be placed in context. What investors wish to know is how this expense ratio compares with comparable investment opportunities. Learning that you rate a nine on a scale of ten in a competition is much more informative than to receive a numerical score when the boundaries of the scale are unknown. Thus, much like unit pricing information for grocery products, providing operating expense and return disclosures in a truly comparative framework is much more likely to elicit an informed choice on the part of investors than if operating expenses or return disclosures are made in isolation.[62]

---

56   *See* **Consolidated Disclosure of Mutual Fund Expenses, Investors Company Act Release No. 16,244, 53 Fed. Reg. 3192 (1988) (amending Item 3 of Form N-1A to require disclosure of the fund's expense ratio). The SEC-mandated disclosure received poor marks.** *See* **Robert A. Robertson,** *In Search of the Perfect Mutual Fund Prospectus,* **54 BUS. LAW. 461, 475 (1999).**

57   **Shareholder Reports and Quarterly Portfolio Disclosure of Registered Management Investment Companies, Exchange Act Release No. 33-8393 [2003-2004 transfer binder] Fed. Sec. L. Rep. (CCH) ¶ 87,148 at 89,253 (May 10, 2004) [hereinafter SEC Fund Expense Adopting Release].**

58   **U.S. GEN. ACCOUNTING OFFICE, GAO-04-317T, MUTUAL FUNDS: ADDITIONAL DISCLOSURES COULD INCREASE TRANSPARENCY OF FEES AND OTHER PRACTICES 3 (2004), http://www.gao.gov/new.items/d04317t.pdf.**

59   *Id.* **at 8.**

60   *See* **SEC Fund Expense Adopting Release,** *supra* **note 58, at 89,253 (relying on a 2000 industry estimate that individualized disclosure would entail on-going costs of $65 million while the procedures adopted by the SEC would entail costs of $16 million annually).**

61   *See* **James D. Cox & John W. Payne,** *Mutual Fund Expense Disclosures: A Behavioral Perspective,* **83 WASH. U. L.Q. 907, 929 (2005).**

62   *Id.* **at 935–36.**

Of course, this makes sense. But the SEC (like the fund boards it oversees) seems more concerned with industry sensibilities than protection of fund investors. True regulatory reform to empower fund investors (and endanger industry profitability) remains off the table.

2. Federal Judicial Oversight

The 1940 Act does not create a comprehensive system of fiduciary duties and gives federal courts only narrow authority to oversee fund boards.[63] In the one area where the 1940 Act explicitly permits fund investors to seek judicial review—the compensation of the fund's management firm—the federal courts have refused to involve themselves in valuing management services and effectively shunned an oversight role.[64]

Under the articulated standard, management compensation fails review only if it is "so disproportionately large that it bears no reasonable relationship to the services rendered and could not have been the product of arm's-length bargaining."[65] This means that fee comparisons become largely irrelevant and that fund directors need not bargain for the least expensive investment advisory services for the fund. Fee comparisons are left to fund investors.[66]

Federal courts reviewing allegations of excessive fees have focused on director qualifications and the board's fee-setting process.[67] Fund directors who meet the statutory standards of independence need only show they followed a prescribed script: frequent meetings (some

---

63   The 1940 Act carefully cabins federal judicial review of fund boards. Section 36(a) permits the SEC (but not explicitly fund investors) to bring actions challenging "a breach of fiduciary duty involving personal misconduct" by fund directors. 15 U.S.C. § 80a-35(a) (2000). Section 36(b) authorizes the SEC and fund investors to sue the management firm and fund board with respect to compensation paid the management firm, which is deemed to have federal fiduciary duties with respect to the compensation. *Id.* § 80a-35(b). Congress, however, deftly avoided defining the standards of "reasonableness" for reviewing management compensation. *See* Cox & Payne, *supra* note 62, at 922–23 (citing INVESTMENT COMPANY AMENDMENTS ACT OF 1969, S. REP. No. 91- 184 (1969); INVESTMENT COMPANY AMENDMENTS OF 1970, H.R. REP. No. 91-1382 (1970)). The § 36(b) action, although procedurally a derivative suit, is not subject to a demand requirement. Daily Income Fund, Inc. v. Fox, 464 U.S. 523, 527 (1984). Nonetheless, it is burdened by a host of impediments: (1) plaintiffs are not entitled to a jury trial; (2) plaintiffs have the burden of proof, reversing the usual common law burden on self-dealing fiduciaries to prove fairness; (3) damages are limited to the year before the action was instituted; (4) damages are limited to those resulting from the fiduciary breach, thus preventing punitive damages; and (5) federal courts have exclusive jurisdiction. *See* Freeman & Brown, *supra* note 52, at 642.

64   Gartenberg v. Merrill Lynch Asset Mgmt., Inc., 694 F.2d 923, 928 (2d Cir. 1982) (eschewing comparative analysis of fund fees, but then adopting deferential "disproportionately large" test).

65   *Id.*

66   During the hearings on the 1940 Act, the Chief Counsel of the SEC testified, "There is not a single provision in section 15 [requiring board approval of the management firm's advisory and underwriting agreements] which even remotely assumes to fix what [the management firm] should be paid as compensation. We feel that is a question for the stockholders to decide." *Investment Trusts and Investment Companies: Hearings on S. 3580 Before a Subcomm. of the Senate Comm. on Banking and Currency*, 76th Cong., 3d Sess. 252 (1940) (statement of David Schenker, Chief Counsel, SEC Investment Trust Section).

67   Krinsk v. Fund Asset Mgmt., Inc., 715 F. Supp. 472 (S.D.N.Y. 1988), *aff'd* 875 F.2d 404 (2d Cir. 1989) (rejecting contentions that § 36(b) of the 1940 Act requires fund directors to negotiate the "best deal" possible and that excessive profitability alone proves a breach of duty).

without representatives of the management firm), fulsome information (including presentations, documents, and legal advice from separate counsel), and documentation of their efforts (negotiation position and strategy, and evaluation of data).[68]

In a critique of federal judicial review under the 1940 Act, Professors Freeman and Brown point out the consistent reluctance of federal courts to engage in any comparative fee valuation:

> Post-*Gartenberg* courts have improperly denied the relevance of advisory fee structures actually set by arm's-length bargaining (as in the pension fund advisory fee analogy). Low-cost fee structures charged by other funds (like Vanguard's) are likewise found essentially irrelevant, if for no other reason than the fact that, because fund advisors refuse to compete against each other for advisory business, lower prices are not available to the fund. . . . The absence of a competitive market has not become a reason for enhanced scrutiny, but a justification for fitting the judiciary with blinders.[69]

Not surprisingly, fund boards (and their management firm sponsors) have a perfect record in more than twenty years of litigation challenging fund fees. No management firm, much less a fund director, has been assessed damages in a case alleging excessive fees.[70] Although some cases have been settled, with payments coming from the management firm or fund-paid D&O insurance, the settlements only reinforce the prevailing view that fund directors are not subject to meaningful federal judicial oversight. The courts have declared the question of "value" to be intractable, and left it to the professional judgment of fund directors—and the marketplace.[71]

Recent attempts to open other avenues of federal judicial review have fallen on deaf ears. Federal courts have refused to imply private actions for the "breach of fiduciary duty involving personal misconduct."[72] Leaving no doubt that the door is closed, some lower courts have explained that

---

68   Stanley J. Friedman, *The Role of Outside Directors in Negotiating Investment Company Advisory Agreements,* 24 REV. SEC. & COMMODITIES REG. 49 (1991).

69   Freeman & Brown, *supra* note 52, at 651.

70   *Id.* at 642 n.116.

71   *See* Castillo v. Dean Witter Discover & Co., 1998 U.S. Dist. LEXIS 9489, at *10, *23 n.10 (S.D.N.Y. June 25, 1998) (refusing to require disclosure, comparing fund fees, and chiding fund investors for not being more careful in the face of conflicts created by the management firm).

72   Section 36(a) of the 1940 Act authorizes the SEC to bring an enforcement action for such fiduciary breaches, but does not explicitly foreclose private actions. 15 U.S.C. § 80a-35(a) (2000). Some courts have implied a private action under the section. *See* Fogel v. Chestnutt, 668 F.2d 100 (2d Cir. 1981). More recent courts, however, have held that the section's failure to mention private plaintiffs forecloses a private action. *See* Olmstead v. Pruco Life Ins. Co., 283 F.3d 429, 432–36 (2d Cir. 2002); Mutchka v. Harris, 373 F. Supp. 2d 1021, 1025–27 (C.D. Cal. 2005); Davis v. Bailey, 2005 U.S. Dist. LEXIS 38204, at *7–16 (D. Colo. Dec. 22, 2005) (No. 05-cv-00042- WYD-OES). The cases reflect a jurisprudential shift in implying private actions. *See* Alexander v. Sandoval, 532 U.S. 275, 287 (2001) (announcing abandonment of "*ancien regime*" for implying private actions and instructing lower federal courts to focus on statutory intent, principally as found in statutory text). *See also* Arthur Gabinet & George Gowen III, *The Past and Future of Implied Causes of Action under the Investment Company Act of 1940,* 3 VILL. J. L. & INV. MGMT. 45, 45 (2002). The refusal to imply a private action flies in the face of legislative urgings. H.R. REP. NO. 96-1341, at 28–29 (1980), *as reprinted in* 1980 U.S.C.C.A.N. 4800, 4810–11. Amending the 1940 Act in 1980, the House Report stated, The Committee wishes to make plain that it expects the courts to imply private rights of action under this legislation, where the plaintiff falls within the class of persons protected by the statutory provisions in question. . . . In appropriate instances, for example, breaches of fiduciary duty involving personal misconduct should be remedied under Section 36(a) of the Investment Company Act. *Id.*

even if a private action could be implied it would not cover board nonfeasance that did not involve self-dealing or bad faith.[73]

Federal courts asked to imply greater federal judicial oversight have pointed to the availability of SEC enforcement and the existing judicial review of advisory fees as foreclosing broader judicial intervention.[74]The Supreme Court has given its blessing to this judicial state of affairs, regularly and uniformly denying review of lower court decisions that deny review of fund boards.[75] It seems the Court believes its "watchdog" rhetoric.

3. State Judicial Oversight

State courts, responsible for enforcing state-based fiduciary duties, have adopted an even more deferential approach than their federal counterparts. Imposing a demand requirement on investor derivative suits, state courts have refused to even hear cases of board nonfeasance.[76] Plaintiffs bear the nearly insuperable burden of showing that a majority of the board—and thus some of the independent directors—have personal conflicts that would prevent them from deciding a shareholder demand in good faith.[77]

Otherwise, the fund board receives the benefit of the doubt under the business judgment rule.[78] Since independent directors, by definition, do not have *direct* financial interests in management fees, the chances of overcoming the business judgment presumption are close to nil. Absent a showing of payola (beyond regular board compensation) or other corrupt behavior, state law effectively disavows fiduciary review of mutual fund activities.

---

73   *See* **Davis, 2005 U.S. Dist. LEXIS 38204, at *15 n.1 (stating that even if § 36(a) authorized private actions, it would not reach a claim for nonfeasance—namely, the failure of mutual funds to collect settlement moneys in securities fraud class actions— since the section only reached "personal misconduct"). Some have pointed out the inconsistency of this cautious judicial attitude and the 1940 Act policy of protecting fund investors.** *See* **William K. Sjostrom,** *Tapping the Reservoir: Mutual Fund Litigation under Section 36(a) of the Investment Company Act of 1940,* **54 KANSAS L. REV. 251, 278–82 (2006) (arguing for broad interpretation of "personal conduct" beyond self-dealing and personal impropriety, to encompass any board decision not made on an informed basis, in good faith and in the honest belief that the action taken was in the best interests of the fund).**

74   *See* **Gabinet & Gowen,** *supra* **note 73, at 58–59.**

75   *See, e.g.,* **Kalish v. Franklin Advisors, Inc., 928 F.2d 590, 591 (2d Cir. 1991),** *cert. denied,* **502 U.S. 818 (1991); Schuyt v. Rowe Price Prime Reserve Fund, Inc., 835 F.2d 45 (2d Cir. 1987),** *cert. denied,* **485 U.S. 1034 (1988); Grossman v. Johnson, 674 F.2d 115 (1st Cir. 1982),** *cert. denied,* **459 U.S. 838 (1982); Gartenberg v. Merrill Lynch Asset Mgmt., Inc., 636 F.2d 16 (2d Cir. 1980),** *cert. denied,* **451 U.S. 910 (1981).**

76   *See* **Werbowsky v. Collomb, 766 A.2d 123, 144 (Md. 2001) (dismissing derivative litigation unless plaintiff can show that "majority of the directors are so personally and directly conflicted or committed to the decision in dispute that they cannot reasonably be expected to respond to a demand in good faith and within the ambit of the business judgment rule"). The standard is the same whether the question is demand futility or board termination of derivative litigation.** *See* **Langevoort,** *supra* **note 28, at 1029.**

77   *Werbowsky,* **766 A.2d at 144.**

78   **Navellier v. Sletten, 262 F.3d 923 (9th Cir. 2001) (affirming jury finding that fund trustees had not violated their fiduciary duties in terminating the investment advisory contract).**

The faith generally placed in independent directors under corporate law rests on justifications that are inapposite to the mutual fund. In the corporate context, efficient capital markets price corporate governance and react to board governance failures; executive compensation is tied to stock performance and aligns management interests with those of shareholders; institutional investors can use (or threaten to use) their voting rights; and markets in corporate control serve as a backstop if the other mechanisms fail.[79]Although each mechanism has shortcomings, they nonetheless have served to justify a judicial attitude of abstention.

None of the justifications for judicial abstention, however, applies in the mutual fund context. Mutual funds do not operate in efficient markets in which investors price the value of fund management services. Management compensation is based on asset size and directors are paid in cash, thus compensation for neither is linked (given the dysfunctional investor market) to the value of the services provided. Since institutional investors purchase their management services independently of retail investors, they do not modulate pricing of retail fund services. Other intermediaries, such as Morningstar and the financial press, have not been effective in informing investors and valuing fund management services. To the contrary, they have exacerbated investor biases. And no control market exists for mutual funds, since any change of management firms would require board approval or a shareholder insurgency.[80]

4. Professional Oversight

Fund directors have lately been viewed as a professional corps—with special professional, though largely aspirational, responsibilities. The mutual fund industry has promoted this view.

Proposals for fund governance reform have come from various quarters, most tellingly, the industry itself. For example, in 1999 an ICI advisory group recommended:

1) at least two-thirds of each fund board be independent directors, and independent directors designate one of their own as "lead" independent director;

2) former officials of the management firm or its affiliates not serve as independent directors, independent directors be selected and nominated by incumbent independent directors, independent directors complete an annual questionnaire on their business, financial and family relationships with the management firm and other service providers, and fund boards adopt policies on retirement of directors;

3) independent directors establish director compensation, fund directors invest in funds on whose boards they serve, and fund boards obtain D&O insurance and/or indemnification from the fund "to ensure the independence and effectiveness of independent directors;"

---

79   *See, e.g.*, RONALD J. GILSON, TRANSPARENCY, CORPORATE GOVERNANCE AND CAPITAL MARKETS 4 (The Latin American Corporate Governance Roundtable 2000), *available at* http://www.oecd.org/dataoecd/55/45/1921785.pdf.

80   As Professor Langevoort points out: "Thinking about mutual funds by imagining them simply as a species of 'corporations' in a way that is directly informed by contemporary corporate law theory is completely misguided." Langevoort, *supra* note 28, at 1032.

4) independent directors meet separately from management when considering the fund's advisory and underwriting contracts, and independent directors have qualified independent counsel and have express authority to consult with the fund's independent auditors or other experts, as appropriate;

5) fund boards establish an audit committee (composed entirely of independent directors) that would supervise the fund's independent auditors; and

6) fund directors evaluate periodically the board's effectiveness, new fund directors receive appropriate orientation, and all fund directors keep abreast of industry and regulatory developments. [81]

Many of the "best practices" proposals, however, simply call for conduct that is already the industry norm.[82] For example, many fund groups have moved on their own to increase the proportion of independent directors on their boards. The SEC estimates that at least 60% of fund boards meet the 75% independent-directors threshold.[83] The shift to independent chairs has been even more pronounced, with 43% of fund boards led by an independent chair, up from less than 20% only a few years ago.[84]

Has the director professionalism movement borne fruit? The industry says yes. For example, in 2005 fees were reduced on 808 mutual funds, while they rose on 263 funds. In comparison, fees rose on 417 funds and fell on 367 in 2003.[85] But the net 545 funds that reduced fees in 2005 represent less than 10% of the 8000-fund industry.

Ultimately, gains in independent board membership and more active negotiation of fund fees do not change the essential dynamic of mutual fund governance. Fund boards can negotiate only at the margin. The threat to buy fund services elsewhere, always present in a real negotiation, is mostly empty (sometimes even ludicrous) in a negotiation of fund fees or other terms of the management contract. Moreover, the composition of fund boards with executives sympathetic to the profit motives of the management firm, cemented by the high levels of compensation for many fund directors, is hardly a harbinger of reform. For example, the $3 million in fee reductions wrangled by the AIM board in 2005 came at a not insignificant cost.[86] In 2005, the AIM independent trustees received total pay, including deferred retirement benefits, of approximately $4.4 million, with the independent chair receiving $359,000 for his board service.[87]

---

81   INVESTMENT COMPANY INSTITUTE, REPORT OF THE ADVISORY GROUP ON BEST PRACTICES FOR FUND DIRECTORS iii–iv (1999), http://www.ici.org/pdf/rpt_best_practices.pdf. *See also* Freeman & Brown, *supra* note 52, at 658–59 n.200 (summarizing ICI advisory group recommendations).

82   *See* Freeman & Brown, *supra* note 52, at 659 n.221.

83   Lauricella, *supra* note 32, at R4 (reporting end-of-year 2004 data from the Investment Company Institute).

84   *Id.*

85   *Id.* at R1 (reporting data from Lipper, Inc.).

86   *Id.* at R4.

87   *See* AIM INVESTMENT SECURITIES FUNDS, STATEMENT OF ADDITIONAL INFORMATION, APPENDIX D, TRUSTEE COMPENSATION TABLE (2006), https://www.aiminvestments.com.

II. EVALUATION OF OUTSOURCING

Has outsourcing to the mutual fund board worked? The mutual fund industry has argued that mutual fund boards, and the funds they supervise, operate in a "vigorous and highly competitive" market.[88] But many outside the industry, including the SEC, have questioned the power of the market and the effectiveness of fund boards in supervising management firms— primarily as relates to fees and costs. More recently, some have also pointed to the failure of the board in reining in aggressive and misguided marketing practices devised by management firms that prey on investor cognitive biases.[89]

Consider the assumptions that undergird the regulatory outsourcing to mutual fund boards and the evidence of how that outsourcing has worked.

A. DEBATE OVER THE FUND BOARD

Oversight of mutual fund boards is built on certain hopeful assumptions. The fund industry regularly trumpets its efficiency and the market pressure that fund investors can wield. To the extent there are market inefficiencies, the SEC has sought to empower the fund board by reforming the rules governing fund board composition. Thus, courts reviewing the performance of fund boards have been inclined to use the same standards of deferential review applied to corporate boards, on the assumptions that market discipline by investors and regulatory oversight by the SEC make judicial intervention unnecessary.

1. Market Efficiency

At first glance, the mutual fund industry shows the classic hallmarks of market competitiveness. The supply side of the market has low barriers to entry and has shown great fluidity, with small funds regularly displacing larger funds.[90] The demand side is characterized by potent information

---

88   *How the Financial System Can Best Be Shaped to Meet the Needs of the American People, Financial Deregulation: Hearing on H.R. 5734: The Financial Institutions Equity Act of 1984 Before the House Comm. on Banking, Finance and Urban Affairs,* **98th Cong., 2d Sess. 1359 (1984) (statement of David Silver, President, Investment Company Institute).**

89   **JOHN C. BOGLE, THE BATTLE FOR THE SOUL OF CAPITALISM 164–65 (2005) (arguing that salesmanship triumphed over stewardship).**

90   **WILLIAM J. BAUMOL, STEPHEN M. GOLDFELD, LILLI A. GORDON & MICHAEL F. KOEHN, THE ECONOMICS OF MUTUAL FUND MARKETS: COMPETITION VERSUS REGULATION 117 (Karl Brunner & Paul W. MacAvoy eds., 1990) (finding that under the Justice Department's antitrust guidelines, mutual fund advisers compete in an unconcentrated market, with the 30 largest complexes experiencing a declining market share, and new smaller entrants taking market shares from larger rivals).**

and liquidity rights that allow fund investors easily to ascertain fund performance and to redeem their shares and move to better-performing or lower-cost funds.[91]

The industry's argument for market efficiency, repeated by some finance theorists, has superficial appeal.[92] SEC disclosure rules arm investors with extensive information about fund investment policies, returns, management fees, and other costs.[93] And for those investors unwilling to wade through the disclosure documents, information intermediaries (such as Morningstar, newsletters, financial press) provide "extensive coverage and analysis of mutual funds."[94] The asset-based compensation structure, which allows the management firm to share in superior investment results as the asset base increases, provides incentives to both attract and retain fund investors.

The industry, until the late-trading and market-timing stories broke in 2003, regularly trumpeted its mostly scandal-free record. By all appearances, portfolio securities seemed to be in safe hands and management firms (under the watchful eye of majority-independent boards) complied with the rules of the game—multitudinous and ample as they are.

Ultimately, the proof is in the pudding. The record of mutual fund fees, expenses, portfolio turnover, investment strategies, fund design, and marketing has received a good deal of attention in the finance literature. The picture that emerges (described below) is not flattering for the industry. At almost every level, it seems that fund management firms have been systematically taking advantage of the informational and cognitive deficiencies of fund investors. Market efficiency, plausible in theory, seems not to have functioned in practice.

2. Structural Critique

The SEC, on a regular basis, has questioned the *structural* effectiveness of the board and, specifically, its independent members.[95] The SEC's solution to the fund board's perceived weaknesses has been to strengthen the board's structural independence and authority.[96]

---

91   SEC, Invest Wisely: An Introduction to Mutual Funds, *available at* http://www.sec.gov/investor/pubs/inwsmf.htm.

92   *See* Paula A. Tkac, Federal Reserve Bank of Atlanta, *Mutual Funds: Temporary Problem or Permanent Morass?*, 98 ECON. REV. 1, 15 (2004), *available at* http://www.frbatlanta.org/filelegacydocs/erq404_tkac.pdf ("The mutual fund industry is . . . no different than any other competitive industry. [Fund investors] exert their power via their aggregated purchasing decisions in a marketplace replete with choices."). Edward B. Rock, *Foxes and Hen Houses?: Personal Trading by Mutual Fund Managers*, 73 WASH. U. L.Q. 1601, 1641 (1994) ("[P]roduct markets that are as competitive as the market for mutual funds . . . provide firms with strong incentives to adopt optimal personal trading policies.").

93   Advertising by Investment Companies, Investment Company Act Release No. 16,245, 53 Fed. Reg. 3,868 (Feb. 10, 1988).

94   Wang, *supra* note 3, at 965–66.

95   SEC Staff Report Protecting Investors, *supra* note 25, at 266 (examining existing governance model to increase board effectiveness, and concluding that board governance is "fundamentally sound").

96   *See* SEC REPORT ON PUBLIC POLICY IMPLICATION OF INVESTMENT COMPANY GROWTH, H.R. REP. NO. 89-2337 (1966) (finding inadequate the independence standard under the 1940 Act, since independent directors are often close to the adviser through business or family relationships). In response, Congress amended the 1940 Act in 1970 to tighten the standards of independence and to permit fund investors to seek judicial review of management compensation. 15 U.S.C.A. § 80a-2(a)(19) (West 2006) (defining "interested person"); *Id.* § 80a-35(b) (providing a private action to remedy fiduciary breaches involving fees paid management firm).

Most recently, the SEC has proposed rules that would effectively require that the board be composed of 75 percent independent directors and that the board chair be an independent director.[97] The SEC proposal, which has met judicial resistance, reflects the long-standing regulatory belief (even faith) in the ability of independent directors to serve the interests of fund investors unable themselves to discipline wayward or faithless fund management.

Observers have long noted the structural bias inherent in the fund board, given the method by which non-management directors are selected and their professional and personal ties of directors to the management firm.[98]

In a recent study of fees charged by mutual funds, Professors Freeman and Brown concluded:

> Scholarly articles published by finance academics have ridiculed board approved 12b-1 fees paid by fund shareholders. Law review commentators offer uncomplimentary evaluations of those who control fund management and policies. The SEC has weighed in, questioning "whether changes are needed in the current system." Another federal agency, the General Accounting Office, recently issued a detailed report finding that mutual funds generally do not attempt to compete on the basis of costs (i.e., price competition is muted). . . . [D]ecades of SEC-commissioned studies, rulemaking, and jawboning have led to a system that, for the most part, works beautifully for those who sell funds to the public, or sell services to funds, but much less admirably for the industry's investors.[99]

In the end, fund directors may perceive their role as supercilious. Fund investors receive disclosure, have available comparative information, and can move their mutual fund investments as they choose. On the assumption of consumer sovereignty, the board is at most a bureaucratic compliance office.

3. Doctrinal Critique

More recently, academic commentators have identified the *doctrinal* deference to fund boards, even when composed by a majority of independent directors.[100] They have criticized the judicial approach of federal courts (which defer to state law on questions of board demand and termination of investor suits) and state courts (which defer to independent directors under the business judgment rule).

---

97   **Investment Company Governance, Investment Company Act Release No. 26,520, 83 SEC Docket 1384 (July 27, 2004). Curiously, the SEC has stated that its rule mandating an independent board chair was not adopted "as a means of enhancing fund financial performance or reducing fund expenses." SEC Staff Report on Independent Chair,** *supra* **note 27, at 2. Instead, the change was said to improve compliance and ensure fund boards focus on the long-term interests of fund investors.** *Id.* **One is left to wonder why improved compliance and an investor focus should not produce financial results.**

98   *See* **Brudney,** *supra* **note 45, at 612.**

99   **Freeman & Brown.** *supra* **note 52, at 611–13 (citations omitted).**

100   *See* **Langevoort,** *supra* **note 28, at 1017–18.**

The transliteration of traditional corporate governance norms to the mutual fund context is simplistic—and misplaced. Unlike their counterparts in operating companies, fund directors are not subject to the threat of shareholder insurgencies or takeover pressures; they lack the realistic power to replace fund management; and they generally rely on the management firm for information, direction, and compensation. And the linking of compensation to performance—as with stock-based compensation in operating companies or performance-based compensation in hedge funds— is diluted by the asset-based compensation in mutual funds.

The doctrinal gap, rather than narrowing, has been widening. Recently, courts have largely sidestepped the wave of investor litigation arising from the spate of late-trading and marketing-timing scandals. Federal courts have refused to imply federal fiduciary duties, and state courts have refused to relieve investors of the board demand and termination procedures of state corporate law.[101]

Summarizing the sad state of the fund board, Professor Wang in a comprehensive article on the board-centric structure of U.S. mutual funds concluded:

> To evaluate the institutional competence of the board, it is essential to inquire into the board's independence and informational advantage. . . . Because directors are not truly independent, they are vulnerable to coalition politics. In addition, because directors have a limited informational advantage over investors, it may not be realistic to expect them to strike the best deals for investors. In this respect, traditional monitoring devices such as fiduciary duties and incentive-compatible contracts are not effective devices to discipline the performance of the board.[102]

B. EMPIRICAL DATA ON MUTUAL FUND MARKETS

How has the mutual fund market performed? Rather than consider the *structural* and *doctrinal* effectiveness of the fund board, the more relevant question is how fund directors have *measurably* fulfilled their role as "watchdogs" for fund investors. Viewing fund governance as a black box, the question is how well fund boards have performed their functions.

Even if fund governance (the supply market) is not working, it is possible that fund investors (the demand market) have exercised their informational and liquidity rights to protect

---

101   Federal judicial abstention in this area is not new. In a line of Supreme Court cases on whether fund boards are bound by federal law or state law, the resounding answer has been in favor of state law. *See* Burks v. Lasker, 441 U.S. 471, 472 (1979) (finding that state law governs termination of derivative suit, unless inconsistent with policies of 1940 Act); *see generally* Kamen v. Kemper Fin. Servs. Inc., 500 U.S. 90 (1991) (finding that state law controls question of board demand). Only when there is clear federal policy, such as the express private action under § 36(b) to overcome the perceived inability of independent directors to control overreaching management, does federal law control. Daily Income Fund, Inc. v. Fox, 464 U.S. 523, 527 (1984) (finding no demand requirement under § 36(b)). Even if the federal courts were to expand their currently cabined view of implied private actions under the 1940 Act, fund investors would face the daunting challenge of bringing derivative claims in the face of board demand and dismissal tools available under state law— primarily, Delaware and Maryland where most mutual funds are organized. *See* Scalisi v. Fund Asset Management L.P., 380 F.3d 133, 142 (2d Cir. 2004) (applying Maryland's approach that demand and termination by independent directors is subject to review under the business judgment rule).

102   Wang, *supra* note 3, at 1008.

themselves. Again, the question is whether fund investors have exercised their buy/sell rights to demand good performance at low cost. The rich finance literature on the functioning of the mutual fund markets over the past several years provides some answers. The studies reveal a largely dysfunctional supply market with fund boards performing poorly nearly all the tasks assigned to them.[103] The same is true for the demand market, where fund investors by and large possess neither the information nor acumen to protect themselves. Although some recent data suggest greater consumerism among fund investors, the change appears to be at the margin.

1. Board Performance

Academic studies tell a consistent and disturbing story of the failure of fund boards to negotiate lower fees in the face of economies of scale generated by rising fund assets and enhanced computer and tele-communications technologies. After reviewing some of the academic literature, the General Accounting Office (GAO) concluded that fund boards "may be keeping fees at higher levels because of [a] focus on maintaining fees within the range of other funds."[104]

Fund boards have also failed investors in the supervision and approval of marketing by management firms. The studies surveyed by the GAO found that "the information currently provided does not sufficiently make investors aware of the level of fees they pay."[105] As one study concluded, perhaps kindly, "funds do not compete primarily on the basis of their operating expense fees."[106] Instead, funds seem to compete on the basis of marketing—with advertisement focused on recent performance results.

Board hiring/retention of management firm

- Business connections between fund directors and advisory firms affect hiring, compensation, and performance. Fund boards preferentially hire advisory firms having more business relationships with fund directors. Fund advisors receive higher pay when more connected to the fund directors. Preferential hiring and pay is not compensated by higher performance. In fact, greater connections correspond to a decrease in fund return, before and after advisory fees, of about 1% per year.[107]

---

103   To date, no studies look at the performance of fund boards in supervising late-trading and market-timing practices. The brazen nature of the practices in some fund families raises questions about the effectiveness of fund boards at this, their most basic, task. Nonetheless, whether because of board pressure or management firm response to the SEC's and Attorney Elliot Spitzer's enforcement actions, there is reason to believe the industry has responded to ameliorate the practices.

104   U.S. GEN. ACCOUNTING OFFICE, MUTUAL FUND FEES: ADDITIONAL DISCLOSURE COULD ENCOURAGE PRICE COMPETITION 8, 47 (2000) [hereinafter GAO Mutual Fund Disclosure Report] (noting that some studies "found that fees had been rising").

105   *Id.* at 7, 76 ("[A]cademic researchers [and others] saw problems with the fee disclosures" by mutual funds).

106   *Id.* at 62.

107   Camelia M. Kuhnen, *Social Networks, Corporate Governance and Contracting in the Mutual Fund Industry* 6 (Unpublished Working Paper, 2006), *available at* http://ssrn.com/abstract=849705 [hereinafter Kuhnen, *Social Networks*].

Board negotiation of advisory contracts and fees

- Expense ratios have risen, even as fund assets have grown and fund management has become more efficient. Weighted average expense ratios for *all mutual funds* (stock and bond funds) rose from 0.73% in 1979 to 0.94% in 1999—a nearly 30% increase.[108] Weighted average expense ratios for *equity funds* grew from 0.64% in 1980 to 0.92% in 2004—an increase of more than 40%—even as equity fund assets rose from $45 billion to $4,034 billion.[109]

- Negotiation of advisory contracts appears to be perfunctory. Contractual renegotiations are "rare event[s]" that happen in only 10% of funds.[110] When they do happen, they produce lower fees for bottom and mid-performing funds that correlate to later positive performance, as well as net inflows. It is "puzzling" that fund boards do not actively renegotiate advisory contracts, given the apparent benefits.[111]

- Fund boards accept higher expense ratios for high-performance funds.[112] Although overall management fees decline somewhat as fund size increases, administrative costs decline more rapidly. That is, advisory fees constitute a profit center for management firms.[113]

- Advisory fees charged mutual funds are not competitive with advisory fees charged pension funds. Advisory fee ratios for public pension clients are roughly half of that for comparable actively managed equity mutual funds—even though the average such mutual fund has assets that are nearly three times larger than the average pension portfolio.[114] On a size-standardized basis, the average actively managed mutual fund pays advisory fees of 0.67%, compared to 0.28% paid by pension portfolios.[115]

---

108   **SEC Division of Investment Management: Report on Mutual Fund Fees and Expenses 20 Table 2 (2000), http://www.sec. gov/news/studies/feestudy.htm. The report determined that the increase in average expense ratios was primarily due to greater use of 12b-1 fees to pay for fund distribution costs.** *Id.* **at 21.**

109   **BOGLE,** *supra* **note 90, at 155 Box 7.2 (finding that unweighted expense ratios have risen even faster than weighted expense ratios, from 0.94% in 1980 to 1.56% in 2004).**

110   **Camelia M. Kuhnen,** *Dynamic Contracting in the Mutual Fund Industry* **8–9 (Unpublished Working Paper, 2005),** *available at* **http://ssrn.com/abstract=687530.**

111   **Kuhnen,** *Social Networks,* **supra note 108, at 1 (discussing a study of negotiations of advisory contracts from 1994–2002).**

112   **Jerold B. Warner & Joanna Shuang Wu,** *Changes in Mutual Fund Advisory Contracts* **2 (Simon Graduate School of Business Administration, Working Paper No. FR 05-14, 2005), http://ssrn.com/abstract=841565 ("[H]igh asset growth increases the likelihood of a contract change."). Advisory "contract changes often shift the percentage fee up or down by more than a fourth, with fee increases and decreases roughly equally likely."** *Id.* **"[F]unds with superior market-adjusted performance are able to raise fees," yet "[r]ate decreases reflect economies of scale associated with growth."** *Id.* **at 6, 2.**

113   **Freeman & Brown,** *supra* **note 52, at 625 (using a sample of 2161 funds in 1999, with a total market value of $2.2 trillion, finding that "advisory and administrative costs decline as fund size increases, but with administrative costs declining much more rapidly"). The authors calculated that if advisory costs had declined by the same percentage as administrative costs, average advisory fees for funds with assets above $5 billion would have been 28 basis points, rather than 46 basis points. Thus, assuming equal economies of scale for advisory fees and administrative fees, the larger funds charge excess advisory fees of about $2.5 billion annually.** *Id.*

114   **Management firms charge retail mutual funds "systematically higher" advisory fees than they charge their pension fund clients, for essentially the same service. Freeman & Brown,** *supra* **note 52, at 628, 630–32 (analyzing fee data collected in 1999 from 36 public pension funds that had placed 220 equity portfolios under active management with outside investment advisers, representing $97.5 billion in assets, finding that comparable mutual funds pay about twice as much as the pension fund clients, with the difference more pronounced as the fund/portfolio size increases). The disparity has existed over time. A Wharton study conducted in 1962, looking at a sample of 54 management firms with both mutual fund clients and other clients, found that fee rates charged mutual funds were at least 50% higher in 39 out of the 54 cases, 200% higher in 24 of the cases, and 500% or more higher in 9 of the cases.** WHARTON SCHOOL OF FINANCE & COMMERCE, A STUDY OF MUTUAL FUNDS, H.R. REP. NO. 2274-87, at 489–94 (1962).

115   **Freeman & Brown,** *supra* **note 52, at 633. The findings are dramatic for largecapitalization funds, where mutual funds pay weighted average advisory fees of 52 basis points, compared to 21 basis points for comparable pension fund portfolios. The fee differential is further exacerbated in view of average fund size, with the average large-cap mutual fund ($2 billion) almost four times larger than the average pension fund portfolio ($555 million).** *Id.* **at 635. That is, management firms charge the average large cap mutual fund $10.4 million, while they charge the average pension fund portfolio $1.2 million—for essentially the same service.**

- Higher advisory fees do not buy better performance. High-fee funds under-perform low-fee funds—even before factoring in fees. Advisory fee levels, generally a percentage of fund total net assets, *increase* as a result of recent superior fund performance.[116]

- Actively managed mutual funds are more expensive than they appear. Most actively managed funds engage in shadow indexing, while charging fund investors for active management. On average, most of the variance between the fund's stated active managed assets and the fund's actual shadow indexed assets is explained by the fund's benchmark index.[117] Separating active assets from passive assets, the mean expense ratio for the active portion of the portfolio of actively managed large-cap equity mutual funds of "5.14% runs more than 500% higher than the published expense ratio of 0.77%."[118]

Board approval of loads

- Nearly two-thirds of equity funds impose distribution fees, as load charges paid directly by fund investors or as annual marketing fees paid pursuant to Rule 12b-1. The true cost of distribution fees to investors is hard to measure because "fund companies have developed distribution arrangements that differ in both the magnitude and timing of fees paid."[119]

- While 12b-1 fees (paid from fund assets) increase the fund's market share, there is "no evidence" current or new investors derive any benefit from 12b-1 fees.[120] Funds with 12b-1 fees have higher expense ratios and are more likely to fail. Fund investors pay for additional marketing, but garner no additional investment returns—a "dead weight cost."[121]

- The number of funds with 12b-1 fees is growing, as is the level of 12b- fees.[122] Increasingly, 12b-1 fees are charged in funds closed to new investors, "almost all of which are load funds."[123]

- Load funds, which directly charge investors for marketing expenses, do not out-perform no-load funds. Even before adjusting for loads in returns, no-load funds beat their load counterparts. When loads are figured in, no-

---

116   Warner & Wu, *supra* note 113, at 26–27. Also finding that advisory fee rates decrease when economies of scale exist and they are associated with growth. *Id.* at 6.

117   Ross M. Miller, *Measuring the True Cost of Active Management by Mutual Funds* 11 (Unpublished Working Paper, 2005), *available at* http://ssrn.com/abstract=746926.

118   *Id.* at 12.

119   Miles Livingston & Edward S. O'Neal, *The Cost of Mutual Fund Distribution Fees*, 21 J. FIN. RES. 205, 206 (1998). The study produced a "simple methodology" that expresses "present value of distribution costs as fraction of original investment for multiple-class fees" during any potential holding period, allowing direct comparison of the effect on investors of distribution fees for different sales arrangements. *Id.* at 214.

120   Ajay Khorana & Henri Servaes, *Conflicts of Interest and Competition in the Mutual Fund Industry* 1–2 (Unpublished Working Paper, 2004), *available at* http://ssrn.com/abstract=240596 (studying the period from 1979 to 1998, when mutual fund industry assets grew enormously, the number of active funds tripled, and the market share of each fund declined).

121   Stephen P. Ferris & Don M. Chance, *The Effect of 12b-1 Plans on Mutual Fund Expense Ratios: A Note*, 42 J. FIN. 1077, 1082 (1987) (describing 12b-1 fees as "a dead-weight cost"); Robert W. McLeod & D.K. Malhotra, *A Re-examination of the Effect of 12b-1 Plans on Mutual Fund Expense Ratios*, 72 J. FIN. RES. 231, 239 (1994) (stating that 12b-1 fees are "a dead weight cost" to fund investors that has been increasing over time); Antonio Apap & John M. Griffith, *The Impact of Expenses on Mutual Fund Performance*, 11 J. FIN. PLAN. 76, 80 (1998) (concluding that for variety of equity funds, 12b-1 fees do not add to funds' performance).

122   William P. Dukes, Philip C. English II & Sean M. Davis, *Mutual Fund Mortality, 12b-1 Fees, and the Net Expense Ratio*, 29 J. FIN. RES. 235, 236 (2006).

123   Todd Houge & Jay Wellman, *The Use and Abuse of Mutual Fund Expenses* 13 (Unpublished Working Paper, 2006), *available at* http://ssrn.com/abstract=880463.

load funds perform much better than load funds. And comparing load funds, there is no significant difference in performance between high-load funds and low-load funds even after adjusting for loads.[124]

- Load funds target less-knowledgeable investors and charge higher expenses. The average annual expense ratio of load equity funds has widened since the early 1990s and by 2000–2004 was 50 basis points higher than no-load equity funds.[125]

- In the 1990s, most funds with front-end loads added new share classes, which allowed investors instead to pay annual fees and/or back-end charges. Multiple-class funds attracted shorter-horizon investors, resulting in an increase in fund volatility and a significant drop in fund performance.[126]

- Expensive load funds, without minimum-balance requirements, are targeted at investors in less affluent, less educated, and ethnic minority neighborhoods—a kind of "predatory" money management.[127]

Board supervision of fund marketing

- Fund investors who purchase through brokers or financial advisors pay unjustified" higher costs. Broker customers are often directed to hard to- find funds, which charge substantially higher fees and provide lower

- risk-adjusted returns than directly placed funds. "[B]roker-channel funds exhibit no superior asset allocation. . . . While we cannot seem to locate tangible benefits delivered by brokers, we remain open to the possibility that substantial intangible benefits exist." [128]

- Fund families create the illusion of high-rated funds by merging low performing funds into high-performing funds—marketing the survivor's healthy past performance. Funds disappear at a rate of approximately 3.6% a year primarily because of multi-year poor performance.[129] The resulting "survivor bias" results in overstatement of fund family performance, by air-painting out below-average funds from the family portrait.[130]

- Fund boards rarely close funds to new investors, even when the fund has reached an optimal size. For actively managed funds, returns (both before and after fees and expenses) decline with lagged fund size. The relationship is most pronounced in funds that invest in small and illiquid stocks, where scale adversely affects liquidity.[131]

---

124   **Matthew R. Morey,** *Should You Carry the Load? A Comprehensive Analysis of Load and No-Load Mutual Fund Out-of-Sample Performance,* **27 J. BANKING FIN. 1245 (2003)** (using sample of funds free of survivorship bias, evaluating performance across different performance metrics and different ages and styles of funds; finding differences to be statistically significant at one percent level across different performance metrics).

125   **Houge & Wellman,** *supra* **note 124, at 3.**

126   **Vikram K. Nanda, Z. Jay Wang & Lu Zheng,** *The ABCs of Mutual Funds: A Natural Experiment on Fund Flows and Performance* **3 (Unpublished Working Paper, 2003),** *available at* **http://ssrn.com/abstract=510325.**

127   **Christopher J. Malloy & Ning Zhu,** *Mutual Fund Choices and Investor Demographics* **1 (Eur. Fin. Ass'n 2004 Maastricht Meetings, Working Paper No. 3377, 2004),** *available at* **http://papers.ssrn.com/sol3/papers.cfm?abstract_id=556225.**

128   **Daniel B. Bergstresser, John M.R. Chalmers & Peter Tufano,** *Assessing the Costs and Benefits of Brokers in the Mutual Fund Industry* **36 (Unpublished Working Paper, 2006),** *available at* **http://ssrn.com/abstract=616981. The paper found that investors buying brokered funds underperform direct-channel funds, even before deduction of distribution-related expenses.** *Id.*

129   **Mark M. Carhart, Jennifer N. Carpenter, Anthony W. Lynch & David K. Musto,** *Mutual Fund Survivorship,* **15 REV. FIN. STUD. 1439, 1443–45 (2002). "[The survivor bias is] 0.07% for one-year samples, but a significantly larger 1% for samples longer than 15 years."** *Id.* **at 1460.**

130   *Id.* **at 1439.**

131   **Joseph S. Chen, Harrison G. Hong, Ming Huang & Jeffrey D. Kubik,** *Does Fund Size Erode Mutual Fund Performance? The Role of Liquidity and Organization,* **94 AM. ECON. REV. 1276 (2004). The study found that even after adjusting returns by various performance benchmarks, fund performance "increases with the size of the other funds in the same family."** *Id.* **at 1293.**

- Funds with front-end loads have recently introduced additional share classes, "allowing investors to replace front-end loads with higher annual fees and/or back-end charges."[132] While increasing fund cash flows by attracting shorter-horizon investors, the result has been a significant drop in fund performance. In fact, fund performance drops and volatility rises as funds increase the proportion of short-horizon investors.[133]

Board supervision of fund investment strategies

- Morningstar ratings, on which fund investors irrationally rely, skew the behavior of fund managers. Funds that achieve high ratings tend to increase their risk levels, resulting in a "significant fall off" in performance as managers are unable to "load on momentum stock" after the fund receives the initial five-star rating.[134]

- Fund managers adapt their investment strategy in the last part of a calendar year according to their performance in the first part, in particular taking greater risk to keep a high Morningstar rating from the beginning of the year.[135]

- Annual trading costs for equity funds average 0.78% of fund assets. Trading costs are negatively related to fund returns, and there is no evidence that average trading costs are recovered in higher overall fund returns. Trading appears to have a greater drag on fund returns than turnover.[136]

- Fund over-trading often occurs because of the presence of short-term investors in long-term funds. Fund managers can use observable investor characteristics to predict investment horizons when investors open an account. The pooling in the same fund of long-term investors and short-term investors costs long-term investors 0.51% in foregone annual returns.[137]

- Larger fund families aggressively market their "winning" funds (the previous year's best performers) and allocate extra manager resources to these funds.[138] In fact, an investment strategy that purchases a fund family's past-year winners and shorts its past-year losers produces abnormal positive returns. The strategy is particularly successful in larger fund families, suggesting the latitude of larger families to allocate resources unevenly between funds.[139]

- Fund families strategically allocate performance across member funds to favor those more likely to generate future inflows and higher fee income. Strategic cross-fund subsidization of "high" funds at the expense of "low" funds is between 6 to 28 basis points of extra net-of style performance per month.[140] This preferential allocation occurs

---

132   **Nanda, Wang & Zheng**, *supra* **note 127, at 1.**

133   *Id.* **at 22.**

134   **Matthew R. Morey**, *The Kiss of Death: A 5-Star Morningstar Mutual Fund Rating*, **3 J. INV. MGMT. 41 (2005) (examining effect 5-star Morningstar mutual fund rating has on fund performance, strategy, risk-taking, expenses, and portfolio turnover during three-year period after initial 5-star rating; findings "robust across different performance measures and different samples of funds").**

135   **Alexei P. Goriaev, Frederic Albert Palomino & Andrea Prat**, *Mutual Fund Tournament: Risk Taking Incentives Induced by Ranking Objectives* **(Ctr. for Econ. Policy Research Discussion Paper No. 2794, 2004),** *available at* **http://ssrn.com/abstract=270304.**

136   **John M.R. Chalmers, Roger M. Edelen & Gregory B. Kadlec**, *An Analysis Of Mutual Fund Trading Costs* **(Unpublished Working Paper, 1999),** *available at* **http://ssrn.com/abstract= 195849.**

137   *See* **Woodrow T. Johnson**, *Predictable Investment Horizons and Wealth Transfers among Mutual Fund Shareholders*, **59 J. FIN. 1979, 2012 (2004).**

138   *See* **Donald W. Glazer**, *A Study of Mutual Fund Complexes*, **119 U. PA. L. REV. 205, 228 (1970) (finding investors are more concerned with the relative performance of aggressive mutual funds).**

139   **Ilan Guedj & Jannette Papastaikoudi**, *Can Mutual Fund Families Affect the Performance of Their Funds?* **24 (Unpublished Working Paper, 2003),** *available at* **http://ssrn.com/abstract=467282 (study of funds in large fund families).**

140   **José-Miguel Gaspar, Massimo Massa & Pedro P. Matos**, *Favoritism in Mutual Fund Families? Evidence on Strategic Cross-Fund Subsidization*, **61 J. FIN. 73, 102 (2006),** *available at* **http://ssrn.com/abstract=557078.**

with respect to IPO deals and opposite trades (sometimes actual cross trading) among "high" and "low value" funds in the same fund complex.[141]

- Fund boards with a greater proportion of independent directors seem to supervise the management firm more diligently than low-proportion funds. Fund performance and the likelihood of replacing underperforming fund managers increases as the proportion of independent directors increases.[142]

2. Empirical Data on Investor/Market Effectiveness

Not only does the finance literature raise doubts about fund governance, it also reveals the investor market to be informationally inefficient—the same finding that motivated the 1940 Act and its outsourcing of fund supervision to the fund board.[143] Recent studies show fund investors continue to lack the investment acumen, relevant information, and ability to protect their own interests.[144] The notion, powerful in theory, that mutual fund investors can discipline wayward management firms by exercising their easy "entry/exit" rights has proved mostly empty in practice. Study after study makes clear that most fund investors are unable to fend for themselves.[145]

Investor response to fund fees

- Investors are often ignorant of expenses charged by their funds. According to a survey of fund investors, fewer than 20% could estimate expenses for the largest fund they held.[146] Even sophisticated fund investors lack a good understanding of the historical returns of their fund investments.[147]

- Investors are often unaware that higher fund expenses are a drag on fund performance. In one survey, about 20% of surveyed investors believed that high-fee funds produced better results; more than 60% believed funds with higher

---

141   *Id.*

142   **Bill Ding & Russ R. Wermers**, *Mutual Fund Performance and Governance Structure: The Role of Portfolio Managers and Boards of Directors* **4 (Unpublished Working Paper, 2005)**, *available at* **http://ssrn.com/abstract=687273 (performing a comprehensive analysis of the relationship between performance and governance structure of open-end, domestic-equity mutual funds from 1985–2002).**

143   **From the beginning, it has been understood that disclosure to investors is not enough. As SEC Commissioner Robert Healy testified in the hearings on the Investment Company Act, "there are certain practices that have happened in connection with investment companies that I think everybody agrees . . . ought to be stopped, and they cannot be stopped by mere disclosure." SEC Staff Report on Independent Chair,** *supra* **note 27, at 28 n.14.**

144   *See generally,* **Stephen Choi**, *Regulating Investors Not Issuers: A Market Based Proposal*, **88 CAL. L. REV. 279 (2000) (proposing a system regulating investors based on their sophistication).**

145   **Reviewing the academic literature, the General Accounting Office came essentially to the same conclusion. GAO Mutual Fund Disclosure Report,** *supra* **note 105, at 7, 76 ("[Academic studies] indicated that the information currently provided does not sufficiently make investors aware of the level of fees they pay," and some academic researchers and others "saw problems with the fee disclosures [by mutual funds].").**

146   **Gordon J. Alexander, Jonathan D. Jones & Peter J. Nigro**, *Mutual Fund Shareholders: Characteristics, Investment Knowledge, and Sources of Information*, **7 FIN. SERV. REV. 301, 309 (1998) (joint study of fund shareholders conducted by the Office of the Comptroller of the Currency and the SEC),** *summarized in* **Freeman & Brown,** *supra* **note 52, at 665.**

147   *See generally* **Dan A. Moore, Terri R. Kurtzberg, Craig R. Fox & Max H. Bazerman**, *Positive Illusions and Forecasting Errors in Mutual Fund Investment Decisions*, **79 ORG. BEHAV. & HUMAN DEC. PROCESSES 95 (1999).**

expenses produced average results; and fewer than 16% believed higher expenses led to lower than average returns.[148] In another survey, 84% of respondents believed that higher fund expenses correlate with higher fund performance.[149]

- Fund investors are relatively insensitive to advisory fees, paying some attention when they buy, but not as they hold. Funds that reduce their fees gain market share, but only if their fees were above average to start. Low-cost funds do not lose market share by charging higher fees.[150]

- Fund investors have become more sensitive to front-end loads and commissions, but remain insensitive to operating expenses. Over the last 30 years, front-end loads (as well as commissions charged by brokerage firms) have had a consistently negative relation to fund flows.[151] There is no relation (or even a perverse positive relation) between operating expenses and fund flows. Investors purchase "funds that attract their attention through advertising and distribution. . . . mutual fund advertising works."[152]

- In relatively homogenous fund sectors, such as S&P index funds, investors find it difficult to identify bargains. Investors tend to go with recognized "name brands" based on fund age and family size, with a marked shift in sector assets to more expensive (often new entry) funds.[153]

Investor response to market changes

- Fund investors over-trade. In turn, investor short-termism drives the short investment horizons of fund managers, not the other way around.[154]

- Fund investors systematically engage in a "buy high, sell low" trading strategy. Monthly data from 1984-2003 show a negative relationship between aggregate net flows into and out of the funds and the returns of the funds in subsequent periods.[155] As a result, fund investors realize lower long-term accumulated return than the "long-term accumulated return on a 'buy and hold' position in these funds."[156]

- Fund investors over-react to market volatility—the "grass is greener" phenomenon. Stock fund investors withdraw assets in response to market volatility—both concurrently and based on past semi-annual and annual volatility.[157] Fund

---

148   *See* **Alexander, Jones & Nigro,** *supra* **note 147, at 310.**

149   *See* **Neil Weinberg,** *Fund Managers Know Best: As Corporations are Fessing Up to Investors, Mutual Funds Still Gloss Over Costs, Hide Top-Dog Pay and Keep Secret How They Cope When Self-Interest Conflicts With Duty,* **FORBES, Oct. 14, 2002, at 220.**

150   **Khorana & Servaes,** *supra* **note 121, at 3–4.**

151   **Brad M. Barber, Terrance Odean & Zheng Lu,** *Out of Sight, Out of Mind: The Effects of Expenses on Mutual Fund Flows,* **78 J. BUS. 2095, 2097 (2005).**

152   *Id.* **at 2099.**

153   **Ali Hortacsu & Chad Syverson,** *Product Differentiation, Search Costs, and Competition in the Mutual Fund Industry: A Case Study of S&P 500 Index Funds,* **119 QUARTERLY J. ECON. 403 (2004). Fund investors also have difficulty identifying the advantage of index investing.** *See* **Moore, Kurtzberg, Fox & Bazerman,** *supra* **note 148, at 96 (hypothesizing that common traits of over-optimism and framing of choices against past performance contribute significantly to investors eschewing index funds, which over time outperform actively-managed funds).**

154   **Li Jin,** *How Does Investor Short-termism Affect Mutual Fund Manager Short-termism* **2 (Unpublished Working Paper, 2005),** *available at* **http://ssrn.com/abstract=675262.**

155   **Oded Braverman,** *Shmuel Kandel & Avi Wohl, The (Bad?) Timing of Mutual Fund Investors* **5 (Unpublished Working Paper, 2005),** *available at* **http://ssrn.com/abstract=795146.**

156   *Id.*

157   **Dengpan Luo,** *Market Volatility and Mutual Fund Cash Flows* **3–4 (Yale ICF Working Paper No. 03-21, 2003),** *available at* **http://ssrn.com/abstract=418360. In the period from 1984– 1998, the paper found different results for bond fund investors, who did not respond to past stock market volatility at the aggregate level.** *See id.* **at 7–8.**

investors over-react both to downside volatility and upside volatility. Stock fund flows, in turn, contribute to   market volatility—as "noisy traders" destabilize the overall stock market.[158]

- Fund investors follow the crowd. Net aggregate equity fund flows typically track general investor sentiment. Moreover, there is a selfreinforcing aspect to investor sentiment as higher equity fund flows induce newsletter writers to become more bullish.[159]

Investor response to past performance

- Fund investors respond to the heuristic "past is prologue."[160] Past performance is at best a weak predictor for anticipating fund performance. While one-star and two-star Morningstar ratings generally predict relatively poor future performance, Morningstar's five-star funds generally do not outperform four-star and three-star funds.[161] In fact, a 5-star Morningstar rating may be a "kiss of death."[162] Three years after a fund receives its initial 5-star rating, fund performance severely falls off across different performance measures and different samples of funds.[163]

- Fund directors, contrary to anecdotal evidence, often hold shares in the funds they oversee.[164] But there is evidence that directors chase performance in their ownership choices, just like other fund investors.[165]

- The "past is prologue" mentality extends to the financial press. Fund rankings by the leading financial publications (Barron's, Business Week, and Forbes) based on past performance do not predict superior future performance.[166] Most ranked funds (65%) have lower performance in the post-ranking period compared to the pre-ranking period.[167]

---

158   *Id.* at 8.

159   **Daniel C. Indro,** *Does Mutual Fund Flow Reflect Investor Sentiment?*, **5 J. BEHAV. FIN. 105, 112 (2004) (using weekly flow data and sentiment indicators from the American Association of Individual Investors and Investors Intelligence).**

160   **The heuristic, valuable in other consumer activities, reflects the likelihood that fund performance (like that of any randomly constructed stock portfolio) regresses to the mean. This is not true for other consumer goods. For example, a five-star automobile safety crash rating (based on the performance of a sample car in a controlled crash test) is a useful predictor that other cars of the same model and year will perform well in real-life crashes.** *See* **Consumer Reports, Annual Auto Issue: Safety Feature Comparison 35–38 (Apr. 2006), http://www.consumerreports.org/cro/index.htm.**

161   **Christopher R. Blake & Matthew R. Morey,** *Morningstar Ratings and Mutual Fund Performance* **20–21 (Unpublished Working Paper, 1999),** *available at* **http://ssrn.com/abstract=168668 (using data set free of survivorship bias and adjusted for load fees). Most studies confirm this result.** *See, e.g.*, **Andrea Frazzini & Owen A. Lamont,** *Dumb Money: Mutual Fund Flows and the Cross-Section of Stock Returns* **(NBER Working Paper No. W11526, 2005),** *available at* **http://ssrn.com/abstract=776014 (concluding that fund flows are "dumb money" as heavy fund demand predicts low future returns at long horizons). But some studies come to contrary results.** *See, e.g.*, **Russ R. Wermers,** *Is Money Really 'Smart'? New Evidence on the Relation Between Mutual Fund Flows, Manager Behavior, and Performance Persistence* **3 (Unpublished Working Paper, 2003),** *available at* **http://ssrn.com/abstract=414420 (finding that when consumers invest heavily in last year's winning funds, managers of these winners invest these inflows in momentum stocks to continue to outperform other funds for at least two years following the ranking year).**

162   **Morey,** *supra* **note 135, at 41.**

163   *Id.* **at 49–50.**

164   **Qi Chen, Itay Goldestein & Wei Jiang,** *Directors' Ownership in the U.S. Mutual Fund Industry* **2 (Unpublished Working Paper, 2006),** *available at* **http://ssrn.com/abstract=713462.**

165   *Id.* **at 38.**

166   **Miranda L. Detzler,** *The Value of Mutual Fund Rankings to the Individual Investor* **4 (Unpublished Working Paper, 1999),** *available at* **http://ssrn.com/abstract=170851 (looking at 757 funds that were ranked between 1993–1995; finding that ranked funds had higher excess returns compared to peer funds during the pre-ranking period, but similar excess returns in the postranking period; finding also that ranked funds had higher risk, measured by standard deviations, in both the pre- and post-ranking periods).**

167   *See* **Miranda L. Detzler,** *The Value of Mutual Fund Rankings to the Individual Investor*, **8 J. BUS. & ECON. STUD. 48, 50 (2002).**

Investor response to scandals

- Response by fund investors to mutual fund scandals has been mixed. Funds affected by scandals experience significantly greater outflow of assets, with the outflow greater the more severe the scandal (as measured by size of regulatory settlement/fine, press coverage, and filing of formal charges). Outflows are greater where the scandal involved a penalized entity, as opposed to individual wrongdoers no longer associated with the fund. But fund scandals first discovered by the SEC do not result in significant outflows. Lastly, strengthened corporate governance controls have no impact on the amount of outflows from a scandal fund.[168]

C. EVALUATION OF DATA

The data paint a dismal picture of fund board performance. Fund boards have failed in their function to negotiate management fees. In fact, the recent slowing growth of *weighted average fees* (compared to the continuing growth in *unweighted average fees*) highlights the inability of fund boards to lower fees, even as some fund investors have moved to lower-cost funds. That is, fund boards have been less effective in lowering fund fees than fund investors. Even worse than their performance on negotiating management fees, fund boards have achieved nothing for their investors by approving loads—especially 12b-1 fees.

The data tell an equally sad story about fund investors. Fund investors are often ignorant of fund expenses and unaware of their relation to performance. They suffer from cognitive biases, for example that "past is prologue"—a belief they share with the financial press and even fund managers. Fund design and marketing pander to this belief and overemphasize high Morningstar ratings, which studies show represent a statistical guarantee the fund will regress to the mean. Many fund investors shun index funds, even though they are a proven long-term investment vehicle. Instead, they engage in pathological "buy high, sell low" trading strategies that over-optimistically aim to out-perform the market. Fund managers mirror (or induce) a "grass is greener" bias in their over-trading of portfolio assets and widespread belief that they too can beat the market. Not everyone can be above average.

Even those studies that suggest independent directors provide some value—that is, that fund performance and the likelihood of replacing underperforming fund managers increases as the proportion of independent directors rises—do not establish a causal relationship between board independence and fund results. Instead, it seems more likely that investor friendly management firms (i.e., those that adopt strategies of low fees, long-term investment policies, responsiveness to failed investment strategies, and investor-appropriate marketing) are more likely to have truly independent directors advising on these matters. In fact, the studies that suggest funds with independent chairs out-perform their management-chaired counterparts lead only to the

---

168   **Stephen J. Choi & Marcel Kahan,** *The Market Penalty for Mutual Fund Scandals* **9, 24–26 (NYU, Law and Economics Research Paper No. 06-07, 2006),** *available at* **http://ssrn.com/abstract=877896 (reviewing mutual fund scandals from 1994–2004).**

conclusion that management firms focused on their own profits under-perform firms with an investor focus.[169]

III. OPTIONS FOR REFORM

Can the fund board be rehabilitated? The mutual fund industry has strong reasons to resist having the board structure dismantled. Outsourcing of regulatory supervision to an internal monitor gives the industry great freedom—particularly when compared to the alternative of external regulation.[170] In areas of fund management subject to board oversight, management firms have the discretion to test the limits of the market.

Not surprisingly, there is no impetus for fundamental reform. The mutual fund industry is quite pleased with the fund board and the results it has produced. Fund directors, without questioning their own value, have supported calls for greater independence and greater role clarity. The SEC willingly parrots the mantra that the fund board is an essential component of fund regulation, particularly since the job falls outside the agency. Perhaps the only mutual fund constituents that might have reservations about the fund board—fund investors—are mostly unaware that there is a fund board or that it has failed them.

After surveying the data on the higher investment advisory fees charged mutual funds compared to pension plans, Professors Freeman and Brown concluded:

> The fund industry is over-regulated and under-policed. The absence of a strong corrective influence should not be surprising. Those in control of an industry boasting over $7 trillion in liquid assets can afford superb lawyers, lobbyists, and public relations specialists. . . . Congress has not shown interest in improving investors' remedies and cannot be counted on to alter the way the fund industry chooses to conduct itself. The SEC generally has contented itself with presenting proposals destined to have little impact on the way most mutual funds do business.[171]

To the extent that some mutual funds have shown a "reform mentality"—lowering management fees, offering life-cycle funds intended to encourage proven long-term investment strategies, and cautioning investors against over-trading—the new attitudes seem driven more by greater investor sophistication than by awakened fund boards. The industry recognizes the scandal-

---

169   In fact, the SEC has been unable to point to any evidence that greater board independence has been effective under the SEC's exemptive rules. Bullard, *Comments on Corporate Governance*, *supra* note 47, at 1106. Indeed, there is "no evidence that the Commission knows whether the independent directors have been effective in the context of the operation of the exemptive rules . . . ," and there is "no evidence that the Commission knows if the exemptive rules themselves have been effective in protecting investors." *Id.* at 1096.

170   Wang, *supra* note 3, at 958–59.

171   Freeman & Brown, *supra* note 52, at 641–42 (citations omitted).

induced skepticism about its product and has every reason to show that its house is in order and that the current regulatory structure is adequate.

But given the long-standing failure of the fund board and the continuing inability of investors to discipline industry excess, the time is ripe for a fundamental re-appraisal of the fund board.

A. ALTERNATIVES TO BOARD-CENTRIC STRUCTURES

The recent mutual fund scandals and a slowing stock market have led many to question the efficacy of the fund board. Reform proposals, most of which seek to create additional structures to compensate for the board's failure, have become a cottage industry.

Consider some recent proposals:

New SRO. Some reformers have proposed a new self-regulatory organization to oversee mutual funds, thus augmenting fund boards and taking pressure off limited SEC resources. Rather than the current reliance on internal mechanisms, the SRO could engage in more focused rule making, with the SEC (and state attorneys general) using their enforcement powers as a "residual mechanism."[172]

New oversight board. Others have suggested a Mutual Fund Oversight Board, modeled on the Public Company Accounting Oversight Board, which would be responsible for (and only for) establishing uniform minimum standards for fund governance. The new board would perform an investigative and rule-making function, providing the flexibility that the SEC lacks to keep standards current.[173]

New "expert" directors. Others would seek to make the fund board more independent and qualified by mandating that the board include a certified financial analyst (CFA)[174]—much

---

172   Joel Seligman, *Should Investment Companies Be Subject to a New Statutory Self-Regulatory Organization?*, **83 WASH. U. L.Q.** **1115, 1126 (2005) (arguing for consideration of self-regulatory organization to oversee mutual funds).**

173   *Review of Mutual Fund Industry Investigations: Hearing Before the S. Comm. on Banking, Housing, and Urban Affairs,* **108th Cong. 2 (2004) (statement of Mercer Bullard, President and Founder, Fund Democracy, Inc.).** *See generally* **Patrick McGeehan,** *With Critics at the Door, Funds Propose Cleaning Own House,* **N.Y. TIMES, Oct. 31, 2003, at C1 (discussing critics' view of the current system and the need for reform).** *See* **Mutual Fund Investor Protection Act of 2003, S. 1958, 108th Cong. § 201 (2003) (Senator John Kerry proposed a bill which would have created a Mutual Oversight Board).**

174   **Tobe,** *supra* **note 19, at 28 (suggesting CFA, a designation awarded by the Association for Investment Management and Research; also pointing to studies showing that public pension plans with CFA officers have lower fees).**

like the Sarbanes-Oxley requirement of a financial expert on the audit committee of public companies.[175] The CFA would presumably be better able to recognize excessive fund fees.[176]

Invigorate mutual fund litigation. Others would call on courts to make derivative litigation a "serviceable mechanism for serious judicial review in cases of fiduciary breach."[177] Given the deficiencies of investor market oversight, courts should look at the merits of fund over-pricing.

More investor-usable disclosure. Others have urged the SEC to mandate greater disclosure of fund expenses—as is required in other financial service industries and consumer markets. Some would require individualized disclosure in account statements that show actual fund expenses, with a break down of fees and other expenses.[178] Some would require that the statements also include how the actual expenses compared with industry ranges and averages.[179]

But others—mostly practicing lawyers—doubt whether the board can be salvaged. Some assert that the SEC's initiatives to buttress board independence are of "questionable efficacy" and implicitly conclude that the board cannot fulfill its watchdog function.[180] A few have called for the fund board to be eliminated, describing it as "paraphernalia."[181] As one reform proponent pointed out a fund without directors would not make "an awful lot of difference and would be cheaper to operate."[182]

Even the SEC has imagined mutual funds without directors. In a 1992 study the SEC staff considered a board-less fund structure, called a unitary investment fund (UIF), as part a comprehensive review of existing fund governance.[183] The concept was a mutual fund that would be treated as a proprietary financial product sold by a sponsor and governed by the terms of a trust indenture. As proposed, the UIF would have a corporate trustee (the sponsor/management firm) that would sell interests in the trust to investors. The trust indenture would spell out fundamental

175   *See* **Sarbanes-Oxley Act § 407, 15 U.S.C. § 7265 (Supp. II 2002).**

176   **Tobe,** *supra* **note 19, at 28.**

177   **Langevoort,** *supra* **note 28, at 1043.**

178   *See* **U.S. Gen. Accounting Office, Mutual Fund Fees Additional Disclosure Could Encourage Price Competition 97–98 (2000), http://www.gao.gov/archive/2000/gg00126.pdf (proposing disclosure of total dollar amount of expenses in quarterly statements); Freeman & Brown,** *supra* **note 52, at 669–670 (proposing that mutual funds be required to itemize their different fund expenses, such as: advisory fees, operating costs, and trading costs).**

179   *See* **Cox & Payne,** *supra* **note 62, at 929. The proposal is similar to one considered by the SEC staff in 1992.** *See* **SEC Staff Report Protecting Investors,** *supra* **note 25, at 337 (outlining Unified Fee Investment Company (UFIC), which would have a simplified fee computed as a percentage of fund assets, permitting ready comparison to other similar funds; the fee would cover all fund expenses other than extraordinary expenses and brokerage commissions on the fund's own transactions).**

180   **Martin Lybecker,** *Enhanced Governance for Mutual Funds: A Flawed Concept that Deserves Serious Reconsideration,* **83 WASH U. L.Q. 1045, 1085–87 (2005).**

181   **Phillips,** *supra* **note 23, at 903.**

182   **Karen Damato, David Reilly & Karen Richardson,** *Do Mutual Funds Really Need Directors?,* **WALL ST. J., June 7, 2004, at R1 (reporting comments of Sheldon Jacobs, editor of the No-Load Investor newsletter).**

183   **SEC Staff Report Protecting Investors,** *supra* **note 25, at 283–84. The idea of a UIF, which was first floated by Stephen West of Sullivan & Cromwell, led to the SEC requesting public comment on the UIF in 1982. Advance Notice and Request for Comment on Mutual Fund Governance, 47 Fed. Reg. 56,509 (Dec. 10, 1982).**

investment policies and the management fee, and could be changed only with some difficulty. A single management fee would cover all fund-related expenses and would be subject to a statutory maximum. The UIF would have no board of directors or shareholder voting, nor would there be judicial review of fund fees. The 1940 Act prohibitions against self-dealing transactions would apply, without exception.[184]

Ultimately, the staff rejected the UIF concept as not offering an adequate substitute for board review of fees and other fund operations. The SEC staff seemed unwilling to imagine a model without an independent monitor. Instead, the staff concluded that the board-centric governance structure is fundamentally "sound" and should be retained.[185]

But the idea of a board-less mutual fund is not far-fetched. In fact, the fastest-growing mutual funds in the United States—private hedge funds and some exchange traded funds organized as unit trusts—do not have board structures.[186] Like registered mutual funds, these financial intermediaries pool money that investors entrust to professional managers to make investments on their behalf. Fee setting is a matter of contract, and regulatory compliance is an internal responsibility of the management firm.

Even though hedge funds are subject to nearly identical internal conflicts as *registered* mutual funds, the idea of a fund board to ensure hedge fund compliance and to regulate management activities were not even considered in the recent SEC rule-making to require hedge fund registration.[187] Instead, the SEC rules (which were recently invalidated) would have required that hedge funds registered with the SEC have a compliance officer.[188] The compliance officer, unlike the mutual fund board, would have no authority to validate self-interested activities of the fund manager. The compliance officer—whose functions were to parallel those performed by in-house legal departments and compliance offices in brokerage firms, banks and insurance companies—would have simply been charged with establishing control systems to ensure legal compliance.

The SEC explained the compliance officer's function in much the same terms as it has described the mutual fund board:

---

184   *See* **Wang**, *supra* **note 3, at 1024–25 (summarizing UIF proposal).**

185   *See* **SEC Staff Report Protecting Investors**, *supra* **note 25, at 283.**

186   **Insurance separate accounts are also exempt from the board requirements. The performance of equity funds managed by insurance companies gives reason to pause. In a recent study, insurance funds under perform non-insurance peers by more than 1% in average annual returns. Perhaps, as speculated by the authors of the study, this is due to insurance industry conservatism or lack of investor-driven incentives to pursue superior performance. Or perhaps, a possibility not mentioned by the authors, the weak performance is due to the absence of a fund board.** *See* **Xuanjuan Chen, Tong Yao & Tong Yu,** *Prudent Man or Agency Problem? On the Performance of Insurance Mutual Funds* **1–3 (Aug. 28, 2004),** *available at* **http://ssrn.com/abstract=589801.**

187   **Registration Under the Advisers Act of Certain Hedge Fund Advisers, 69 Fed. Reg. 72,054 (Dec. 10, 2004) (to be codified at 17 C.F.R. pts. 275 and 279),** *invalidated by* **Goldstein v. SEC, 451 F.3d 873 (D.C. Cir. 2006).**

188   *See* **Investment Advisors Act of 1940, 17 C.F.R. § 275.206(4)-7 (2006),** *invalidated by* **Goldstein v. SEC, 451 F.3d at 874.**

> Hedge fund advisers . . . must develop and implement a compliance infrastructure. . . . Our examination staff resources are limited, and we cannot be at the office of every adviser at all times. Compliance officers serve as the front line watch for violations of securities laws, and provide protection against conflicts of interests.[189]

For hedge funds, external regulatory oversight ultimately resides with the SEC under its powers to regulate securities fraud and the fiduciary responsibilities of investment advisers under federal and state law, as well as with investors through contractual protections and their ability to "enter" and "exit" the fund.

B. MUTUAL FUND STRUCTURES OUTSIDE OF THE UNITED STATES

Mutual fund boards are largely a U.S. phenomenon. Most other countries treat mutual funds as an investment "product" offered by investment management firms. The regulatory focus elsewhere is on the management firm, not the investment pool or its legal supervisor. Regulation of product terms (fees and management services), custodial responsibilities, and fund marketing is a matter of government agency supervision, with residual oversight by self-regulatory organizations and courts under a regime of fiduciary duties that fall on the management firm.

Consider the regulation of mutual funds in Germany, Japan and Britain. In Germany mutual funds are not separate entities, but instead segregated asset pools managed by an investment management firm that is regulated by the German Federal Banking Commission (BAKred).[190] Investors enter into a contract with the management firm and acquire participatory units in the segregated assets, with the management firm obligated to repurchase the units if redeemed by the investor. The assets must be kept with a custodian bank, which is obligated to supervise the management firm on behalf of fund investors. Thus, protection of fund investors in Germany is primarily the responsibility of the management firm, which has a statutory duty to act in the interests of fund investors. The management firm, in turn, is supervised by the custodian bank and the BAKred, both of which may bring suit against the management firm for failures to act. The BAKred may dismiss a fund manager who is unfit professionally or who violates the mutual fund rules.

In Japan mutual funds exist as investment trusts, with a trustee that must be a trust company or bank.[191] The trustee enters into a "contract of trust" with an investment trust management company, which must be licensed and is subject to statutory standards. The management company gives advice with respect to trust assets and has fiduciary duties in relation to the assets, though not necessarily to fund investors. The trustee keeps custody and administers the trust assets. Fund

---

189   *See* **Registration Under the Advisers Act of Certain Hedge Fund Advisers, 69 Fed. Reg. at 72,063.**

190   **Wang,** *supra* **note 3, at 951. The BAKred, among other things, specifies the qualifications for the mandatory managing directors of the management firm.** *Id.* **at 951–52.**

191   *Id.* **at 953–55.**

investors have beneficial interests in the trust. The Ministry of Finance regulates the trustee, as well as the terms of the trust contract entered into with the management company. The management company is subject to the rules of a selfregulatory group, the Investment Trust Association.

In Britain mutual funds are unit trusts, constituted under trust law.[192] The trustee contracts with a manager (a firm or individual) that manages the trust assets, though the trustee retains custody and control of the assets. The trustee oversees the manager, though the manager typically appoints the trustee. To qualify as an authorized unit trust, the trust must comply with detailed regulations that cover its constitution, the power and duties of the trustee and manager, investment and borrowing powers, and pricing and valuation. The trustee and manager are both subject to regulation by selfregulating organizations. Government oversight comes from the Department of Trade and Industry, which has delegated most of its powers to the non-governmental Securities and Investment Board.

In addition, since 1997 mutual funds in the United Kingdom can be operated as open-ended investment companies (OEICs), which can be marketed elsewhere in the European Union.[193] An OEIC is established under company law rather than trust law. The OEIC owns the underlying assets and investors own shares that reflect their interests in those assets.

The OEIC must have a board, though the only board member required is the authorized fund manager. Although independent directors are permitted, in practice nearly all OEIC boards are comprised of the manager alone. In addition, there must be a depository who has the same responsibilities for custody and oversight that the trustee has in the unit trust.

OEICs were designed to replicate the characteristics of unit trusts but with a corporate structure. For all practical purposes, the two are identical from the investor's standpoint. The OEIC provides a vehicle recognized in continental Europe; there were no other advantages seen to the corporate form. In both the OEIC and unit trust, the authorized fund manager makes the day-to-day investment decisions of the fund, prices portfolio assets, and maintains financial records. The role of the trustee and the depository are essentially identical, to safeguard portfolio assets, oversee the manager's activities, and ensure compliance with FSA rules. FSA regulation is the cornerstone of investor protection in the United Kingdom.

Investors in each country have, at best, a minimal role in fund governance. In Germany and Japan, investors have no voting rights.[194] In the United Kingdom, investors of unit trusts can vote on only four matters: changing the trust deed, approving departures from stated investment policy, removing the manager, and approving trust mergers.[195]

---

192   *Id.* at 955–56.

193   American Enterprise Institute, The Regulation and Structure of Collective Investment Vehicles Outside the United States (May 2006), http://www.aei.org/events/filter.all,eventID.1318/summary.asp# (summary of a presentation by Richard Saunders, Chief Executive of U.K. Investment Management Association).

194   Wang, *supra* note 3, at 962.

195   *Id.*

The "product" structure, compared to the "board" structure, of mutual fund regulation makes clear that investors are purchasing services from an investment management firm. The buck stops with the government regulator, who has collateral support from courts that enforce the fiduciary duties of the management firm and (in some countries) from self-regulatory organizations that set standards of professional conduct.

IV. CONCLUSION

At the time of the 1940 Act, it was inconceivable that the fund board would oversee fund families with hundreds of different funds, spanning the full range of modern investment styles, some with over $1 trillion in assets under management. Equally unimaginable was the reality that mutual funds would become the primary investment vehicle for private retirement savings—surpassing company pension plans, bank accounts, and brokerage investments. And still more far-fetched was the likelihood, or so it seems, that mutual funds would supplant or even absorb the federal social security system as the funding vehicle for retirement income.

Regulatory outsourcing was an innovation of the 1940 Act—in marked contrast to the multi-faceted regulatory approach applied to public offerings under the 1933 Act and the nod to self-regulation of securities firms and stock exchanges under the 1934 Act. Rather than external supervision by the SEC or a self-regulatory organization (none existed), Congress delegated supervision to an internal regulator.

At best, the mutual fund board is an anachronism, a throw back to the time that the mutual fund was seen as an investment holding company (on the model of Berkshire-Hathaway) and the fund board a servant of investor interests. But the board suffers from fundamental structural flaws. Independent directors are neither independent of the management firm nor truly capable of being directors. They are selected by the management firm, rely on it for information and direction, and are paid (sometimes handsomely) not according to the results for fund investors, but based on currying continuing favor with the firm they are supposed to supervise. They are effectively limited in their power to fire the management firm, to revamp the business or sell it to outside buyers, or to enter into tough negotiations on behalf of fund investors.

The evidence bears out the fund board's inherent weakness and leads to the unavoidable conclusion that internal regulation cannot but fail. In a market that lacks effective arbitrage mechanisms to bring fund expenses into line, the board has no effective means to truly regulate management fees and ensure that fund marketing is in the interests of fund investors. Not surprisingly, as the mutual fund industry has exploded in size, and during a period of unparalleled advances in computer and telecommunications technology, the economies of scale and operational efficiencies have rebounded to the benefit of management firms, not fund investors. Likewise, fund boards have approved loads and marketing fees that increase market share, thus boosting fees for the management firm, but without any benefit for fund investors. Rather than focusing fund marketing on investor education, the fund board has permitted advertising that exploits the informational defects and cognitive foibles of fund investors.

It is remarkable that in an industry widely described as heavily regulated, the board-centric structure faces so little accountability. Each of the potential sources of board monitoring—the SEC, federal courts, state courts—has adopted the attitude that somebody is doing the job. The

SEC ultimately assumes that fund investors acting in markets will discipline wayward boards; the federal courts defer to the investor market and the regulatory function of the SEC; and state courts apply the business judgment rule, which assumes that markets are more discerning than judges.

At worst the fund board creates an illusion of investor protection. It allows the industry to tell the appealing story (however false) that the board serves as a "watchdog" against internal malfeasance, while fund investors exercise their powerful "entry/exit" rights to discipline management firm over-charging, over-trading, and over-marketing. The very existence of an internal monitor may actually be counter-productive. Rather than constraining management excesses, the presence of the supposedly independent board may actually embolden management firms to disregard their responsibility to fund investors, on the glib belief that the board performs its functions. Behavioral studies show that fiduciaries led to believe that someone else is protecting the interests of their beneficiaries tend to minimize and slacken their own fiduciary performance.[196] A lackadaisical watchdog may be worse than no watchdog at all.

Look again there.

---

[196]   **Daylian M. Cain, George Loewenstein & Don A. Moore,** *The Dirt on Coming Clean: The Perverse Effects of Disclosing Conflicts of Interest,* **34 J. LEGAL STUD. 1, 9 (2005) (finding that when subjects asked to guess the amount of money in a jar, with the help of an "adviser" who had disclosed conflicting interests, the subjects were more likely to trust the adviser on the theory disclosure evidences good faith, and the adviser feels greater moral freedom to act selfishly on the theory the subject has been put on notice).**

Appendix B

Glossary of Commonly Used Mutual Fund Terms

Account: A mutual fund account or open account. It reflects the record of investments, together with reinvestments of distributions and/or withdrawals and charges; an open account is open to further investment.

Acquisition Cost: The load, or sales commission charged.

Adjustable Rate Mortgage Fund: A fund that invests in adjustable rate mortgage (ARM) securities issued and guaranteed by the U.S. government or its agencies. These funds are designed for conservative, income-oriented investors who are willing to accept minimal fluctuations in the funds' share prices. ARMs generally have lower yields which vary frequently since their dividend rates are periodically reset. (See ARMs.)

Adjustable Rate Preferred: A bond or preferred stock whose dividends are adjusted periodically to maintain a yield within some designated range of a benchmark Treasury security. The dividend is also fixed between floor and ceiling yields, and the stock can be redeemed before maturity.

Advisor: The organization employed by a mutual fund to give professional advice on its investments and management of its assets.

Advisory and Service Fee (contract): The fee charged to an investment company (mutual fund) by its investment advisor under a contract approved by vote of a majority of the company's shares. The fee is computed as a percentage of the average net assets, and may also provide for an additional bonus or penalty based on performance.

Aggressive Growth Fund: A mutual fund which seeks maximum capital appreciation through the use of investment techniques involving greater than ordinary risk, which may include such techniques as borrowing money in order to provide leverage, short selling, hedging, options and warrants.

All-Weather Fund: A fund that long-term investors can hold relatively safely throughout a complete market cycle. Low volatility and asset allocation funds may be all-weather funds.

Alpha: A statistical measure representing the difference between the actual and expected performance of a fund given its characteristic volatility. A positive alpha is often considered a measure of management's ability.

Alternative Minimum Tax (AMT): A substitute computation of tax, which ensures that those taxpayers with substantial deductions and credits pay at least some income tax.

Annuity Contract: A contract issued by an insurance company that provides payments for a specified period, such as for a specified number of years or for life. (See Variable Annuity.)

Arbitrage: The purchase of an asset in one market accompanied by a simultaneous sale of the same (or a similar) asset in a different market to take advantage of the difference in price.

ARMs: Adjustable rate mortgages. The index rate on the loan is periodically reset relative to a base rate. (See Adjustable Rate Mortgage Funds.)

Asked or Offering Price: The price at which a mutual fund's shares can be purchased. The asked or offering price is the current net asset value per share plus a sales charge.

Asset-based Charge: A charge deducted from the net assets of a mutual fund under the terms of a 12b-1 plan.

Asset Value: Either total or per share. Total net assets of a fund represent the market value of holdings plus any other resources such as cash, minus liabilities. Per share is determined by dividing the total assets by the number of shares outstanding.

Automatic Reinvestment: The option available to mutual fund shareholders whereby fund income dividends and capital gains distributions are automatically used to buy new shares at no charge and thereby increase holdings.

Back-end Load: A redemption charge paid when withdrawing money from a fund. In the case of a 12b-1 fund, it is designed to recoup sales expenses not collected by the periodic 12b-1 fee, due to withdrawal(s) prior to a pre-determined period.

Balanced Fund: A mutual fund that has an investment policy of always balancing its portfolio, generally by including relatively fixed portions of bonds, preferred stocks and common stocks.

Bankers' Acceptances: Short term credit arrangements designed to enable a business to obtain funds to finance commercial transactions. Generally, an acceptance is a time draft drawn on a bank by an exporter or an importer to obtain a stated amount of funds to pay for specific merchandise. The draft is then "accepted" by a bank that, in effect, unconditionally guarantees to pay the face value of the instrument on its maturity date.

Basis Point: A unit used to measure changes in interest rates and bond yields, i.e., 100 basis points equal 1%. One basis point equals .01% (or 1/100 of 1%).

Bear Market: A market cycle in which stock prices are generally declining.

Beta: A coefficient that measures a fund's volatility relative to the total market, usually as represented by the S&P 500. It is the percentage performance of a fund which has historically accompanied a 1.00% move up or down in the S&P 500. High beta funds have price fluctuations greater than the broad market; low beta funds fluctuate less than the market as a whole. Funds with high betas are consequently riskier than the market, those with low betas are less risky.

Bid or Redemption Price: The price at which a mutual fund's shares are redeemed (bought back) by the fund. The bid or redemption price usually means the current net asset value per share.

Big Board: Another name for The New York Stock Exchange.

Blue Chip: The common stock of well established companies with a stable record of earnings and dividends.

Blue Sky Laws: Rules and regulations of the various states governing the securities business, including mutual funds, broker/dealers and salesmen.

Bond Fund: A mutual fund whose portfolio consists primarily of fixed-income securities. The emphasis of such funds is normally on income rather than growth.

Bookshares: A share recording system that gives the fund shareowner a record of his holdings. Used in lieu of share certificates.

Break Point: A quantity of securities purchased at which a lower sales charge takes effect; also, an aggregate amount of investment company assets in excess of which a lower rate of investment advisory fee is applicable.

Broker: A person who executes securities transactions for others, receiving a commission for his or her services.

Broker-Dealer (or Dealer): A firm which sells mutual fund shares and other securities to the public.

Bull Market: A market cycle in which stock prices are generally rising.

Call Option: The right to buy 100 shares of a particular stock or stock index at a predetermined price before a preset deadline, in exchange for a premium.

Capital Gain or Loss: Profit or loss resulting from the sale of property or securities.

Capital Gains Distributions: Payments to mutual funds shareholders of gains realized on sales within the fund's portfolio securities.

Capital Growth: The increase in the market value of securities held, which is the long term objective of many funds.

Cash Equivalent: Receivables, short-term bonds and notes.

Cash Position: Cash plus cash equivalents minus current liabilities in a fund's portfolio.

Certificate: Printed evidence of ownership of securities including mutual fund shares.

Certificates of Deposit: Negotiable certificates evidencing the indebtedness of a commercial bank to repay funds deposited with it for a definite period of time at a stated or variable interest rate.

Closed End Investment Company: Unlike mutual funds (known as open end funds), closed end companies issue only a limited number of shares and do not redeem them (buy them back). Instead, closed end shares are traded in the securities markets, with supply and demand determining the price. Also called publicly traded funds.

CMO: A security where a group of mortgage pass-through securities have been put together, and the cash flows are paid out in a specific order or preference to different buyers in order to give structure to the uncertain cash flows of mortgage pass-through securities.

Commercial Paper: Unsecured short term notes issued in bearer form by large well known corporations and finance companies and certain governmental bodies. Maturities on commercial paper range from a few days to nine months.

Commission: A fee paid to a broker or mutual fund salesmen for the buying or selling of securities.

Common Stock: A security representing ownership in a corporation's assets.

Common Stock Fund: A mutual fund whose portfolio consists primarily of common stocks. The emphasis of such funds is usually on growth.

Compounding: The process that occurs through the reinvestment of interest, dividends, or profits. Growth thus occurs at the same rate that the investment itself earns, allowing the reinvested money to multiply, rather than simply adding to the investment.

Conduit: The nature of a fund, which permits it to channel investment dividend income or capital gains to fund shareholders for tax purposes, and avoid being taxed within the fund.

Contingent Deferred Sales Charge: A sales fee payable when the shareholder redeems shares, rather than when shares are purchased, and which is frequently reduced each year that the shares are held.

Contrarian: An investor who does the opposite of what most investors are doing at a particular time. A contrarian fund generally invests in out-of-favor securities, whose price/earnings ratio may be lower than the rest of the market or industry.

Conversion Privilege: See Exchange Privilege.

Convertible Securities: A preferred stock or bond providing the right for the owner to exchange it for another security, such as common stock of the company, under specified or unspecified conditions of time, price and/or number of shares.

Corporate Obligations: Bonds and notes issued by corporations and other business organizations, including business trusts, in order to finance their long term credit needs.

CUSIP: The Committee on Uniform Securities Identification Procedures – it assigns identifying numbers and codes to all securities. These CUSIP numbers are used when recording all buy and sell orders. Each fund has a CUSIP number.

Custodian: The organization (usually a bank) that holds in custody and safekeeping the securities and other assets of a mutual fund.

Cycle: A pattern of swings and reversals in a trend that recurs over a period of time.

Daily Dividend Fund: A fund that declares its income dividends daily. The fund usually reinvests or distributes them daily or monthly. (See Money Market Funds.)

Deflation: A fall in the general price level of goods and services.

Direct Marketed Fund: A no-load or low-load fund whose shares can be bought directly from the fund, without going through a dealer, thus avoiding all or most of the sales commissions. Investors purchase fund shares through the mail or by telephone in response to advertising or publicity.

Discount: The percentage below asset value at which a closed end investment company sells in the open market.

Disinflation: A slowdown in the rate of inflation without turning into deflation.

Distributions: The payments of dividends or realized capital gains that a fund determines to pass along to shareholders, who can take them in cash or in additional shares.

Distributor: An organization that purchases mutual fund shares directly from the issuer for resale to other parties.

Diversification: The mutual fund policy of spreading its investments among a number of different securities to reduce the risks inherent in investing.

Diversified Investment Company: A fund that complies with statutory requirements of the Investment Company Act of 1940, which specifies that such a fund have at least 75% of its assets represented by cash, government securities, securities of other investment companies, and other securities limited in respect to any one issuer in an amount not greater than 5% of a fund's assets and not more than 10% of the voting securities of a single issuer.

Dividend: As distinct from a capital gains distribution, represents earnings from investment income.

Dollar-Cost-Averaging: Investing equal amounts of money at regular intervals regardless of whether the stock market is moving upward or downward. This reduces average share costs to the investor who acquires more shares in periods of lower securities prices and fewer shares in periods of higher prices.

Economics: The study of how people use limited resources – personal, commercial, national or international – to achieve maximum well-being.

Efficient Market: Theory that market prices reflect the knowledge and expectations of all investors. Believers of the theory hold that any new development is quickly reflected in a company's stock price, making it impossible for an investor to beat the market over the long run.

Equity: In investments, an ownership interest by shareholders of a corporation. Stock is equity, as opposed to bonds, which are debt.

Equity Fund: A common stock mutual fund.

Eurodollar CDs: Certificates of Deposit issued by a foreign branch (usually London) of a domestic bank, and as such, the credit is deemed to be that of the domestic bank.

Exchange Privilege: Enables a mutual fund shareholder to transfer his investment from one fund to another within the same fund group generally at no cost, if his needs or objectives change.

Ex-Dividend: For mutual funds (but not for securities listed on a stock exchange), that date on which declared distributions are deducted from total net assets. On the day a fund goes ex-dividend, its closing net asset value per share is calculated minus the distribution.

Expense Ratio: Annual expenses of a mutual fund (not including interest and income taxes paid) divided by average net assets.

Family of Funds: A group of mutual funds under the same management.

FANNIE MAE: Nickname for the Federal National Mortgage Association.

Fed: Nickname for the Federal Reserve System.

Fedwire: A computerized communications network connecting the Federal Reserve banks, their branches and other governmental agencies. It enables banks to transfer funds for immediate available credit.

Fiduciary: A person vested with legal power to be used for benefit of another person.

Fixed Income Fund: A mutual fund investing all or a major portion of its assets (normally 75% or more) in fixed income securities.

Fixed Income Security: A debt security such as a bond or a preferred stock with a stated return in percentage or dollars.

Flexibly Diversified: In contrast to a balanced fund whose portfolio at all times must be diversified among a generally stated minimum or maximum percentage of bonds/preferred/common stocks. Flexible diversification means that management, at its discretion, may allot the percentage for each type of security.

Float: The period between the writing of a check and the debiting of an account for that amount. Money fund shareholders earn interest on the float when they write checks on their accounts.

401(k) Plan: A plan by which an employee may elect, as an alternative to receiving taxable cash as compensation or bonus, to contribute pretax dollars to a qualified tax-deferred retirement plan.

FREDDIE MAC: Nickname for the Federal Home Loan Mortgage Corporation, and also the mortgage-backed securities it issues.

Front End Load: Sales charge applied to an investment at the time of initial purchase.

Fully Managed Fund: A term generally used when a fund's prospectus permits assets to be converted to debt securities or all cash at management's discretion, for timing purchases and sales.

Fundamental Analysis: Analysis of corporate balance sheets, income statements, management, sales, products and markets in order to forecast future stock price movements.

Futures Contracts: Obligations to buy or deliver a quantity of the underlying commodity or financial instrument at the agreed-upon price by a certain date. Most contracts are simply nullified by an opposite trade before they come due.

General Obligation Securities: The obligations of an issuer with taxing power that are payable from the issuer's general, unrestricted revenues. These securities are backed by the full faith, credit and taxing power of the issuer for the payment of principal and interest; they are not limited to repayment from any particular fund or revenue source.

Global Asset Allocation Fund: A broadly diversified fund that typically invests across a number of markets to provide a hedge against declines in the U.S. stock market. Their holdings may include U.S. stocks; international stocks; U.S. bonds, often governments; international bonds; gold or gold mining shares; cash equivalents, and sometimes real estate securities. They seek satisfactory performance in almost all foreseeable economic climates – inflation, deflation, stability.

Global Fund: A fund that invests in the securities of the U.S. as well as those of foreign countries.

GNMA Fund: A fund investing in GNMA securities issued by the Government National Mortgage Association, a corporation that helps finance mortgages.

Growth Fund: A mutual fund whose primary investment objective is long term growth of capital. It invests primarily in common stocks with growth potential.

Growth - Income Fund: A mutual fund whose aim is to provide for a degree of both income and long term growth.

Hedge: To offset. To safeguard oneself from loss by making compensating arrangements on the other side. For example, to hedge one's long positions from short sales, so that if the market declines the loss of the positions will be offset by profit on the short positions.

Hedge Fund: A fund whose policy is to hedge long positions with short positions. Occasionally used to describe an aggressive fund.

Illiquid Securities: According to SEC regulations, open-end investment companies (mutual funds) can invest no more than 15 percent of their capital in illiquid investments. This rule is aimed at assuring that the funds will be able to redeem their shares on demand.

Incentive Compensation: The fee paid to a fund manager based upon performance in relation to a specific index.

Income Dividends: Payments to mutual fund shareholders of dividends, interest and short term capital gains earned on the fund's portfolio securities after deduction of operating expenses.

Income Fund: A mutual fund whose primary investment objective is current income rather than growth of capital. It usually invests in stocks and bonds that normally pay higher dividends and interest.

Index Fund: A mutual fund whose investment objective is to match the composite investment performance of a large group of publicly-traded common stocks represented in a stock market index.

Individual Retirement Account (IRA): A retirement program for working individuals. An individual may contribute and deduct from his or her income tax a dollar amount subject to current IRS limits. An Individual Retirement Account is often funded with mutual fund shares.

Institutional Investor: A bank, insurance company, mutual or pension fund that invests other people's money on their behalf. It typically trades securities in larger volume than individuals.

Industrial Group Index: The grouping of stocks comprised of a specific industry group.

Investment Advisor (Manager): Under the Investment Company Act of 1940, a company providing investment advice, research and often administrative and similar services for an agreed-upon fee, as a percentage of net assets.

Investment Advisors Act of 1940: Covers the registration and regulation of most persons who provide investment advice to individuals or institutions, including investment companies, for compensation.

Investment Advisory Agreement: An agreement between an investment company (mutual fund) and an investment manager, contracting with the investment manager to provide investment advice to the investment company for a fee.

Investment Company: A corporation, trust or partnership in which investors pool their money to obtain professional management and diversification of their investments. Mutual funds are the most popular type of investment company.

Investment Company Act of 1940: The federal law governing the registration and regulation of mutual funds.

Investment Objective: The goal – e.g., long-term capital growth, current income, etc. – of an investor or a mutual fund.

Junk Bonds: Low-quality, high-risk bonds that typically offer above average yields.

Legal List: A list published by a state government authority enumerating or setting standards for securities appropriate for money held in trust.

Letter of Intent: An agreement by which a shareholder agrees to buy a specified dollar amount of mutual fund shares, usually over 13 months, in order to receive a lower sales charge provided the agreed amount is invested.

Letter Stock: A form or restricted security so-called because it is generally accompanied by a letter stating that the stock has been purchased only for investment and will not be offered to the public until registered. (See Restricted Securities.)

Leverage: The use of borrowed money.

Liquidity: The ease of converting an asset to cash. (See Illiquid Securities.)

Liquid Asset Fund: A money market fund.

Load: The sales charge or commission for buying a mutual fund.

Load Fund: A fund whose shares are sold by a broker or salesman with a sales charge.

Long Term Funds: An industry designation for all funds other than short term funds (money market and short term municipal bond). The two broad categories of long term funds are equity and bond/income funds.

Management Company: The entity which manages a fund, as distinct from the fund itself. Officials of both, and even of a company distributing shares or acting as a broker may be the same persons.

Management Fee: The amount paid by a mutual fund to the investment advisor for its services. Fees vary and depend on the nature of the fund's investment objective and its total assets.

Market Timer: An investor who attempts to time the market so that shares are sold before they decrease in value and bought when they are about to increase in value. Sometimes the strategy calls for frequent buy and sell decisions.

Money Managers: Professionals employed by mutual fund companies to invest the pool of money in accordance with the fund's investment objectives. Also called portfolio managers.

Money Market Fund: A mutual fund whose primary objective is to make higher interest securities available to the average investor who wants safety of principal, liquidity, and current income. This is accomplished through the purchase of short term money market instruments such as U.S. Government securities, bank securities, bank certificates of deposit and commercial paper.

Money Market Instruments: Include the following types of short term investments: U.S. Government securities, certificates of deposit, time deposits, bankers acceptances, commercial paper and other corporate obligations; also included within such term are short term repurchase agreements backed by any of the foregoing instruments.

Mortgage-backed Securities: Pass-through securities created from pools of mortgages that are packaged together and sold as bonds. The monthly payments of interest and principal on the underlying mortgage debt are passed through to investors.

Municipal Bond Fund: A mutual fund which invests in a broad range of tax-exempt bonds issued by states, cities and other local governments. The interest obtained from these bonds is passed through to shareholders free of federal tax. The fund's primary objective is current tax free income.

Municipal Securities: Include a wide variety of debt obligations issued for public purposes by or on behalf of the States, territories and possessions of the United States, their political subdivisions, the District of Columbia, and the duly constituted authorities, agencies, public corporations and other instrumentalities of these jurisdictions. Municipal Securities may be used for numerous public purposes, including construction of public facilities, such as airports, bridges, highways, housing, hospitals, mass transportation, schools, streets, water and sewer works and gas and electric utilities. Municipal Securities may also be used to obtain funds to lend to other public institutions and to certain private borrowers. Municipal Securities are generally classified as either the general obligation, revenue, or industrial type.

Mutual Fund: An investment company that pools investors' money and is managed by a professional advisor. It ordinarily stands ready to buy back (redeem) its shares at their current net asset value; the value of the shares depends on the market value of the fund's portfolio securities at the time. Most mutual funds continuously offer new shares to investors.

NASDAQ: An automated information network which provides brokers and dealers with price quotations on securities traded over-the-counter. NASDAQ is an acronym for National Association of Securities Dealers Automated Quotations.

National Association of Securities Dealers, Inc. (NASD), now known as FINRA, Financial Industry Regulation Authority: A Self Regulatory Organization (SRO) charged by federal law with policing the SEC regulations applying to mutual funds and over-the-counter securities, but not those traded on stock exchanges.

Nest Egg: Assets put aside to provide for a secure standard of living after one's retirement.

Net Assets: A fund's total assets less current liabilities such as taxes and other operating expenses.

Net Asset Value Per Share (NAV): A fund's total assets – securities, cash and any accrued earnings – after deduction of liabilities, divided by the number of shares outstanding.

Net Investment Income Per Share: Dividends and interest earned during an accounting period (such as a year) on a fund's portfolio, less operating expenses, divided by the number of shares outstanding.

Net Realized Capital Gains Per Share: the amount of capital gains realized on sale of a fund's portfolio holdings during an accounting period (such as a year), less losses realized on such transactions, divided by the number of shares outstanding.

No-Load Fund: A mutual fund selling its shares at net asset value, without the addition of sales charges. In some cases, the fund may have a nominal 12b-1 or redemption fee.

Non-Diversified Investment Company: A fund whose portfolio does not meet the requirements of the Investment Company Act of 1940 to qualify as a diversified investment company. For example, a fund which (as to 50% of its assets) may invest up to 25% in the securities of one company.

Offering Price: Same as asked price, which is net asset value per share plus an applicable sales commission.

Open End Investment Company: The more formal name for a mutual fund, indicating that it stands ready to redeem its shares (buy them back) on demand.

Over-the-Counter Market: A trading network composed of dealers nation-wide who trade issues on other than the regular stock exchanges.

Payment Date: The day on which a distribution is mailed to shareholders. Usually later than the declaration date, which is the day the distribution is announced by the board of directors; and usually follows the record date, which is the date the distribution goes ex-dividend. Only shareholders as of the record date are entitled to the payment.

Performance Results: The percentage change in a fund's per share value over a specified period of time. As used in the mutual fund industry, it generally includes the value of the income and capital gains dividends distributed during the specified period.

Portfolio: The group name for securities owned by a fund.

Portfolio Managers: (See Money Managers.)

Portfolio Turnover: Generally stated in a percentage of total assets in a year. For example, 80% of the dollar value of a portfolio's holdings were changed in a year. (See Turnover Ratio.)

Preferred Stock: An equity security generally carrying a fixed return in percentage or dollars, which must be paid before common stock holders can share in earnings or assets.

Premium: The percentage above asset value at which a closed end investment company sells in the open market. Applies to closed end funds whose shares must be purchased or sold only through a broker and not through the fund.

Prospectus: The official document which describes the mutual fund and offers its shares for sale. It contains information required by the Securities and Exchange Commission on such subjects as the fund's investment objectives and policies, services, investment restrictions, officers and directors, how shares can be bought and redeemed, its charges and its financial statements. A more detailed document known as "Part B" of the prospectus or the Statement of Additional Information is available upon request.

Proxy: Enables shareholders not attending a fund meeting to transfer their voting power to another person, usually fund management, to vote on fund business at the meeting.

Prudent Man Rule: The rule which enables a trustee to use his own judgment in making investments as long as he acts conservatively. This rule comes from an 1830 court decision.

Publicly Traded Investment Company: A closed-end fund.

Qualified For Sale: Qualified by reason of registration with the SEC or in accordance with a state's regulations.

Real Estate Investment Trust: (REIT). An investment company that specializes in real estate holdings. Cannot be a mutual fund because investments are considered illiquid. (See Illiquid Securities.)

Record Date: The date on which declared distributions are set aside (held separate, for payment to shareholders at a later date, payment date) and deducted from total net assets.

Redemption Fee: The charge levied by some funds when shares are redeemed.

Redemption Price: The amount per share the mutual fund shareholder receives when he cashes in his shares. The value of the shares depends on the market value of the fund's portfolio securities at the time (less any redemption fees).

Red Herring: A preliminary prospectus.

Registrar: The organization, usually a bank, that maintains a registry of the share owners of a mutual fund, and the number of shares they own.

Reinvestment Privilege: A service provided by most mutual funds for the automatic reinvestment of a shareholder's income dividends and capital gains distributions in additional shares at NAV.

Repos: Abbreviation for repurchase agreements.

Repurchase Agreements: A sale of securities with the concurrent agreement of the seller to repurchase the securities at the same price plus an amount equal to interest at an agreed-upon rate, within a specified time.

Restricted Security: One which requires registration with the SEC before it may be sold to the public. Because of this restriction, the security may not be considered a liquid asset and therefore may be priced at a substantial discount from market value.

Revenue Securities: Securities repayable only from revenues derived from a particular facility, local agency, special tax, facility user or other specific revenue source; certain revenue issues may also be backed by a reserve fund or specific collateral.

Reverse Repurchase Agreements: Ordinary repurchase agreements in which a Fund is the seller of securities, rather than the investor in securities, and agrees to re-purchase them at an agreed-upon time and price. Use of reverse repurchase agreements may be preferable to a regular sale and later repurchase of the securities.

Right of Accumulation: The right to combine a current mutual fund share purchase with shares previously acquired and currently owned to qualify for a quantity discount that reduces the sales charge on that purchase.

Rule 12b-1: A rule under Section 12 of the Investment Company Act of 1940 that permits the use of a fund's assets to pay distribution-related expenses subject to certain conditions.

Sales Charge: An amount charged to purchase shares in a mutual fund. The charge varies based on the amount invested. The charge is added to the net asset value per share in the determination of the offering price. Also known as a front-end sales charge. (See Contingent Deferred Sales Charge and 12b-1 Plan.)

Sales Force Marketing: A method of distribution whereby funds sell their shares to the public through brokers, financial planners, and insurance agents. Some fund organizations sell shares through a captive sales force – salespeople employed by the fund organization to market only the shares of its associated funds.

Sector: Particular group of stocks, usually found in one industry.

Sector Funds: A number of separate industry portfolios grouped under the umbrella of one fund. The advisor usually provides easy switching by phone between portfolios and a related money fund.

Securities and Exchange Commission (SEC): The agency of the U.S. government which administers Federal securities laws.

Senior Securities: Notes, bonds, debentures or preferred stocks, which have a prior (senior) claim ahead of common stock to assets and earnings.

Series Fund: An investment company that offers multiple segregated portfolios of common stock.

Service Fee: A payment by a fund to brokers, financial planners, and money managers for personal service to shareholders and/or the maintenance of shareholder accounts. Transfer agent, custodian and similar fees are not considered service fees. (Also see Trailing Commissions, 12b-1 Plan.)

Short Sale: The sale of a security which is not owned, in the hope that the price will go down so that it can be repurchased at the lower price. The person making a short sale borrows stock in order to make delivery to the buyer and must eventually purchase the stock in the open market, for return to the lender.

Short Term Fund: An industry designation for money market and short term municipal bond funds.

Single-state Funds: Funds that invest in the tax-exempt securities issued by governmental organizations of a single state. Investors receive earnings free from both federal and any state tax. Single-state funds can be both short and long term.

Social Conscience Fund: A fund that invests in the securities of companies that do not conflict with certain social priorities. For example, some social consciences funds do not invest in tobacco stocks or defense stocks.

Special Fund: A mutual fund specializing in the securities of certain industries, special types of securities or in regional investments.

Split Funding: A program which combines the purchase of mutual fund shares with the purchase of life insurance contracts or other products.

Stability: Relatively low volatility in a declining market. For example, a fund rated above-average for stability, is one that declines relatively the least.

Stock-index Arbitrage: Buying or selling baskets of stocks while at the same time executing offsetting trades in stock-index futures or options. Traders profit by trying to capture fleeting price discrepancies between stocks and the index futures or options. If stocks are temporarily cheaper than futures, for example, an arbitrageur will buy stocks and sell futures.

Target Fund: A fixed income fund whose portfolio matures within a given year. Often structured as a series fund with each series maturing in a different year depending on an expected retirement date.

Tax Anticipation Notes: Issued by governmental entities in anticipation of specific future tax revenue, such as property, income, sales, use, and business taxes. Some such notes are general obligations of the issuer, and others are payable only from specific future taxes.

Technical Analysis: Research into the supply and demand for securities based on trading volume and price studies. Technical analysis uses charts or computer programs to identify price trends in an attempt to foretell future price movements. Unlike fundamental analysts, technical analysts do not concern themselves with the financial position of a company, such as earnings, etc.

Telephone Switching/Exchange: Process of selling one mutual fund and buying another at the same time by telephone. Switching is often between stock, bond, or money market funds within the same fund family.

Total Return: A performance calculation that includes capital gains and dividend distributions. (See Performance.)

Total Return Fund: A fund whose objective is to obtain the highest possible total return, i.e., a combination of ordinary income and capital gains. Funds usually invest in a combination of dividend paying stocks and bonds.

Trailing Commission: Also called a trail, it is a small commission periodically paid to a broker or a financial planner to service an existing shareholder as long as money remains in the fund. A typical trail might be one quarter of one percent per year. It is often paid out of the 12b-1 fee. (Also see Service Fee.)

Transfer Agent: The organization which is employed by a mutual fund to prepare and maintain records relating to the accounts of its shareholders.

Treasury Bills: Marketable U.S. Government securities with an original maturity of up to one year.

Treasury Bonds: Marketable U.S. Government securities with an original maturity of ten years or more.

Treasury Notes: Marketable U.S. Government securities with an original maturity of from two to ten years.

Turnover ratio: The extent to which an investment company's portfolio is turned over during the course of a year. Calculated by dividing the lesser of purchases or sales of portfolio securities for the fiscal year by the monthly average of the value the portfolio securities owned by the mutual fund during the fiscal year. Excluded from the numerator and denominator are all U.S. Government securities and all other securities whose maturities at the time of acquisition were one year or less.

12b-1 Plan: Allows the fund to pay a percentage of its assets to cover the distributor's sales and marketing costs. The payment is a direct deduction from a fund's total assets. (See Asset-based charges.)

Underwriter or Principal Underwriter: The organization which acts as the distributor of a mutual fund's shares to broker-dealers and the public.

Unit Investment Trust: An investment company with an unmanaged portfolio that is liquidated after a specific time period.

Unrealized Appreciation or Depreciation: The amount by which the market value of a security or a portfolio of securities, at any given time, is above (appreciation) or below (depreciation) the cost price.

U.S. Government Obligations: Debt securities (including bills, notes, and bonds) issued by the U.S. Treasury or issued by an agency or instrumentality of the U.S. government which is established under the authority of an act of Congress. Such agencies or instrumentalities include, but are not limited to, the Federal National Mortgage Association, the Federal Farm Credit Bank, and the Federal Home Loan Bank. Although all obligations of agencies and instrumentalities are not direct obligations of the U.S. Treasury, payment of the interest and principal on these obligations is generally backed directly or indirectly by the U.S. government. This support can range from the backing of the full faith and credit of the United States to U.S. government guarantees, or to the backing solely of the issuing instrumentality itself. In the latter case of securities not backed by the full faith and credit of the United States, the investor must look principally to the agency issuing or guaranteeing the obligation for ultimate repayment and may not be able to assert claim against the United States itself in the event the agency or instrumentality does not meet its commitments.

Variable Annuity: An annuity having a provision for the accumulation of an account value, for benefit payments, or both, that vary according to the investment experience of the separate account to which the amounts paid for the annuity are allocated. The holdings may consist of one or more open end mutual funds.

Volatility: The relative rate at which a fund's shares tend to move up or down in price as compared to the change in the price of a stock market index or a mutual fund average. For example, a highly volatile fund is one that usually rises or declines far more than the average fund.

Voluntary Plan: A flexible share accumulation plan in which there is no definite time period or total amount to be invested.

Withdrawal Plans: Many mutual funds offer withdrawal programs whereby shareholders receive payments from their investments at regular intervals. These payments typically are drawn from the fund's dividends and capital gains distributions, if any, and from principal to the extent necessary.

Yield: Income received from investments, usually expressed as a percentage of market price, also referred to as return. Usually computed on the basis of one year's income.

Yield to Maturity: The yield earned on a bond over its full life. Includes capital gains if the bond was bought at a discount from its face value.

Zero Coupon Bond: A bond that is bought at a price that is below par with no coupons. The return is the difference between the purchase and the sale price, or par if held to maturity. Zeros accumulate and compound interest at the same rate that prevailed when the bond was purchased.

Appendix C

Mutual Fund Investor's Information Sources

Websites

Coalition of Mutual Fund Investors (Fund investor advocacy site)	**www.investorscoalition.com**
Financial Industry Regulatory Authority (Securities industry self regulatory organization)	**www.finra.org**
Fund Alarm (Fund analysis/research site)	**www.fundalarm.com**
Investment Company Institute (Mutual fund advisor's trade/ lobbying organization)	**www.investmentcompanyinstitute.com**
Investopedia (Financial "encyclopedia" of investment terminology)	**www.investopedia.com**
John C. Bogle (John Bogle's blog and information site)	**www.johncbogle.com**
Morningstar, Inc. (Mutual fund rating service)	**www.morningstar.com**
Mutual Funds Bureau ("Mutual Funds Today" site)	**www.mutualfundsbureau.com**
Mutual Fund Directors Forum (Independent mutual fund director's site)	**www.mfdf.com**
Retirement Dictionary (Retirement plan information and updates)	**www.retirementdictionary.com**
U. S. Securities & Exchange Commission (Federal securities regulatory agency)	**www.sec.gov**

Publications

Forbes Magazine	**www.forbes.com**
Investors Business Daily	**www.investorsbusinessdaily.com**
Kiplinger's Personal Finance	**www.kiplingermagazine.com**
The Wall Street Journal	**www.wsj.com**

Notes: